THE SENSE OF LIFE
IN THE MODERN NOVEL

BY ARTHUR MIZENER

The Far Side of Paradise
The Sense of Life in the Modern Novel

EDITED BY ARTHUR MIZENER

Afternoon of an Author, by F. Scott Fitzgerald
The Fitzgerald Reader
Modern Short Stories

THE
SENSE OF LIFE

IN THE MODERN NOVEL

BY ARTHUR MIZENER

The Riverside Press Cambridge

HOUGHTON MIFFLIN COMPANY BOSTON

1964

The author wishes to thank the following publishers for permission to quote passages from the works cited:

Harper & Row, Publishers, Incorporated, and Victor Gollancz, Ltd.: "Knob" and "The Population of Argentina" in The Carpentered Hen and Other Tame Creatures *by John Updike. Copyright © 1958 by John Updike.*
Houghton Mifflin Company: "American Letter" in Collected Poems: 1917–1952 *by Archibald MacLeish.*
New Directions: The Cantos of Ezra Pound. *Copyright 1934, 1948 by Ezra Pound.*
Charles Scribner's Sons and Eyre & Spottiswoode (Publishers), Ltd.: "Ode to the Confederate Dead" in Poems *by Allen Tate.*

First Printing

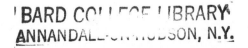

For R. P. M.

With Love

THIS book is not a history of the novel, nor is it an attempt to make an inclusive analysis of the novel as a literary form or to cover completely any writer it discusses. Its purpose is to examine one aspect of the novel. Its starting point, as I have tried to suggest in the first chapter, is a conviction that our ideas about the novel are confused and contradictory and that the best thing we can do at present is to concentrate on certain immediate questions raised by novels. Subjects of this kind are necessarily limited in scope and the results of considering them will be, at best, modest; but they have what is, under existing circumstances, a striking advantage: they are specific and definable subjects.

One such subject is the relation of the represented life in the novel to "nature," and the effects this relation has on the novel's expression of values. This problem is omnipresent in the novel, but it is often lost sight of because it is treated as a minor aspect of the large and confused subject usually called realism. The argument of this book is directed to this question of the novel's relation to nature. It deals with other subjects, such as the lives of novelists or the social histories of their times, only as an understanding of these subjects appears to help us understand the novel and nature.

To the best of my ability I have selected for discussion novelists whose work raises in interesting ways questions about the novel and nature. I believe all these novelists are important, worth considering for themselves. But the selection of them rather than other, equally gifted novelists depends primarily on their usefulness for a discussion of the subject of this book; by the same token, the omission of a novelist from the discussion is not meant as a reflection on his general merits; it only means that, as far as I could see, he was less useful for my purpose than the novelists I have chosen.

One considerable qualification of this general statement is necessary. I have devoted what is perhaps an inordinate amount of attention to the American novel of the twentieth century, partly, to be sure, because the relation of the novel and nature has been acutely disturbing to the American novel. But it would be less than honest not to admit that I have also done so because of my own interest in and familiarity with the American novel.

What I have tried to do, then, is to begin, in the first chapter, with a general discussion of the novel and nature and, in the next three chapters, with a discussion of the ways in which this relation has been dealt with by two representative, though very different novelists of the nineteenth century and two twentieth-century novelists who are in their different ways, I hope, equally representative. These first four chapters are, in short, intended to define and illustrate the subject. The next three chapters describe the peculiarly troubled relation between the representation of nature and the expression of values in the American novel, again first in the nineteenth century and then in the twentieth century. The five chapters that follow attempt to show the various ways in which important American novelists of the twentieth century, from Faulkner to John Updike, have dealt with it. The final chapter discusses an unusual, perhaps in some sense even un-American novel of great intelligence and skill that seems to have found a solution to this conflict.

I very much hope this brief outline makes clear the limited objective of this book and will prevent readers from supposing it says, or intends to say, more than it does. Its purpose is to deal with a specific and limited aspect of the novel. I believe this aspect is an important one and that until we can see it — and a number of others of the same kind — clearly, we cannot hope to deal effectively with the novel as a whole. But I am under no illusion that a consideration of this aspect of the novel can provide either a theory or a history of the novel as a whole, and I am anxious that no reader should suppose I am.

It is hardly necessary to say that I owe a great deal to other writers; enough of them are mentioned during the course of the discussion to indicate how great my debt is. Much of the material of this book has appeared in other forms elsewhere; for permission to use it here I am indebted to the editors of *Harper's Magazine, The Times Literary Supplement, The Kenyon Review, The Sewanee Review, The Southern Review, Perspectives, The Spectator, From Jane Austen to Joseph Conrad* (The University of Minnesota Press, 1958), and *The Great Experiment in American Literature* (Heinemann, 1961).

ARTHUR MIZENER

Cornell University
September, 1963

CONTENTS

Foreword   vii

I The Novel and Nature   I

II The Realistic Novel in the Nineteenth Century:
Trollope's Palliser Novels   25

III The Novel of Doctrine in the Nineteenth Century:
Hardy's *Jude the Obscure*   55

IV The Novel and Nature in the Twentieth Century:
Anthony Powell and James Gould Cozzens   79

V The American Novel and Nature in the Nineteenth
Century   105

VI The American Novel and Nature in the Twentieth
Century   119

VII The Dilemma of the American Novelist   139

VIII The American Hero as Gentleman: Gavin Stevens   161

IX The American Hero as Entrepreneur: Monroe Stahr   183

X The American Hero as Leatherstocking: Nick Adams   205

XI The American Hero as Poet: Seymour Glass   227

XII The American Hero as High-school Boy: Peter Caldwell   247

XIII The Realistic Novel as Symbol   267

Index   289

THE NOVEL AND NATURE

THERE are not very many things critics can say about fiction that are not debatable, as Wayne Booth's *The Rhetoric of Fiction* — that landmark in the study of fiction — shows. There is perhaps one, that we have less confidence in the relevance of what we say about novels than we have in the relevance of what we say about poems or plays. At the lowest level, the sheer size of novels has something to do with this. Poems and even plays are small enough so that it is possible for us to hold in our minds with relative ease all that is in them and thus select with some confidence the things we want to emphasize. It is far more difficult to do that with fictions at once so bulky and so coherent as *Emma* or *Bleak House* or *Ulysses*. By a mighty effort of reading and rereading we can perhaps achieve the full knowledge of a novel that seeing it as a whole requires, but that kind of effort is necessarily rare.

In any event, problems of this kind, though of great practical importance, are essentially mechanical or administrative, problems of the way to do certain things. They assume that we know what we want to do. But the assumption that we know what we want to do with the novel is not easily justified. We have no established theory of the novel; we can hardly be said to have several alternative theories. What we do have is a number of incomplete and incompatible theories, some of them of such dubious standing and such imperfect logical development that we all too easily convince ourselves we ought not to adopt any one of them. But the notion that you have no theory of the novel when you read, though no doubt stimulating to openness of mind, is a delusion. It is impossible to read at all without a theory, and to ignore it is only to be unaware of how the theory you have unconsciously elected in making your judgment at one point of the novel affects your reading at another.

Thus the problem of what theory of the novel to adopt is a real and unavoidable problem. But so far as the general reader is concerned we are — with *The Craft of Fiction* and *Aspects of the Novel* — still living critically in the age of Sir Arthur Quiller-Couch and A. C. Bradley; which, in fact, we are not. Nor is this difficulty merely a remote theoretical one of concern only to the aesthetician; it is immediate and practical. We need an adequate theory of the novel, not primarily because of any passion we may have for an orderly aesthetic, but because critics have to talk about novels all the time, in a way they do not have to talk about poetry or the drama. Under these circumstances it is particularly awkward not to know what kind of talk is relevant and what kind is not.

We have to talk about novels all the time because novels are the part of literature in which professional and common reader share an interest, though whatever the grounds for the common reader's interest may be, they probably do not include everything about novels that concerns the professional reader. They probably do not include, for example, the contemporary critic's intense, post-Jamesian concern for the techniques of the novel. Probably no one would want to question the importance of the Art of the Novel, and Henry James's prefaces are certainly the best kind of talk about that art that we have. We cannot do without it, whatever else we may need to say about the novel. Perhaps it is not enough to say that the novel, as largely practiced in English, is a perfect paradise of the loose end, or even, with a later authority, that the novelist goes forth to encounter the reality of experience with no better means of communion with it than silence, exile, and cunning. But neither is it enough if we omit to say and do these things. Whatever there is to be said, for example, for Hardy as a novelist, what James said against him is also to be said.

But if we cannot do without the Art of the Novel, neither can we do with it alone, and we are thus, as critics, forced to choose between a kind of talk about novels that seems to us acute and relevant but inadequate — and dangerously misleading if its inadequacy is not recognized — and a kind of talk that will get at what a discussion of the techniques of the novel does not. But the second of these choices is known to us only as something we have not got or as a discouraging confusion of sprightly remarks about Gentle Jane's charm and Hardy's pessimism and Dos Passos' communism which is usually trivial and frequently downright false.

Moreover, this is not simply a problem for the critic and his reader. It is also a problem for the practicing novelist. Nearly every novelist nurses a grudge against critics, often justified by his personal experience with reviewers. But though it is true that good novelists are not writers who put into practice the theories of the novel dear to the critics of their time, as novelists usually imagine critics believe them to be, it is also true that novelists are much more likely to be influenced by models that are analyzed and given prominence by the criticism of their time than by other models, even those that may be far more congenial to their talents. Even more important is the fact that the climate of doctrine and attitude that has so much to do with shaping the critical theories of a period is equally powerful in shaping the minds of novelists. Thus even though we ignore entirely the indirect influence of criticism on novelists, we must still recognize that the problems that preoccupy theorists of the novel are in large part the same problems that trouble novelists. For this reason, if for no other, any discussion of the form of the novel has to try to get at the elements of doctrine and attitude in our world that appear to influence both our theories of the novel and the practices of our novelists.

The most widespread conception of the novel in our time is that of the well-made novel, a theory much influenced by James's prefaces to the New York edition of his work. So eloquent is James in these prefaces that we seem hardly yet to have realized the extent to which he fails to talk, at least directly, about what matters most to him in his novels, very much as he fails in his autobiographical volumes to talk directly about what matters most to him in his life. How long it has taken us to discover the plain facts about that important accident of James's; how many marvelous and wild theories of castration and the like his indirectness has given rise to. No doubt the cause of James's excessive restraint in speaking about what was personally important to him in both his life and his work was connected with his conception of the decency of a gentleman, a feeling perhaps a little like the one Hamlet experienced when he found himself, to his embarrassment, complimenting Horatio to his face.

James's deprecatory air when he is talking about his own novels has led critics who have been influenced by his prefaces — and what critic has not, to some degree, been influenced by them — to concentrate on the structure of the novel, on its architecture and ordination, on what it is logical to include and exclude once one has committed himself to a certain mode of attack on the subject. Richard Blackmur once remarked wryly of criticism of this kind that "the Henry James novel, the Joyce novel, the Kafka novel, the Mann novel and the Gide novel together will kill us yet if we do not realize soon that these novelists do not depend on what we think of as their 'novels' except in the first instance." The critic who depends for his view of novels on "the James novel" in this way is all too likely barely to glance at the problems of character delineation, and of the concrete presentation of the appearance and gestures that distinguish the society in which characters live and move and have their being.

Nor do such critics touch, except vaguely, on what is usually called "meaning," the novel's implied judgment of the characters and of the represented world as a whole, though surely it is obvious from his novels that James himself had a highly developed sense of character and of social circumstances, just as it is obvious that he had deep feelings about both, feelings so deep that they substantially determine the whole course of a novel's action. Almost the first thing a reader notices about novels like *The Ambassadors, The Wings of the Dove,* and *The Golden Bowl,* for example, is how strongly affected their actions are by James's feelings about the oddly linked subjects of sex and money.

Who really doubts that what makes a novelist select a subject in the first place and develop it as he does is that this subject manifests a particular way of conducting life that has supreme value for him? As we watch Henry James fixing, for example, on that dinner-table anecdote that he eventually transformed into *The Spoils of Poynton* with what he himself so beautifully called a renewal "in the modern alchemist [of] something like the old dream of the secret of life," we see clearly how his feeling for particular values of conduct has determined his interest in the story. This power of seeing in a chance anecdote an opportunity to create a verisimilar image of what is for him significant conduct is all the more remarkable when we consider how unpromising for James's sense of the heroic life the anecdote would appear to anyone but James. All that survives from that anecdote as motive in the novel are the spoils themselves and Mr. Gereth's not strictly relevant indignation about the treatment of dowagers in Chapter V. As James himself observed, "the first thing to be done for the communicated and seized idea is to reduce almost to naught the form. . . ."

This element of value, of "meaning," so lightly touched on by theorists of the well-made novel, is the main preoccupation of a second popular conception of the novel, the theory that stresses the importance of the symbolized meaning of novels and is more interested in what a character or an event "stands for" than in whether it stands at all, as a realized object, in the fiction. There are many varieties of this theory, depending on whether the critic believes that, for example, the essential meaning of experience is embodied in myths, Christian or classical, or in the dramatis personae of psychoanalysis, or even in the icons of some home-made "philosophy." It makes some difference, to be sure, whether the critic fancies that the old man in Hemingway's *The Old Man and the Sea*, struggling up the hill with his sail over his shoulder, is Christ carrying the Cross or everyman carrying a phallic symbol.

But the critical theories that encourage these interpretations are at bottom much the same. Both assume that what really matters is a truth that exists independently of the story and is definable in terms other than the author's; for them a story matters, not because of what it is, but because something it alludes to matters. When a novelist makes this assumption, it is often revealed by the appearance in the novel of essays or sermons on the true doctrine. As Jane Austen, with her characteristic mock humility, observed a long time ago, doubtless *Pride and Prejudice* could easily have been improved by the insertion of "an essay on writing, a critique on Sir Walter Scott, or the history of Buonaparté."

The most familiar version of this theory is, as a theory, now somewhat out of fashion, but it is used by reviewers and followed by both practicing novelists and readers a great deal of the time. This is the theory that novels justify themselves by expressing some social or moral doctrine, are novels of "social consciousness," as, for example, *The Grapes of Wrath* is. This theory assumes that what common sense observes is not what is "really" there, that the abstracting intelligence of the socially conscious observer, guided by a doctrine that is The Truth, sees through the ordinary appearances of things to the reality that his doctrine adumbrates. In the 1930's, for example, critics were everywhere announcing that *King Lear* was meaningless in the twentieth century because Lenin had demonstrated that the family was no longer a viable institution, and that all sorts of novels were untrue because they failed to show the working class behaving as Marx had said in the nineteenth century it was going to behave in the twentieth century. Though this kind of comment is a gross parody of the thought of sensitive social critics, it has the advantage for our purposes of revealing in all its naked glory the central assumption that underlies all social theories of the novel, the assumption that it is the doctrine the novel explicates or alludes to, not the life of the novel itself, that counts.

All theories of this kind are thus reductive. The mythological theory judges a novel by the completeness with which it can be reduced to an accepted myth, the psychoanalytical theory by the degree to which its characters conform to the grotesque personae of a psychoanalytical pantheon, the social theory by the completeness with which its implications can be reduced to orthodox doctrine.

The most troublesome thing about these theories is that they all point to something that is in novels; they are not talking about something wholly unrelated to them. There can hardly be any doubt that the doctrines these theories are committed to affect novelists and often play a considerable part in releasing their imaginations. Even though we may agree that dogma presented as sermon or essay has no place in a novel (and the early example of *Tom Jones* suggests that even this agreement may be a mistake), we still have to consider that significant aspects of the novelist's imaginative grasp of his subject often appear to have been made possible by a preoccupation with

dogma. In novelists the discursive intelligence often seems to
interact in all sorts of odd, unexpected ways with the imaginative understanding; perhaps it does in everyone. With some
novelists — possibly all good social novelists — it is hard to
avoid the conviction that insight can be released from the depths
of imagination only by an intellectual commitment to some
dogma.

What is certainly one of the great novels, *War and Peace*, is
an instructive case. There was a serious split in Tolstoy between
his thought-out conception of experience as social history and
his habitual sense of life; it eventually came close to destroying
him as a novelist. The explanatory historical interchapters in
War and Peace that readers frequently skip show how seriously Tolstoy took his own historical doctrine. "There are," he
says in one of them, "two aspects to the life of every man, the
personal life, which is free in proportion as its interests are abstract, and the elemental life of the swarm, in which a man must
inevitably follow the laws laid down for him." Much of the
beautifully imagined life represented in *War and Peace* ac-
cords with this doctrine. Bagration dominates the battle of
Hollabrun, not by directing its course — he is as helpless to do
that as Stendhal's Fabrizio is to direct the battle of Waterloo
— but by consciously submitting to the course of events. His
wisdom consists in recognizing what is happening and acceding
to it. Kutuzov deals with the retreat to Moscow in the same
way. "Instead of an intellectual grasping of events and working
plans," Prince Andrey says of him, he "had only the capacity
for the calm contemplation of the course of events." But this
capacity made him "confident that all would be as it should
be," since if whatever is is not necessarily right according to the
standards of the free individual whose interests are abstract, it
is unavoidable. This attitude is in strong contrast with the attitude of Napoleon, who suffers from a silly delusion that he
can control and direct the course of events: Tolstoy delights in

scenes that show Napoleon's vain and blustering efforts to dominate things, and his eventual defeat is a kind of grand demonstration by life itself that the only wisdom is to "follow the laws laid down for [every man]" insofar as he must participate in the "elemental life of the swarm."

Dreiser is in some ways an even more instructive case because his "peculiar and ever-changing philosophy," as he himself called it (apparently without irony) is in itself incredibly silly. But if it is arguable that the expressions of this "philosophy" constitute what is worst in Dreiser's work, it is also arguable that only his interminable "thinking" about it could bring to the surface of his consciousness those powerful feelings that give his best work its awkward impressiveness. All his life he "philosophized" in his inimitable way over "the sensitive and seeking individual in his pitiful struggle with nature." Yet it was apparently the painstaking elaboration of this doctrine that released from the depth of his imagination all his best characters — Sister Carrie, Jennie Gerhardt, Clyde Griffiths, Aileen Butler — and his best fables.

The superior truth of science had been early impressed on him by a reading of Herbert Spencer, but the only result of this conviction was to make him a lifelong victim of pseudo-scientific cranks, from the people who discover new authors for Shakespeare's plays or diagnose diseases from handwriting to "biologists" like Charles Fort, in whom Dreiser fancied he found support for his religious notions. His speculations along lines suggested by such people are so awful as to have a kind of fascination. Here is one on the sapping idea of "chemism" that keeps popping up in his novels like an insane clown:

> . . . our sensorially perceived personal lacks and surplusages have given rise to the thoughts and final words of good and evil as related to us, our mood in regard to that which befalls us — i.e., lack of balance and proportion in our life (philogenetically

developed, of course). And association and comparison, forced
on us by the chemic sensitiveness of plasma itself, to harm or
help, causes us to contrast our sensitiveness at times of either
harms or helps to us with those of others, as manifested by them
at times of harm or help. These harms or helps . . . are due to
chemico-physical rearrangements and readjustments which related principally to this planet, and this our chemico-physical
race, and accompanied by earthly or chemico-physical wear
and tear.

In this way, the surface of Dreiser's mind was as busy as a
savage's or a child's with "my philosophy" and with observations of the world that he ludicrously misinterpreted in the light
of it; and because his mind was also as unselective as a child's,
nearly all his "philosophy" got into his novels, either directly, as
argument, or indirectly as interpretation — in the absurdly mis-
judged particulars of upper-class life, the movie-magazine heroines he mistook for great ladies, the impossible dialogue. Cow-
perwood, who is supposed to be a man of the world, addresses
his wife as "my fine big baby" and "my red-headed doll" and
convinces supposedly shrewd businessmen that he is a financial
genius by wearing a "light-brown suit picked out with strands
of red, [a] maroon tie, and small cameo cufflinks." We
hardly need to be told that Dreiser was himself a deadly serious
snappy dresser.

Clearly ideas as absurd as these could hardly have survived
even in a mind like Dreiser's had they been only ideas. They
must have had some more powerful source of support than
that, and in fact it is evident that they are rationalizations of
the one thing in Dreiser that is wholly convincing, the fantasy
world of his powerful, primitive imagination. It was the
strength of this fantasy that made Dreiser impervious to sense
and reason, so that he could not see the absurdity of directing
President Roosevelt, when the world was on the verge of war,
to give his full attention to the shocking failure of the Ameri-

can railroads to provide sleeping cars for the poor, or of advising the director of the Rockefeller Institute for Medical Research to stop fooling around and look into "the true function of the Solar Plexus."

Dreiser's long, long "thoughts" appear really to be an elaborate, and probably necessary, ritual for releasing the powerful but imprisoned life of his imagination. The account of Jennie Gerhardt's childhood, for example, is intensely moving, despite Dreiser's muddling about with his social theories, because that muddling has somehow set free the powerfully imagined experience of his own childhood. In *An American Tragedy*, the description of Lycurgus Society is absurd in itself but magnificent as Clyde Griffith's version of upper-class life, because Dreiser's doctrinaire social indignation has set free his stored memories of the vision of upper-class life that dominated the imagination of Theodore Dreiser when he himself was a naïve poor boy.

The problem for writers like Dreiser is apparently how to release from deep beneath the viscous and muddy surface of their conscious minds their imaginative apprehension of their experience, and the only way they seemed to be able to do so is, paradoxically, by a slow roiling of the muddy surface.

The value of doctrine in stimulating the creative process in this way is not, however, the only reason we cannot discard out of hand doctrinal theories of the novel. An even stronger reason is that such theories have some critical validity. The novel is too much a projection of the archetypal patterns of our civilization for us wholly to ignore its mythological aspects, too minutely descriptive of its characters for us to avoid judging it psychologically, too close to history for us to fail to consider the conception of society implied by it. These theories are all talking about things that are in novels; their limitation is to believe that the only thing in novels is what they are talking about. The worst of such assurance is not, perhaps, that it ex-

cludes the understanding provided by rival theories but that
the doctrine behind each theory is confidently identified with
reality itself, with the result that for each theory novels become
illustrations of its doctrine rather than perceptions of the world.

What criticism of the novel needs is a theory that will put at
the center of our attention the world envisioned by the novel,
which will then serve to limit and discipline the exercise of our
metaphysics upon it. Our lot would very much like to circum-
ambulate the novel's charms for the nearly exclusive purpose of
keeping our metaphysics warm. The only valid source of discipline for this corrupting impulse to metaphysical speculation
is the unique object that is the novel itself.

This is only to say what ought to be very familiar, what is at
least very old, that our theory must start with nature — not,
of course, nature in the popular sense that limits the word to
vague emotions about sunsets or those rocks and stones and
trees which, in earth's diurnal course, Lucy was rolled round
with. Wordsworth himself did not mean nature in this limited
sense, much as he cared for it, but was very much aware of the
larger sense of the word that is still, perhaps unconsciously,
preserved in phrases like "human nature" and was certainly
consciously present in the minds of our ancestors when they
asserted that "Nature entitles a Nation to a separate and equal
station." That was, of course, in the eighteenth century, when,
according to Alexander Pope, nature was "still divinely bright,
One clear, unchang'd, and universal light."

Unfortunately for Pope's belief in the fixity of nature's light,
it was scarcely three decades after the *Essay on Criticism* that
novels like *Pamela* and *Amelia* began to represent a nature not
nearly so clear as Pope's and different from it in important
ways. Embarrassing instances of this sort make it seem that, at
least for critical purposes, we do better not to think of nature as
absolute, though we have to remember that critical purposes
are not the only ones in the world or even the only ones we

have to be aware of in talking about literature. As literary critics, nonetheless, what mainly concerns us is that, in any given period, there is *a* nature, a sense of the way things are. This sense is primarily an habitual common consent to certain ways of thinking and evaluating that are never more than partly conscious. As individuals we all, no doubt, deviate from these ways in this or that respect, often without being fully aware we do, since all the world is mad but me and thee, and thou art (unbeknownst to thyself) a little queer.

But no novelist can, without paying an inordinate price, conceive the nature of things in a way radically different from the way his audience conceives it — though he can of course, use one or another of the established variations of the representation of nature that have a specialized or distorted view of it, as Lewis Carroll does; because this variation is established, it includes an unexpressed understanding with the audience about the way things actually are. A novelist's sense of the nature of things may be slightly "in advance" of his audience's or even behind it, but hardly ever apart from it. Even so, if he is very far ahead or behind, he is usually thought brilliant or mad and often just plain mad, and, like such victims of the Elizabethan malady as Hamlet, he is, in an important sense, truly mad. The difficulties caused by the more or less deliberate cultivation of an alien sense of nature are compounded when it is accompanied — as it often is, because the same impulse lies behind both — by an enthusiasm for dramatic representation and imagism.

The assumption behind these theories of expression is that the set of objects or events that evoked the precise feeling in the author will, if set before the reader in exactly the same way they appeared to the author, evoke the same feeling in the reader. Except where relatively crude responses, firmly established by the social habits of the society, are involved, this is a doubtful assumption; where the feeling is an unusual and eccentric one, highly specialized and long refined, it is unlikely that a reader,

even when he is assisted by concealed hints from the author in
the diction and syntax of the ostensibly dramatic and objective
presentation, will be able to determine what he is meant to feel.
It is difficult enough to do so even when all the expressive resources of presentation are used by an author; when they are
not, we are likely to be left with some uncomfortable feeling
that there is an important attitude, a significant complication of
feeling about the subject, that we cannot with the best will in
the world fathom.

In *The Rhetoric of Fiction* Wayne Booth makes this point by
demonstrating that it occurred to no reader to suppose we
ought to read Joyce's *Portrait of the Artist as a Young Man*
with considerable ironic qualification until the earlier version,
Stephen Hero, made it reasonably clear that it was Joyce's intention we should. "But who," as Mr. Booth says, "is to blame
[readers]? Whatever intelligence Joyce postulates in his
reader — let us assume the unlikely case of its being compara-
ble to his own — will not be sufficient for precise inference of
a pattern of judgments which is, after all, private to Joyce." An
analysis of the more complicated exploitation of Joyce's private
pattern of judgments in *Ulysses* is made in Robert Adams' *Surface and Symbol*. Mr. Adams shows us that the events of *Ulysses* are — to use Spenser's term for it in the *Faerie Queene* —
"intendments" only part of the time and that when they are and
when they are not is determined by some impenetrable, private
standard, or perhaps only whimsy, of Joyce's own. He also
shows us that the historical detail of the novel's surface itself
is often untrue, whether because Joyce simply got it wrong or
because he made it wrong deliberately for some indeterminable
symbolic purpose or, perhaps, simply for some private joke of
his own about Dublin.

What Mr. Adams' magnificently patient reading of *Ulysses*
shows us is that the better we read *Ulysses*, the more clearly we
see the extent to which a pattern of private judgments, not even

suggested to us by the dramatic representation of the novel, is at work in it, determining both the character of its surface and the occasion as well as the content of its intendments. Since this pattern of judgments is not only private — that is, almost on principle different from the sense of nature habitual to Joyce's readers even in his own time — but something Joyce's theory of expression prevents his indicating directly, it is in a very real sense incomprehensible. Thus, beyond a certain point in our understanding of *Ulysses*, we can only know that something complicated and important is going on; we cannot know what it is.

But Joyce is the extreme case, the most gifted writer of an age that set out, with Joyce's enthusiastic agreement, to épater the common reader and his grubby sense of life. Most novelists, even in the twentieth century, have been prepared to take seriously the commonly accepted sense of how things are and what they are that controls their age's habitual observation and judgment. This sense has two aspects that are important for them. The first of these is the set of unconscious major assumptions that are hidden behind key terms, for example, in the eighteenth century, terms like "reason," "fancy," "judgment," and "nature" itself, in the nineteenth century, terms like "imagination," "sincerity," "the heart," and, again, "nature." We understand how powerful these unconscious assumptions are in ages that are far enough behind us to have quite different assumptions from ours. We can now see, for example, that eighteenth-century writers often undermined their nominally Christian position by committing themselves to certain rationalist attitudes, without realizing their ultimate consequences; the fundamental assumption of Christian civilization had such a strong grip on their habitual state of mind that it continued to hold its place there long after it had, logically speaking, no business doing so. We can now see how powerfully something like the argument from design operated in the habitual thinking of the nineteenth century to make the world seem a place in

which good would somehow be the final goal of ill, despite
man's conviction that nature red in tooth and claw with ravine
shriek'd against this creed. Such major assumptions are very
powerful elements in the nature of things, all the more powerful because they will be made only half consciously and will go
largely unexamined.

The nature of things will also consist of a very large number
of more evident conventional judgments, the conscious but
habitual conclusions about what things are and what they are
worth that pass with large numbers of men for their carefully
thought-out personal conclusions. There will be visible behind
these conclusions, in a fragmentary form, the theories that support them, and one of the main occupations of intellectuals in
any age is an attempt to make men more widely conscious of
the systems of thought their clichés logically commit them to
(as, for example, the way many of the clichés of conservative
businessmen logically imply a commitment to certain ideas very
like those of Karl Marx, in whose company they like to believe
they could not be caught dead). These conventional judgments are the small change of human intercourse and have a
large part in making us members of the human community,
and perhaps the best source of information about them in
any age is the work of a great normal novelist of that age, a
novelist like Fielding or Trollope.

There is a kind of recognition of the novel's primary dependence on nature in the way novels have always moved toward an imitation of biography, particularly that rather old-
fashioned kind of biography that used to call itself "The Life
and Times of," whether of Tom Jones or Stephen Dedalus, of
Jake Barnes or Phineas Finn. In the earliest days of the novel
this kind of representation was, quite rightly, often called history, what we call today social history: the exact title of *Tom
Jones* is *The History of Tom Jones/ A Foundling*. The vast
majority of novels, in fact, have always been mainly concerned

to show us people who live in the everyday world and act as we expect such people to. Characteristically, that is to say, the body of the novel has been a representation of "the manners and customs of the times."

Novels may therefore be said to represent nature by representing manners, provided that we understand the word *manners* in its most inclusive sense, the sense in which it is used to refer to the expressive habits of behavior of all kinds and classes of people. In this sense it is, for example, a matter of manners when the Negro cook in Hemingway's story, "The Killers," puts his head through the kitchen door and says, "What was it?" (in a situation where the neutral locution is, "What is it?"), as much as it is a matter of manners when Maria Gostrey in James's *The Ambassadors* dines very daringly alone with Strether at his hotel wearing a red ribbon around her neck that reminds Strether of Mary Queen of Scots, instead of the ruche Mrs. Newsome wore in Woollett when she dressed up, which reminded Strether of Queen Elizabeth. It is equally a matter of manners when the antebellum Southern gentleman in Robert Penn Warren's story, "When the Light Gets Green," rebuked by his daughter-in-law for smoking his old pipe at the breakfast table, says with courtly consideration, "Stinks, don't it?" In cases like these the characters are being exactly placed by the system of manners habitual in their societies and being evaluated by being so placed.

The novel has never found a way to touch this one for the simultaneous achievement of immediacy, perspicuity, and subtlety. We need only think for a moment of famous examples like Mrs. Elton in the Woodhouses' drawing room or Mrs. Proudie in the Bishop's study or Levin cutting hay with the peasants to realize its unequaled value. When the novel operates successfully in this way, it persuades us that what it shows is something life says, not just something the author says about life — and rightly so persuades us. The novel, then, may be said to represent nature by representing manners, so long as we remain clear that the word *manners* is not being used in the rather dreary sense it has in the conventional phrase "the novel of manners," but means the gestures and modes of behavior established by a society for the expression of moral attitudes; manners are the outward and visible manifestation of morals.

But if we have to be careful here about the meaning of *manners* we have also to be careful about the meaning of *nature*. We have constantly to remind ourselves when we are thinking about the novel and nature that *nature* does not mean the way things "really" are. In fact, it means to a considerable extent the opposite, if "the way things really are" implies, as it usually does, the way things are conceived to be in the most advanced philosophical or scientific thought of our time. The difference between the way things naturally seem to be and the way they "really" are may possibly be greater in our time than it has been in the past. At least we spend a good deal of time feeling sorry for ourselves on the assumption that it is, though perhaps we ought to be given pause by the fact that many earlier ages have felt equally strongly that New Philosophy had never brought all in doubt as it had in their time. In any event, there has been in every age a recognized difference between the way things naturally seem and the way they "really" are, and someone like our contemporary physicist has always been about to tell people that no doubt to common sense so-and-so seems thus-and-so, but that really it is not at all. But perhaps not even theoretically physicists perceive life as it "really" is in the normal course of their lives.

Whether they do or not, Aristotle was surely right that in a fiction we must prefer the impossible probability to the improbable possibility, because fiction addresses itself to the nature of things, not to the improbable view of them held by the best thought of an age. To show the very age and body of the time his form and pressure is not to hold the mirror to some theoretical construct that is not an habitual part of our way of perceiving things; it is to hold the mirror to nature, to the commonly held conception of things, to the shared, human view of them.

If we assume that this view of things changes from time to time, we must also recognize that it changes only within limits. To some extent we can still understand Homer and the Greek dramatists, as we probably could not if the conception of nature changed very drastically; if it were capable of unrestricted change, it would certainly have changed beyond recognition over the long stretch of time since the beginning of Western culture. Nevertheless it does change. Homer — and therefore presumably his audience — was quite at home with a world that would seem very queer to us. When Odysseus goes up to have a look at Circe's castle, he observes, "But as I was threading my way through the enchanted glades that led to the witch's castle, whom should I fall in with but Hermes, god of the golden wand." "Whom should I fall in with"! The expression is hardly stronger than "Fancy seeing you here," as if running into Hermes, the god, was a little surprising but wholly natural. It would obviously not seem so to us, though quite possibly the things we would naturally expect to run into in a foreign land are, in some absolute sense, more outlandish than Hermes.

At the same time we can glimpse the limits within which our nature differs from Homer's. Odysseus himself is altogether magnificently natural to us, conformable, that is, to human nature as we conceive it. Even the mysterious irrationality of the gods who are ultimately responsible for things is a very human sort of irrationality, and that is more than we can say for the irrationality behind our world. Homer's first causes puzzle us as men puzzle us, but ours are inhuman, and that perhaps helps to explain why the president of the immortals and even humble members of his assembly so seldom appear effectively in novels.

If we assume that the proper study of the novel is to hold

the mirror up to nature, we must be alert for the different ways in which it does so, for the apparently ineradicable tendency of the imagination to isolate for consideration one aspect of nature, to establish a relation with it and to elaborate a set of conventions and short cuts for dealing with it. The subject of literary conventions is a complicated one, for a writer cannot invent a new convention — or at least he does so at the cost of his work — because a convention depends for its success on a mutual and unselfconscious understanding between author and audience. Yet new conventions do come into existence. Perhaps they do so only when some shift in the conception of nature within the culture makes them possible and desirable.

Nevertheless works of literature tend to divide into categories according to the particular aspect of nature that constitutes the focus of their attention. Our ancestors defined these categories as genres, and though the specific definitions of the genres current in other ages are probably not much use to ours, genres themselves might be. In an almost instinctive way our novelists move toward them. Something like the old pastoral, for instance, is certainly represented by the Western and to some extent by any novel dealing with the frontier. John Steinbeck's *Grapes of Wrath* is very like what that fine old pedant Polonius called historical-pastoral. In much the same way we can see novels fitting into categories not unlike, though not absolutely identifiable with, the various kinds of tragedy and comedy defined by the old theory of the genres. It has lately been maintained with great vigor that we shall not begin to understand the American novel until we recognize that it is a form of romance.

The majority of novelists choose, at least by way of emphasis, an aspect of nature — the way things actually happen or some inward action in the characters' psyches or bodies, in society, or in the universe — that seems to them the "real," the important, the significant aspect of our total awareness of experience. Whichever aspect of nature a novelist fixes his attention on, he

will select, emphasize, and — above all — control rhetorically
our sympathies according to its requirements. Thus, there simply is no such thing as an "objective" novel or a "real-life"
novel in the naïve, literal sense suggested by these popular
phrases.

Nevertheless, it makes a good deal of difference what the
novelist fixes on as real; it is his major act of selection and all his
other acts of selection are restricted if not wholly dictated by
this one. It would be very foolish of us as readers to look in
The Big Money for delicate shifts in the characters' psyches,
just as it would be absurd of us to look for the excitement of
what happens in *Ulysses*. The initial commitments to particular
ideas of what is real that Dos Passos and Joyce make exclude
these effects.

None of us is the ideal reader in the sense that he can enter
with equal delight into the representation of every aspect of
reality. Like authors, we have our temperamental or even ideological limitations. Nonetheless, most serious readers recognize
that almost the first thing required for a successful reading of a
work of literature is an understanding of the "kind" of work
it is, and that to approach *Zuleika Dobson* as if it were the same
kind of work as *Emma* or either of them as if it belonged to the
same category as *Moll Flanders* would be disastrous to understanding.

Works of literature divide into classes of another kind that is
more difficult to deal with if not to understand. No individual's
sense of things is wholly identical with the common sense of his
time, since no individual is wholly "enslaved" by what Tolstoy
called "the elemental life of the swarm," any more than he is
wholly free of it. Consequently, each of us has novelists he
loves in a way that seems to his friends excessive. These are
novelists who exploit a sense of life not widespread in our time
but one that we and these novelists happen to share. That exclusive little group of readers who have a high regard for the

work of Ronald Firbank illustrate this eccentricity. Every age
also has its favorite writer of another age and sees him very dif-
ferently from the way other ages — often including the writer's
own — have, because he exploits some sense of things that was
rare in his age but common in another. The reputation of
Donne is a striking illustration of this phenomenon. In the
eighteenth century, Pope thought Donne's verse "a wild chaos
and heap of wit," though Pope's sensitivity to poetry was as
great as any man's has ever been and, ironically enough, his own
work had been influenced, at least indirectly through Dryden's,
by Donne's verse. In the nineteenth century, Coleridge clearly
respected Donne's verse, but without much enthusiasm — as a
professional, you might say. We in the twentieth century, however, think Donne's verse profoundly penetrating — or at least
we have done so until very recently — quite possibly for reasons that would have surprised Donne as much as they would
certainly have shocked Pope.

Finally, we must always allow for the fact that very few
novelists in any age are wholly at ease with the common sense
of things of their time. The superbly normal writer like the
Shakespeare of the early romantic comedies, the Congreve of
Love for Love, the Pope of the *Essay on Man*, or novelists like
Fielding, Jane Austen, and Trollope — the writer like these is
comparatively rare, because superbly normal people are in general rare, and inevitably even rarer among those who are highly
specialized in talent as all great writers are. Most great works
of art exhibit some strain between the artist's personal sense of
things and his awareness of what is the common sense of them.
When the strain is comparatively slight, we get the self-possessed
irony of Jane Austen; when it is somewhat greater we get the
more serious ambiguity of feeling of the late Henry James or of
his master, Hawthorne; when this strain is severe, we get the
exacerbated and disintegrating ambiguity of attitude of *Troilus
and Cressida* or Melville's *Confidence Man*. This is the point at

which the writer begins to ignore, in spite of himself (as bad writers ignore from the start, out of self-regard), the common sense of things. A controlled deviation from the common sense of things is normal in novels; an uncontrolled one produces that kind of fiction T. S. Eliot once said *Hamlet* is, a fiction in which the hero (or even the author) "is dominated by an emotion which is inexpressible, because it is in *excess* of the facts as they appear" — in excess, that is, of any understanding of them possible to our sense of life.

However freely we allow for and admire controlled deviations from nature that express the writers' personal and eccentric sense of things, these deviations only work when they are deviations. If they become central to the work, the work will have at its heart a mystery such as Eliot finds in *Hamlet*, an emotion that is inexpressible in any terms made available by nature. But to work within the limits of nature is not simply a practical necessity; it is also the way the novel achieves what has generally been recognized as its most magnificent effect, the effect that has often been described as Tolstoy's great achievement — so to work that the reader does not feel that he is reading the work of a particular man at all, but feels that he is, simply, there, in an actual world.

War and Peace is natural in this way over a remarkably wide range of experience. Range of this kind is not, of course, the only measure of a novelist's greatness, but it is amusing to compare a novelist like Henry James with Tolstoy in respect to it. It is perhaps possible to imagine Lambert Strether at one of Anna Pavlovna's soirées and to see James judging Prince Vassily about as Tolstoy does. It is not so easy to imagine Strether or James at the Rostovs' house or at Bleak Hills. They would perhaps manage at these places about as unsuccessfully as James did, according to Edith Wharton's famous anecdote, when he tried to consult an English rustic about the route into Windsor ("My friend, to put it to you in two words, this lady and I have just arrived here from *Slough;* that is to say, to be more strictly accurate, we have recently *passed through* Slough on our way here, having actually motored to Windsor from Rye, which was our point of departure; and the darkness having overtaken us, we should be much obliged if you would tell us where we now are in relation, say, to the High Street, which, as you of course know, leads to the Castle, after leaving on the left hand the turn down to the station"). Certainly the imagination boggles at the thought of Strether at the battle of Borodino. But Tolstoy can take his people to all these places, and can take us to them, too.

Tolstoy's kind of effect is central to the novel. Without it, no amount of wit and wisdom, no ingenuity of symbolic implication or manipulated central intelligence will serve; with it, all sorts of doctrinal longueurs and excessive technical ingenuities become endurable and sometimes — as in *War and Peace* or *The Golden Bowl* — clearly necessary to the achievement of the novel's otherwise magnificently natural life. The theory of the novel that we need but have not got is a theory which will be dominated by a concern for this effect. If we take the term "manners" in its broadest sense, then manners constitute the means by which the novel achieves this effect.

The primary concern of the chapters that follow is with this sense of life in novels, their representation of nature, and as a consequence with the manners by means of which they represent nature — or with the want of manners by which they fail to. It is particularly concerned with American novels, in which the problem is made more complicated and interesting by the fact that American novels are usually to some degree — and sometimes to a very marked degree — romances.

II

THE REALISTIC NOVEL IN THE NINETEENTH

CENTURY: TROLLOPE'S PALLISER NOVELS

IF we are to appreciate the difficulties that have confronted the American novelists of our time, we need some norms with which to compare their work, some examples from among novelists of other times and places, of how realism has worked when it has been used and has been wanted when it has not been. The obvious example for the first of these purposes is Jane Austen, but the very perfection of Jane Austen's novels creates a difficulty for criticism that makes it hard to use them as illustrations of anything, especially if you are as a critic, as we all are today, in the same kind of trouble as the novelists you are examining. Of the criticism of poetry today, Mr. Eliot once observed that it "moves between two extremes. On the one hand the critic may busy himself so much with the implications of a poem . . . — implications moral, social, religious, or other — that the poetry becomes hardly more than a text for discourse. . . . Or if you stick too closely to the 'poetry' and adopt no attitude toward what the poet has to say, you will tend to evacuate it of all significance." This is the problem for the critic of fiction, too, and it makes Jane Austen a very difficult novelist for him to tackle.

Emma, for example, is a great novel, but a novel from which it is practically impossible to abstract either a set of implications for a discourse or the evidence for ingenious speculations on technique, though Professor Garrod tried the first in a famous essay and many have tried the second. What *Emma* says is very clear, but it is so nearly identical with what happens in *Emma* (including what happens in Emma's understanding) that even the delicate surgery of modern criticism has not successfully operated to remove one from the other. Jane Austen did not achieve this purity of effect by following the rules of some carefully worked-out craft of fiction, though her letters — which do not much lend themselves to critical operations either — indicate that she was very aware of what she was doing. One of her major resources was that intrusion of the novelist "on the stage" of the fiction that many modern theorists consider the greatest of offenses against decorum. Everywhere in *Emma* she addresses the reader directly, with ease and assurance.

Trollope does the same thing in his novels and has not escaped criticism, as Jane Austen on the whole has, for doing so. In a well-known passage in "The Art of Fiction" Henry James argues in his high-minded way against Trollope's admission "that the events he narrates have not really happened, and that he can give his narrative any turn the reader may like best." This is, James feels, "a betrayal of a sacred office [that] seems to me, I confess, a terrible crime" because "it implies that the novelist is less occupied in looking for the truth (the truth, of course I mean, that he assumes, the premises that we grant him, whatever they may be) than the historian."

This argument sounds a little like the eighteenth century's defense of the unities, which asserted that the unities were the means of achieving literal credibility for a play, and that such credibility was essential to success. So far as the drama is concerned, Dr. Johnson exploded this argument that plays become literally real for the audience in his *Preface to Shakespeare* during the eighteenth century itself, when he pointed out that "he that can take the stage at one time for the palace of the *Ptolemies*, may take it in half an hour for the promontory of *Actium*" and added that "there is no reason why a mind thus

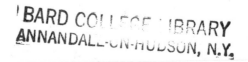

wandering in extasy should count the clock, or why an hour should not be a century in that calenture of the brains that can make the stage a field." "The truth is," as he concluded, "that the spectators are always in their senses, and know, from the first act to the last, that the stage is only a stage, and that the players are only players."

If the dramatist does not have to pay too great a price for observing the unities, they are very convenient devices for giving a play the concentration of action that the limitations of the stage and the need for intensity of effect make so valuable. The devices of the dramatic novel are useful in the same way. But in neither case are these devices necessary parts of the form itself, and it is a mistake to try to make them appear so by arguing that credibility can be achieved only by using them. The novelist who, contrary to the strict rules of the unities, occasionally steps forward to tell the reader that what he is reading is a novel can hardly destroy the truth of his novel, since credibility in a novel, as in a play, is a matter, not of the reader's supposing the events represented are literally happening, but of his supposing it probable that they might happen. The novelist who occasionally jokes with his reader about his story, as Trollope occasionally does, is doing nothing that affects the probability of the novel's action, only something that affects a literal reality it can be supposed a novel will have only for a reader whose mind is "wandering in extasy." Readers of this kind are as undesirable as is the spectator at the play who takes the events on the stage so literally that he cannot resist shouting a warning to the hero when the villain begins to creep up on him from behind.

But even if we accept James's argument that the novelist must never admit "that the events he narrates have not really happened," we must recognize that he is not arguing in general that the novelist ought not to address the reader directly, as critics of Trollope often seem to suppose he is; he is arguing only

against Trollope's occasional assertions that his novels are only
fictions, and may even have meant to argue seriously only
against Trollope's alleged belief "that he can give his narrative
any turn the reader may like best." Trollope would certainly
have agreed with James that the novelist ought not to follow
the whims of his readers in this way; his stubborn refusal, over a
considerable period of time and a number of novels, to respond
to his readers' demands that Lily Dale accept Johnny Eames is a
good example of how little inclined he was himself to give his
novels "any turn the reader may like best."

In any event, James is certainly not attacking the practice of
addressing the reader directly, and Jane Austen's method of narration, to say nothing of that of many other great novelists including James himself, shows that what matters is not whether
the novelist addresses the reader directly but what kind of thing
he says when he does so. What the novelist clearly must not
do in addressing us is to deny or betray what he has established
as the truth in the action of his novel — "the truth, of course I
mean, that he assumes, the premises that we grant him, whatever they may be." If he does not, then what he says to us only
enriches, as it can in many ways, the understanding given us by
the action of the novel. Trollope's novels are like Jane Austen's
in their use of direct address, as they are in other ways.

In a well-known passage in his *Autobiography* Trollope says
he early made up his mind that *Pride and Prejudice* was the best
novel in the English language, and if he later asserted — perhaps partly because of his personal admiration for Thackeray —
that it had competitors for that title in *Ivanhoe* and *Esmond*, his
original choice still defines the general character of his sensibility. Trollope did not, however, so much write novels, in the
narrow sense of the term, as live with characters. This deep-
seated habit of his imagination is what gives him his strongest
resemblance to Jane Austen, who "would, if asked, tell [her
friends] many little particulars about the subsequent career of

some of her people"; she obviously delighted to inform Cassandra of her disappointment at not finding a portrait of Mrs. Darcy at either the Exhibition or Sir Joshua Reynolds' show and to suggest that "Mr. D. Prizes any Picture of her too much to like it should be exposed to the public eye," from a "mixture of Love, Pride & Delicacy." It was her habit to "sit quietly working [sewing, that is] beside the fire in the library, saying nothing for a good while, and . . . suddenly burst out laughing jump up and run across the room to a table where pens and paper were lying, write something down, and then come back to the fire and go on quietly working as before." The social conditions in which Trollope got down the work of his imagination were different (though not less apparently distracting), but not the character of his imagination itself. He too had the habit of living with a group of characters for a long time, and as a consequence his sense of life is best felt in groups of books that deal with the same set of characters.

Critics have usually sought to define Trollope's imagination by examining the Barset novels, but the Barset novels came at the beginning of Trollope's career and the Palliser novels, beginning with *Can You Forgive Her?* (1864), written three years before the last Barset novel, and ending sixteen years later with *The Duke's Children* (1880), were written when Trollope was at the height of his powers. Of the leading characters in these novels Trollope said in the *Autobiography* that "by no amount of description or asseveration could I succeed in making any reader understand how much these characters with their belongings have been to me in my latter life." Characteristically, however, he is not at all sure that this intensity of imagination is not merely a private foible unlikely to be as fully enjoyed by his readers as it is by him. Trollope never assumed that what mattered to him — or anyone else — privately was, or ought to be, important to the world; the source of his most characteristic comedy — as it is the source of Jane Austen's — is rather the assumption that it is not and ought not to be. "Who," he asked himself, "will read *Can You Forgive Her?*, *Phineas Finn*, *Phineas Redux*, and *The Prime Minister* [*The Duke's Children* is omitted from this list because it was written after the *Autobiography*] consecutively in order that he may understand the characters of the Duke of Omnium, of Plantagenet Palliser, and of Lady Glencora? . . . But in the performance of the work I had much gratification. . . ." Perhaps not many people will read these novels consecutively; they constitute a large order, of something over four thousand pages. But they offer the reader much gratification and are the best source of evidence for the kind of greatness Trollope had.

This is a kind of greatness it is not so easy to see as it used to be. All Trollope's weaknesses are in those very aspects of the novel we are now accustomed to scan most attentively and demand the most of. He confessed with almost ostentatious disingenuousness that he scarcely ever knew how a novel was going to end when he started it; he even says of the detective-story plot of *The Eustace Diamonds* that "I had no idea of setting thieves after the bauble till I had got my heroine to bed in the inn at Carlisle." He had so little interest in the delicate cabinetmaking that fascinates artificers of the well-made novel that he hardly ever revised and seldom even read proof with any care (a bad habit in which the publishers of most modern texts have followed him; Trollope at least had the excuse that his typesetters were trustworthy). What he was prone to boast of was that he had never but once (twice, if we count *The Landleaguers*, which was left unfinished at his death) allowed a word of a novel to be printed until it was finished, that he always fulfilled his contracts on the dot, that if his career had any interest it was as an example "of the opening which a literary career offers to men and women for the earning of their bread." The pervasive irony of Trollope's feeling that what matters to him need not necessarily matter to us is at work here, an irony we Americans think of as a peculiarly British sort of swank. But the irony does not make his assertion any less serious so far as it goes. On the contrary.

Trollope was able to say such things because in those respects in which he was a great novelist he was so easily and naturally one and did so much of the work of imagination when he was not at his writing desk that when he sat down he could clock his two hundred and fifty words every quarter of an hour without diminishing the power of his work, just as Jane Austen could compose her novels amid the buzz of conversation in that incredibly tiny library. Moreover, Trollope was, as far as these gifts took him, a novelist of a remarkably pure kind. For better and — in a minor sense — for worse, his gifts were never blurred by abstract ideas, either about the form of the novel or the meaning of life. Trollope had a certain number of opinions, or perhaps only prejudices, that were direct outgrowths of his observations of experience; but he had no ideas in the proper sense. He never reasoned abstractly with any success and, as his remarks in the *Autobiography* show, he seldom analyzed either his own books or others' to any purpose. Another part of his mind, however, understood them with great delicacy as we can see from his occasional observations — for instance, his remark about Dickens that "it has been the peculiarity and the marvel of this man's power, that he has invested his puppets with a charm that has enabled him to dispense with human nature." This part of Trollope's mind is at work everywhere in his novels, and they fail only in those respects in which success depends on abstract reasoning.

About the limitations of these aspects of his work Trollope always displayed that belligerent honesty of his on which critics of his novels have depended heavily for their objections to his work. He thought of a plot as a piece of machinery, something that held together mechanically the characters and incidents, "the most insignificant part of a tale," as he frankly called it.

Because he prided himself on being a conscientious workman, he worked hard over his plots and he was always the first to admit their defects. He says, for instance, in a letter to Mary Holmes that he thinks *The Last Chronicle of Barset* the best novel he has ever written, but he does not hesitate in the *Autobiography* to point out the defects of its plot. He confesses that when he became an experienced novelist he "abandoned the effort to think, trusting myself, with the narrowest thread of a plot, to work the matter out when the pen is in my hand," and he was frank to say that "I am not sure that the construction of a perfected plot has been at any period within my power."

But if the plots of his novels are seldom perfected, they are a good deal better than is usually allowed. The dangers of his procedure are, of course, disproportion, lack of economy, and the possibility that the story may shift direction and be encumbered by awkward commitments made at the start. Trollope knew the dangers: "[*Phineas Finn*] is all fairly good, except the ending, — as to which till I got to it I had made no provision. As I fully intended to bring my hero again into the world, I was wrong to marry him to a simple pretty Irish girl, who could only be felt as an encumbrance on such return." Other instances are easy enough to come by. In *The Last Chronicle of Barset*, for example, we move easily enough from our interest in Grace Crawley to Lily Dale and thence to the old question of Johnny Eames's wooing of Lily and to Johnny's battles with Sir Raffle Buffle. But Mrs. Dobbs Broughton's domestic life and her husband's business career, though they have considerable importance for Trollope's judgment of the way we live now, are much too detailed for the slight connection they have with the main narrative interest. Similarly, though we are interested in Lily and therefore in Adolphus Crosbie's relations with her, the chapters Trollope devotes to Crosbie's efforts to borrow five hundred pounds from Butterwell do not grow logically out of this interest, or lead back to it. But the very cause of Trol-

lope's running these risks, that he started with a group of characters and a situation but no predetermined plot, means that he
seldom imagined a piece of action until he had fully imagined
the movements of thought and feeling in the characters that
produced it. Situations are seldom forced on characters by
the exigencies of plot in Trollope, and this is a considerable
and unusual merit.

To the further dismay of modern critics, Trollope not only
failed to plan his plots in detail; he was also much addicted to
the Victorian custom of starting several stories and running them
alternately throughout the book. In this way, it seems to many
critics, he maximized the occasions for trouble. How are the
narrative links between the stories to be established without awkwardness unless they are planned ahead? How are the large
meanings of the various plots to be unified when Trollope's hit-
or-miss method of composition is followed? A strict interpretation of the unity of action — that it requires a single story —
has its obvious advantages, but as William Empson once pointed
out about plays, "one might almost say that the English drama
did not outlive the double plot"; there is something to be said
for a loose interpretation of the unity of action too, even for
one so loose that it requires no narrative connections between
the stories at all, as in The Second Shepherd's Play.

Trollope does not go that far; he does provide narrative
links between his stories as well as play their meanings off
against one another. *The Prime Minister,* for example, has three
stories or centers of action. There are the Duke and Duchess
of Omnium with their great houses in Carlton Gardens and at
Matching and Gatherum, where the political and social life of
the great world is lived. There are the Whartons in Manchester Square and at Wharton, intermarried with the Fletchers of
Longbarns, living their lives of country gentility and legal dignity. There is Ferdinand Lopez, floating commercially and socially from his very temporary flat in Westminster to Sexty

Parker's office in Little Tankard Yard and thence to The Progress. They are interlocked in innumerable ways, by Arthur
Fletcher's love of Emily Wharton and Lopez's marriage to her,
by the Duchess's taking up Lopez and persuading him to contest
Silverbridge where Arthur Fletcher is running, etc. Each of
them is an independent world with its own integrity and we
know each thoroughly, from inside. But they are not only connected as stories but parallel in character. Trollope had an extremely sharp eye for social differences; perhaps no English
novelist has had a sharper one. But he knew very well that vanity, fear, and lust, unselfishness, courage, and love are much the
same everywhere. It is perfectly obvious that Abel Wharton
and the Duke think and act alike time after time; that Emily
and the Duchess fail in similar ways — and so succeed, too ("I
do not know that she was at all points a lady," said Trollope of
the Duchess in *Can You Forgive Her?*, "but had Fate so willed
it, she would have been a thorough gentleman"); that Lopez
having a dinner brought into Manchester Square from Stewam
and Sugarscraps in Wigmore Street has his resemblance to the
Duchess preparing for her entertainment at Gatherum; and that
Emily's horror at the ostentatious falseness of Lopez's dinner is
like the Duke's feeling that the entertainment at Gatherum is
vulgar. It would not be easy to exhaust the parallels of this
kind in any good Trollope novel; they are one of the main virtues of the multiple-plot structure.

But for Trollope plot construction was nonetheless a second-
ary matter. His main task was to make "the creatures of his
brain . . . speaking, moving" and therefore "living, human creatures"; and he was convinced from his own experience as a
writer that to do so the novelist had to live with these characters
"in the full reality of established intimacy." Though Trollope
put his famous remark about Mrs. Proudie in his usual way, almost as if he were making fun of himself for a silly habit, he
was describing the main secret of his art when he said in the

Autobiography that "I have never dissevered myself from Mrs. Proudie, and still live much in company with her ghost." This was ten years after he had written the last word about Mrs. Proudie. It explains why he wrote Alfred Austin, again in his customary wry way, "My only doubt as to finding a heaven for myself at last arises from the fear that the disembodied and beatified spirits will not want novels," for (as he adds in the *Autobiography*) "I have been impregnated with my own creations till it has been my only excitement to sit with the pen in hand, and drive my team before me at as quick a pace as I could make them travel."

It is easy, much too easy if one wants to convey the full impressiveness of the achieved thing, to generalize the sources of the kind of understanding Trollope possessed. In the first place, he was an indefatigable and fascinated observer. One of his Irish friends once told Escott that Trollope's "close looking into the commonest objects of daily life always reminded her of a woman in a shop examining the materials for a new dress." The comparison is admirable; Trollope's observation was always a homely act of the imagination that found its delight and excitement in the qualities of the thing observed rather than in the qualities of the observer. With this same modesty and quietness he used in his novels the common objects of daily life he observed so lovingly with an almost perfect sense of their relevance to the reader's vision of the action. Objects never exist in Trollope simply for their own sakes; they are always an integral part of the action. Nor does he indulge in trickiness in the way he introduces these objects; nevertheless their effect can be very subtle.

For example, when Phineas Finn meets Lady Laura above the falls of Loughlinter, Trollope gives us a straightforward description of how he was dressed: "At the present moment he had on his head a Scotch cap with a grouse's feather in it, and he was dressed in a velvet shooting-jacket and dark knickerbock-

ers." But the purpose of introducing these particulars is not so
straightforward; Trollope is not telling us how Phineas looked
merely to allow us to see him clearly. He goes on, "[He] was
certainly, in this costume, as handsome a man as any woman
would wish to see." A woman is seeing him, a woman who is
going to love him all her life, whose tragedy is that at this moment she does not even suspect that she cannot conquer her love
for him and marry prudently. This image of Phineas, with his
beauty and his air of breeding, will haunt Lady Laura's imagination for the rest of her life; if we are to feel exactly what she
felt, we must see exactly what she saw.

After Mr. Wharton told Arthur Fletcher that he would
probably have to give in to Emily and allow her to marry
Lopez, Arthur "sat himself down on the river's side and began
to pitch stones off the path in among the rocks, among which
at that spot the water made its way rapidly." Arthur Fletcher
will never forget how the water flowed over those rocks; nor
will Trollope. "*Barchester Towers,*" he once remarked to Arthur Tilley, "was written before you were born. Of course I
forget every word of it! But I don't. . . . I always pretend to
forget when people talk to me about my old books. It looks
modest. . . . But the writer never forgets," because everything he loves, everything he is, is in the actions of those books,
just as everything Lady Laura and Arthur Fletcher are is in
what they saw at the decisive moments of their lives.

Trollope will describe Ullathorne Court to us in detail because it is alive with the innocent passion for blue blood that
guides the Squire of St. Ewold's and is his sister's "favorite
insanity." But the home of that truly insane man, Mr. Kennedy,
will never be more for us than a set of "ionic columns" through
which one passes "to the broad stone terrace before the door,"
because nobody really lives there. In Trollope's novels we always move through the space defined by the characters' consciousnesses, crossing "from Regent Street through Hanover

Square and [coming] out *by the iron gate* into Oxford Street."

This fine imaginative sense of material objects is particularly evident where Trollope wishes to convey emotion, especially if the emotion is artificial or if Trollope, though sympathetic, finds it extravagant. When the moneylender, Mr. Clarkson, attempts to collect from Phineas on Laurence Fitzgibbon's bill, Phineas says, "I can pay no part of that bill, Mr. Clarkson."

> "Pay no part of it!" and Mr. Clarkson, in order that he might the better express his surprise, arrested his hand in the very act of poking his host's fire.

When Mr. Chaffanbrass is accused by Sir Gregory of having "indiscreetly questioned" a witness, he

> would not for a moment admit the indiscretion, but bounced about in his place, tearing his wig almost off his head, and defying every one in Court. . . . The judge looking over his spectacles said a mild word about the profession at large. Mr. Chaffanbrass, twisting his wig quite on one side, so that it nearly fell on Mr. Sarjeant Birdbott's face, muttered something as to having seen more work done in that Court than any other living lawyer, let his rank be what it might. When the little affair was over, everybody felt that Sir Gregory had been vanquished.

Like Mr. Clarkson, Mr. Chaffanbrass is putting on an act, though in both cases the real motives are quite serious, if less marked by moral dignity than the acted ones.

When Tom Spooner proposed to Adelaide Palliser, he first sent back to Spoon Hall for a dark-blue frock-coat and a colored-silk handkerchief and brushed his hair down close to his head. When, thus expressively arrayed, he proposed, Adelaide stopped short in the path in sheer astonishment and Tom Spooner "stood opposite to her, with his fingers inserted between the closed buttons of his frock-coat." After showing us this beautifully revealing scene, Trollope has one of his amused analyses of "why she should thus despise Mr. Spooner, while in her heart of hearts she loved [that more polished and less worthy gentleman] Gerald Maule."

The realization in the form of appearance and manners of characters so continuously significant as Trollope's takes great energy of invention, and it is not the least of Trollope's achievements that he created a whole host of characters and brought them fully to life in this way, in gesture and speech. About the least of them he knows exactly the look and the tone, as he does, for instance, with Major Pountney when the Major is so ill-advised as to approach the Duke with an idea of asking his support at the Silverbridge election.

> "I don't know when I have enjoyed myself so much altogether as I have at Gatherum Castle," [he says by way of working up to the delicate subject]. The Duke bowed, and made a little but vain effort to get on. "A splendid pile!" said the Major, stretching his hand gracefully toward the building.
> "It is a big house," said the Duke.

Because Trollope was involved in the life around him in this fascinated but unself-regarding way, he has what Mr. Cockshut calls an almost "universal pity." He always understands the way the minds of even his worst characters work and sees how they justify themselves to themselves. He also sees the self-regard that makes even the best of his characters comically illogical. "It is amusing," as he once put it, characteristically of himself, "to watch how a passion will grow upon a man. During those two years it was the ambition of my life to cover the country with rural letter-carriers." It was a perfectly respectable ambition and Trollope took real delight in throwing himself into it with all his energy. But no one understood better than he how absurd he must look to the commonsense of those who did not share his passion for so deliciously incongruous an object as covering "the country with rural letter-carriers."

This was the characteristic tone of his mind. His letters are full of it: "My lecture at Bury went off magnificently. I went there in a carriage with a marquis, who talked to me all the way about the state of his stomach — which was very grand." It is very evident in the way he treats his own favorite passions, such as hunting. The great question of Trumpington Woods is a constant concern in the Palliser novels. When Phineas arrives for a visit at Harrington Hall, Lord Chiltern barely has time to greet him because of it.

> "Finn, how are you?" said Lord Chiltern, stretching out his left hand. "Glad to have you back again, and congratulate you about the seat. It was put down in red herrings, and we found nearly a dozen of them afterwards, — enough to kill a pack."

When fine points of hunting are in question, your real devotee recognizes no other claims on his attention.

> "I tell you she didn't. You weren't there, and you can't know. I'm sure it was a vixen by her running. We ought to have killed that fox, my Lord." Then Mrs. Spooner made her obeisance to her hostess. Perhaps she was rather slow in doing this, but the greatness of the subject had been the cause. These are matters so important, that the ordinary civilities of the world should not stand in their way.

Thus it was that Trollope showed how a passion, to say nothing of a habit of life or a fixed conviction, will grow on a man. Even those he hates most, as he hated the parliamentary agents of his unhappy campaign at Beverley, are for him men with their understandable self-justifications; when one of these agents turns up as Grimes in *Can You Forgive Her?* he thinks of himself, however absurdly, as an honest businessman "worth what he'll fetch." When Trollope recalled his own quarrels with Hill at the Post Office, in which "I never scrupled to point out the fatuity of the improper order in the strongest language I could decently employ," he remembered, not only that "I have revelled in these official correspondences, and look back to some of them as among the greatest delights of my life," but that "I am not sure that they were so delightful to others." As a man, Trollope certainly deplored violently such political opinions as were held by Phineas' landlord in Great Marlborough Street. But his imagination gives Bunce a rightness in his conversations and a dignity that only sympathy could create: "He longed to be doing some battle against his superiors, and to be putting himself in opposition to his employers; — not that he objected personally to Messrs. Foolscap, Margin, and Vellum, who always made much of him as a useful man; — but because some antagonism would be manly, and the fighting of some battle would be the right thing to do." One has only to turn the pages of the Geroulds' *Guide to Trollope* to be reminded of how many hundreds of characters he imagined with this understanding.

But if Trollope has almost universal sympathy, he also has almost unfailing good sense. The ironic balance of these two feelings in his work has a delicacy it would be hard to exaggerate. It is what makes us see that so likable a young man as Silverbridge is limited and indeed weak. It is what shows us that so impossible a little man as Major Tifto is touching. When Tifto observes at the Beargarden that " 'By George, there's Silverbridge has got his governor to dinner,' . . . as though he were announcing some confusion of the heavens and earth," and having fortified himself with two glasses of whisky-and-water, engages the Duke in conversation, calling him "my Lord Duke" or "your Grace" a dozen times in as many sentences, we are watching a precise, external show of social uncertainty. But when Silverbridge, in his embarrassment, says, "Tifto, you are making an ass of yourself," and the little man exclaims in outrage and astonishment, "Making an ass of myself!" we are, without ceasing to see how Tifto looks to common sense also seeing how he looks to himself.

The characters Trollope most respected, like Plantagenet Palliser, have some awareness of the distortions of self-regard: "It is the chief torment of a person constituted as [the Duke] was that strong as may be the determination to do a thing, . . . no sooner has it been perfected than the objections of others, which before had been inefficacious, become suddenly endowed with truth and force." In much the same way, Mr. Crawley understands most of his own faults of character, often as he is defeated by them, as he typically is when he tries to tell himself that others have suffered more than he:

> Of what sort had been the life of the man who had stood for years on the top of a pillar? But then the man on the pillar had been honoured by all around him. And thus, though he had thought of the man on the pillar to encourage himself by remembering how lamentable had been that man's suffering, he came to reflect that after all his own sufferings were perhaps keener than those of the man on the pillar.

But it is fundamental with Trollope that even the best men are incapable of seeing themselves with perfect clarity, and one of the finest things he regularly does is to add a shade of self-deception to otherwise admirable characters. Emily Wharton, for instance, is an intelligent, considerate, honest girl. But there is in her just a touch of over-assurance about the rightness of her own judgment. She is not extravagantly overconfident as is Alice Vavasor; nevertheless, her assurance is great enough to lead her, against all advice, into her disastrous marriage with Lopez and — finest of all — to make her cling with just a shade too much self-confidence to her later conviction (an essentially self-regarding conviction) that as Lopez's widow she is not good enough for Arthur Fletcher.

Trollope's greatest delight was to observe the way people's egos and self-interests would lead them quite sincerely to find arguments of principle for what passion or willful prejudice made them believe. Even his villains are only extreme cases

of this sort of self-deception; so Lopez, "to give him his due,
. . . did not know that he was a villain . . . [and] conceived
that he was grievously wronged by [Emily] in that she adhered
to her father rather than to him." The plainly comic version
of such self-deception is the man wholly absorbed by an ob-
session, as are Trollope's imperceptive lovers like Tom
Spooner or Lord Popplecourt or Dolly Longstaff when he woos
Isabel Boncassen, or people like Reginald Dobbes, to whom the
hunting at Crummie-Toddie was everything in life and for
whom "the beauty of the world would be over" if a railroad
were run through that country. When Silverbridge elected to
bring young Gerald to hunt there, Dobbes felt that "Boys who
could not shoot were . . . putting themselves forward before
their time."

But it is the way self-deception will overwhelm normally
reasonable people when self-interest is powerful that fascinates
Trollope most, as when Lady Glencora learns that the old Duke
wishes to marry Madam Max and thinks:

> And to do this for a thin, black-browed, yellow-visaged woman
> with ringlets and devil's eyes, and a beard on her upper lip, —
> a Jewess, — a creature of whose habits of life and manners of
> thought they all were absolutely ignorant; who drank, possibly;
> who might have been a forger, for what any one knew; an ad-
> venturess who had found her way into society by her art and
> perseverance, — and who did not even pretend to have a rela-
> tion in the world!

All this is, of course, fantastically false or distorted. Madam
Max will, indeed, presently become the only intimate friend
Lady Glencora ever makes. But at the moment Lady Glencora
fears the old Duke will marry Madam Max and have a son who
will stand between the dukedom and her own son.

Trollope characteristically gives us both a character's own
view of his conduct and its motives and the commonsense judg-

ment of them. He has two habitual ways of doing so and he often uses them together as he does in presenting Tom Spooner's proposal to Adelaide Palliser discussed earlier. The first is to let us see and hear the character, as we hear Tom Spooner's proposal and see him strike what he conceives to be a manly pose with his fingers inserted between the closed buttons of his dark-blue frock-coat and his hair brushed down close to his head. Here Trollope depends on the reader's own judgment of manners to recognize the ironic qualification of common sense. The second way is to give us the thoughts that accompany the character's actions. It is vital to Trollope's purpose that, however close he keeps to the original thoughts of the character, these passages should be given in summary, in his own words, because it is his own words that here provide the balancing ironic judgment of common sense. This is, of course, also the main reason Jane Austen addresses her readers directly, as the deservedly famous first sentence of *Pride and Prejudice* shows. To understand this motive for addressing the reader directly is to see how blindly doctrinaire it is for critics to rule against it without qualification. Of this form of direct address Trollope was one of the great masters.

The technical achievement of Trollope's novels consists in the right combination of this kind of summary with the direct presentation of action. For example, in *The Prime Minister* Everett Wharton is presented as a pleasant young man who "lacked firmness of purpose."

He certainly was no fool. He had read much, and, though he generally forgot what he read, there were left with him from his readings certain nebulous lights begotten by other men's thinking which enabled him to talk on most subjects. It cannot be said of him that he did much thinking for himself; — but he thought that he thought.

Everett naturally imagines himself perfectly equipped to be a member of Parliament, and when he fails to persuade his father to spend the money necessary to elect him, he feels put upon. But when he learns that his friend Ferdinand Lopez is planning to run, he feels himself really injured. Trollope first lets us hear him on the subject.

> "Upon my word I can't understand you." — he says to Lopez — "It was only the other day you were arguing in this very room as to the absurdity of a parliamentary career, — pitching into me, by George, like the very mischief because I had said something in its favour, — and now you are going in for it yourself in some sort of mysterious way that a fellow can't understand." It was quite clear that Everett Wharton thought himself ill-used by his friend's success.

Trollope knows just what Everett will remember of his previous conversation with Lopez at The Progress; he knows just the tone of Everett's voice ("pitching into me, by George . . ."). But the characteristic touch is Everett's wonderfully irrational conviction that Lopez's greatest offense is "going in for it . . . in some sort of mysterious way that a fellow can't understand."

Having let us see and hear Everett, he then summarizes Everett's thoughts for us with his characteristic combination of sympathy and sense of the absurd way ego translates its needs into principles:

> It was so hard that if a stray seat in Parliament were going a begging, it should be thrown in the way of this man who didn't care for it, and couldn't use it to any good purpose, instead of in his way! Why should any one want Ferdinand Lopez to be in Parliament? Ferdinand Lopez had paid no attention to the great political questions of the Commonwealth. He knew nothing of Labour and Capital, of Unions, Strikes, Lock-outs. But because he was rich, and, by being rich, had made his way

among great people, he was to have a seat in Parliament! . . .
for the moment there came upon him a doubt whether Ferdinand was so very clever, or so peculiarly gentlemanlike or in
any way very remarkable, and almost a conviction that he was
very far from being good-looking.

Like all Trollope's passages of this kind, this one is wonderfully in character, but it is also much more than that. It is
Everett's weakness that he cannot see through Lopez's outward
appearance of gentility and wealth, just as it is Mr. Wharton's
weakness that he distrusts Lopez on quite irrational grounds.
Lopez has got his chance at a seat in Parliament by deceiving
Lady Glencora in the same way he has deceived Everett and
Emily, for he is in fact neither rich nor a gentleman. The opinion Everett expresses in this moment of irritation is quite right,
but it is right for reasons that have nothing to do with his
judgment.

Everett only thinks he thinks about the great political questions of the Commonwealth; moreover, he has never demonstrated the ability to do anything steadily, except to overspend
a generous allowance and to talk authoritatively of how "all
desire for personal property should be conquered and anni-
hilated by a philanthropy so general as hardly to be accounted
as a virtue." His belief in his peculiar competence for Parliament is a comic delusion, bred of a simple desire to have what
he wants: "it was so hard" that someone else should have what
he wanted. Like all of us, Everett moves from annoyance with
a successful rival to a feeling that the rival has no virtues at
all that will justify his success; he is just the man to think cleverness, gentlemanliness, and good looks the major virtues: his
very eagerness to deny Lopez any merit makes more evident his
comic over-evaluation of these qualities. Yet no one knows better than Trollope, who had the outward appearance of none
of them, how useful such qualities are to a man, and how much

they count for in determining the actual loyalties of people a
great deal more intelligent and serious than Everett. Everett is
not appreciably worse than other men; he has only been more
thoroughly exposed. If Trollope makes us feel Everett is ludicrous, he also makes us see how like him we all are.

Nearly everything that is important in Trollope's plots is the
working out of this kind of understanding too — for example,
the melodramatic career and ending of Ferdinand Lopez and
the ironic but delightful conclusion of the novel that establishes Everett as Sir Alrud Wharton's heir. To see this is to see
how much humility there is in such remarks as Trollope's to
Mary Holmes, that "I acknowledge the story of the soi-disant
hero, Lopez, and all that has to do with him, to be bad." The
"happy endings" of Trollope's novels are, as Miss Brown puts
it, "pledges . . . to life, whose demands they have learned to
accept, or to their own integrity which events have taught them
to honour." Trollope is always at pains to show them making
these pledges within the limits of their natures. How perfectly
right in its stupidity and its pathos is Mr. Arabin's unfortunate allusion to Mr. Slope when he first attempts to propose to
Eleanor Bold, how rightly imagined both her knowledge that he
loves her and her irritation at his clumsiness. How exactly adjusted to his character is Chiltern's reply when Phineas con-
gratulates him on his engagement to Violet Effingham after his
long and violent wooing.

> "And is it to be in a month, Chiltern?" said Phineas.
> "She says so. She arranges everything, — in concert with my
> father. When I threw up the sponge, I simply asked for a long
> day. 'A long day, my lord,' I said. But my father and Violet
> between them refused me any mercy."
> "You do not believe him," said Violet.

How precisely imagined is the moment when the Duchess
comes in just as Phineas has proposed to Madam Max and

Madam Max allows herself almost the only fling of extravagance in her life by saying to the Duchess, "I couldn't refuse Mr. Finn a little thing like that." What Trollope said of Mrs. Proudie, that he had a "thorough . . . knowledge of all the little shades of her character," is true of his knowledge of all his characters.

Trollope was, to borrow from Sadleir a figure that was also a fact, a clumsy rider who had "hands." He guided his characters very delicately, showing them moving and speaking in ways that are always perfectly right for them, revealing the exact tone of their minds as they did so. He was not a profound thinker, but he had a profound insight into the way men think. Old Trollope, as Froude said in some irritation (Trollope beat him to the punch with a book on Africa), went banging about the world; but he never missed anything and his imagination was always tirelessly at work, so that both the inner and the outer natures of his characters were "clear to me as are the stars on a summer night." "Mr. Trollope," a London hostess once said to him, "how do you know what we women say to each other when we get alone in our room?" But Trollope always knew everything of that sort.

"I should like of all things," he once wrote Kate Fields, "to see a ghost, and if one would come and have it out with me on the square I think it would add vastly to my interest in life." Of all his characters, the ones Trollope lived with longest and had it out with most on the square were the characters of the five Palliser novels, especially Plantagenet Palliser and Lady Glencora. He thought Plantagenet Palliser "a very noble gentleman," as indeed he is. Who but a great gentleman could have sacrificed himself as he does when he takes his wife abroad? Who could have apologized so nobly as he does to Mrs. Finn? Who could have dealt so gallantly at the Beargarden with the embarrassment of his meetings with Tregear and Tifto? Who — for all his stiffness — could have so beau-

tifully expressed his love for his wife, his sons, his daughter?
Trollope also thought that "Plantagenet Palliser stands more
firmly on the ground than any other personage I have created,"
and he probably does. Of Lady Glencora, he said, "She is by
no means a perfect lady; but if she be not all over a woman,
then I am not able to describe a woman."

Indeed she is all over a woman.

> "Why do you say 'Oh dear'?"
> "Because —; I don't think I mean to tell you."
> "Then I'm sure I won't ask."
> "That's so like you, Alice. But I can be as firm as you, and
> I'm sure I won't tell you unless you do ask." But Alice did not
> ask, and it was not long before Lady Glencora's firmness gave
> way.

She fights with heroic energy against Plantagenet's ignorance
of her feelings and his sisters' advice and gets herself firmly fixed
in a hopeless muddle of mistaken beliefs that she is not going to
give the Pallisers an heir and might therefore just as well run
off with Burgo Fitzgerald. She fights Plantagenet with a flounc-
ing outrageousness that is nevertheless essentially justified.

> "My belief is that [Mrs. Marsham] follows me about to tell
> you if she thinks that I am doing wrong."
> "Glencora!"
> "And that odious baboon [Mr. Bott], with the red bristles
> does the same thing, only he goes to her because he doesn't dare
> go to you."

Nor does she ever forget or forgive. Months later, when the
word reaches them at Basle of the new elections, Plantagenet
says in a melancholy way, "another of my friends in the House
has been thrown out."

> "Who is that unfortunate?" asked Lady Glencora.
> "Mr. Bott," said the unthinking husband.

"Mr. Bott out!" exclaimed Lady Glencora, "Mr. Bott thrown out! I am so glad. Alice, are you not glad? The red-haired man, that used to stand about, you know, at Matching; — he has lost his seat in Parliament. I suppose he'll go and stand about somewhere in Lancashire."

Whenever Plantagenet seeks to remonstrate with her, she says, "I don't want to stop you, Plantagenet. Pray, go on. Only it will be so nice to have it over." He is always trying to mollify her unreasonable extravagance of judgment.

"Since we got out of that horrid boat I have done pretty well. Why do they make the boats so nasty? I'm sure they do it on purpose."

"It would be difficult to make them nice, I suppose," said Alice.

"It is the sea that makes them uncomfortable," said Mr. Palliser.

But such unmodulated reasonableness only strikes her as a disregard of her feelings and makes her more extravagant.

Alice was glad to find [from Mr. Palliser] that a hundred and fifty thousand female operatives were employed in Paris, while Lady Glencora said it was a great shame, and that they ought all to have husbands. When Mr. Palliser explained that this was impossible, because of the redundancy of the female population, she angered him very much by asserting that she saw a great many men walking about who, she was quite sure, had not wives of their own.

When she becomes pregnant and is otherwise quite happy, she is driven nearly frantic by the solicitude of her ludicrously anxious husband. "I wish I had never told him a word about it," she said afterward to Alice. "He could never have found it out himself, till this thing was all over."

These are the husband and wife who, after maturing in

Phineas Finn and *Phineas Redux*, move to the front of the
stage again in *The Prime Minister*. Lady Glencora, now the
Duchess, still has her nimble and often outrageous wit, but she
has matured. There is a faint touch of something that is almost
hardness about her, and she is still incapable of admitting steadily what she can sometimes see, that what she wants her husband to want is only what she wants. Here the serious aspect of
Trollope's irony is at its best. The Duke, with his almost fem-
inine sensitivity and his agonized pride, is always trying to
make the Duchess see his motives —

> but he had come to fear that they were and must ever be unin-
> telligible to her. But he credited her with less than her real in-
> telligence. She did understand the nature of his work and his
> reasons for doing it; and, after her own fashion, did what she
> conceived to be her own work in endeavouring to create within
> his bosom a desire for higher things.

But however clearly she sees his reasons for doing his work, her
conduct is governed by the wonderful self-deception in that
last sentence. When the Duke will not appoint his own wife
Mistress of the Robes, she sulks briefly, and then sets out to
solidify the Duke's ministry in her way, by entertaining
lavishly. It might have worked, for she has great energy and
skill. But not being a perfect lady, she cannot resist making ill-
timed jokes about the ministry to the assembled company at
Gatherum; she will plant her heels about having Sir Orlando
to her parties and thus contributes materially to his resignation;
she cannot quite resist the temptation to say a word to Mr.
Spurgeon, the Duke's agent, about Lopez's candidacy at Silverbridge, despite the Duke's express command that she should not.
Even these errors might not have been fatal had the Duke
had a tougher skin. He is right about the vulgarity of the "assumed and preposterous grandeur [of the Duchess's parties at
Gatherum] that was as much within the reach of some rich

swindler or of some prosperous haberdasher as of himself," but he is too sensitive about it. He is quite right that the Duchess ought never to have laid him open to Quintus Slide's attack on him about Lopez's candidacy and the payment of the five hundred pounds, but he knows that Slide's attack is motivated largely by his own refusal to invite Slide to Gatherum and he ought not to take it so to heart. If the Duchess was small-boy vengeful in her treatment of Sir Orlando, the Duke had already snubbed him with full ducal pride when Sir Orlando first proposed those four ironclads.

Then, to make matters worse, there gradually creeps over him a pride in his political position and a desire to cling to the office of Prime Minister. "He spends one quarter of an hour," as the Duchess says, "in thinking that as he is Prime Minister he will be Prime Minister down to his fingers' ends, and the next in resolving that he never ought to have been Prime Minister at all." She knows, too, how much she has contributed to his difficulties.

> To him a woman, particularly his own woman, is a thing so fine and so precious that the winds of heaven should hardly be allowed to blow upon her [someone ought to study Trollope's skill with Shakespearean echoes]. He cannot bear to think that people should even talk of his wife. And yet, Heaven knows, poor fellow, I have given people occasion enough to talk of me. . . . I could never tell him what I felt, — but I felt it.

She never can because she is always carried away by her energy into acting on the half-truth she understands so much better than he does and then into defending her own actions. When he remonstrates with her about the Lopez episode, he says innocently that other men's wives may do foolish things but that they never interfere in politics, and she cannot resist answering out of the confidence of her short-sighted common sense.

"That's all you know about it, Plantagenet. Doesn't everybody know that Mrs. Daubeny got Dr. MacFuzlem made a
bishop, and that Mrs. Gresham got her husband to make that
hazy speech about women's rights, so that nobody should know
which way he meant to go? There are others just as bad as me,
only I don't think they get blown up so much."

Yet she knows all the time that the Duke cannot endure to believe that his wife is not infinitely finer than Mrs. Daubeny and
Mrs. Gresham — or even to believe that they are not.

Thus they go on, loving one another at cross-purposes, understanding each other without knowing how to say so, until
even the Duke sees he must resign. Even then the Duchess, al-
ternating between the feeling that he is being a coward and
an angry suspicion that he has been egregiously betrayed, refuses to see it. When he soothes himself by a long talk with
Phineas Finn on the theory of liberalism — one of his finest
statements of his political creed — the Duchess cannot resist attacking him.

"Mr. Warburton has sent three messengers to demand your
presence," said the Duchess, "and, as I live by bread, I believe
that you and Mr. Finn have been amusing yourselves!"
"We have been talking politics," said the Duke.
"Of course. What other amusement was possible? But what
business have you to indulge in idle talk when Mr. Warburton
wants you in the library? There has come a box," she said, "big
enough to contain the resignations of all the traitors of the
party." This was strong language and the Duke frowned. . . .

No wonder she loves him and finds him hopelessly inept in
all she counts important; no wonder he loves her and frowns
on her.

Then the Duchess, having committed one more indiscretion
by condoning the secret engagement of Lady Mary and Frank

Tregear (because she remembers how she suffered when she was separated from Burgo Fitzgerald), dies, and the Duke is "as though a man should be suddenly called upon to live without hands or even arms." Like a bunch of firecrackers, the unsuitable engagements of his children explode around him, inducing the comedy of the Duke's inner struggle between his heroic sense of justice and his pride of rank. "If every foolish girl were indulged, all restraint would be lost, and there would be an end to those rules as to birth and position by which he thought his world was kept straight." Remembering how his own Glencora had been separated from Burgo Fitzgerald, he tries his hand, with pathetic clumsiness, at arranging a marriage between Lady Mary and Lord Popplecourt, that foolish young man with "good looks of that sort which recommend themselves to pastors and masters, to elders and betters." At the same time, not knowing that Silverbridge has asked Isabel Boncassen to marry him, he happily lectures her on the democracy of English society, pointing out to her the way in which "our peerage is being continually recruited from the ranks of the people." "But there was an inner feeling in his bosom as to his own family, his own name, his own children, and his own personal self, which was kept altogether apart from his grand political theories."

In the end, however, because he is a just man and Frank Tregear is a gentleman and Isabel not only a lady but perfectly suited to Silverbridge in her goodness of nature and even in her somewhat limited intellect, he comes round; and because he is a great gentleman he comes round with his whole nature: "You shall be my own child, — as dear as my own," he says to Isabel, and we know he means it with all his heart. To be sure, as Silverbridge, with one of those flashes of shrewdness that characterize him, points out, "My belief is that he's almost as much in love with you as I am." Certainly Isabel has her touches of Glencora; when the Duke says with all his solemn dignity, "I almost forgot my own boy's name because the practice has grown up of calling him by a title," Isabel says irrepressibly, "I am going to call him Abraham." More than anything else, perhaps, it is this that makes the Duke give her the ring the Duchess had always worn.

The action Trollope constructs around this central conflict is more perfectly integrated and is carried on with more comic energy than any other in the Palliser series; the book teems with life. "Have you ever read the novels of Anthony Trollope?" wrote Hawthorne. "They precisely suit my taste, — solid and substantial . . . and just as real as if some giant had hewn a great lump out of the earth and put it under a glass case, with all its inhabitants going about their daily business, and not suspecting that they were being made a show of." Trollope described this remark as "a piece of criticism which was written on me as a novelist by a brother novelist very much greater than myself."

III

THE NOVEL OF DOCTRINE IN THE NINETEENTH
CENTURY: HARDY'S *Jude the Obscure*

A READER may grant that Trollope's novels are, within their
limits, "as real as if some giant had hewn a great lump out of
the earth," and still feel their limits are too narrow, that neither
the great issues of life nor the particular social and political
events in which they manifested themselves in Victorian society are included within these limits. Where, he may ask, are
all the problems of Victorian times that critics like Matthew
Arnold dealt with? — the poverty and suffering, the revolutionary mutterings of the working classes, the crass vulgarity
of the prosperous middle class, the pompous irresponsibility and
inefficiency of the aristocracy? They are simply not there, or
are only indirectly there when some individual example of
them — like Adolphus Crosbie or the De Courcys — falls under Trollope's observation.

Such a reader may feel that without a vigorous and direct
concern for such problems, a novelist may be entertaining but
hardly important, may feel that social ideas are necessary to
direct and discipline the novelist's otherwise irresponsible or at
least random imagination and that even a muddled set of social
ideas will be, as perhaps Dreiser's was for him, the means of releasing the powers of his imagination in a useful way. But it
needs to be considered that a serious and responsible commitment to a doctrine may also be a means of preventing such a release. When it is, the signal will probably be a consistent and,

indeed, often ingenious narrative structure that conforms to the
doctrine. Hardy is an interesting writer to consider in the light
of this possibility. He had a powerful and, in the best sense of
the word, primitive imagination; he was also a careful if not
very original thinker who took the ideas he was committed to
with the utmost seriousness.

There is widespread critical agreement that Hardy's essential vision of life was not merely gloomy — a matter of temperament — or pessimistic — a matter of intellectual commitment — but tragic. There appears also to be a widespread feeling that somehow his novels are not wholly successful, are not,
for all their deep sense of the horror of ordinary life, really
tragic. "There is," as E. M. Forster put it, "some vital problem
that has not been answered, or even posed, in the misfor-
tunes of Jude the Obscure." Hardy's deepest and most persistent feeling about experience appears to have been the one he
put in "Seventy-four and Twenty" when he contrasted the
young man who could read life's "very figure and trim" with
"the breezy sire who cannot see/ What Earth's ingrained conditions are."

His failure to realize satisfactorily his tragic sense of "what
Earth's ingrained conditions are" in *Jude the Obscure* may well
have been the consequence of an attitude he shared with his
age rather than of one peculiarly his own, for many Victorian
writers seem to have restrained or even suppressed their deepest
feelings, when these feelings were of a melancholy character —
Tennyson is the obvious example — in the interest of some
doctrine, especially of some religious or social doctrine.

Hardy did not, as did many of the writers of his age, identify
what he called "the ideal life" with the conventional idealism
of his time. He was, on the contrary, often devastating about
this conventional idealism: "How could smug Christian optimism
worthy of a dissenting grocer find a place inside a man
[Browning] who was so vast a seer and feeler when on neutral

ground?" Yet at bottom Hardy's pessimism suffered from the same limitation as Browning's optimism. Browning thought he had to assert that all was right with the world because he believed that God was in his heaven. Hardy convinced himself that there could be no heaven because all was obviously not right with the world. So rigid a commitment to logical consistency of doctrine appears to have restricted Hardy's imagination severely. It needed some hope of heaven; that hope is at the heart of his vision of life, the source of his dissatisfaction with the world as it is. If he cannot locate it somewhere outside time — in some "type of paradise," as he called it, some pastoral world, or Golden Age of Pericles, Elizabeth or the antebellum South — he must place it in time, make it the higher thing to which mankind will inevitably rise, in the course of history, on stepping-stones of its dead selves. As a nineteenth-century agnostic, Hardy thought he was bound to choose the second of these alternatives; he called it meliorism. This commitment to meliorism was at best half-hearted, a desperate remedy resorted to only for want of better. "It may be added here," Florence Hardy says in *The Later Years*, "that the war destroyed all Hardy's belief in the gradual ennoblement of man, a belief he had held for many years. . . . He said he would probably not have ended *The Dynasts* as he did end it if he could have foreseen what was going to happen within a few years."

As a view of man's historical fate, meliorism may conceivably be the best available. But Hardy was clearly trying in his novels to express a tragic feeling about experience, and there is a serious difficulty for the imaginative sense of tragedy in meliorism, just as there is in Browning's optimism. Browning and Hardy alike found it impossible to believe in both "the goodness of God" and in "the horror of human and animal life," as Hardy called them. They thought they had either to see human life as logically consistent with the ideal life, or to see the ideal life as a logical development (sometime in the future, of course) of a human life that is, at present, a horror.

This inability to escape the demands of some kind of doctrinal consistency may have been the major problem for Victorian literature as a whole. "There is the assumption that Truth is indifferent or hostile to the desires of men; that these desires were formerly nurtured on legend, myth, all kinds of insufficient experiment; that, Truth being known at last in the form of experimental science, it is intellectually impossible to maintain illusion any longer, at the same time that it is morally impossible to assimilate Truth," as Allen Tate once summed up the Victorian's difficulty. If this be true, then the doctrine that created such difficulties for Hardy the novelist was largely a product of the Victorian climate of opinion, and it may well be more remarkable that he came as close as he did to escaping it than that he was, finally, trapped.

The doctrine Hardy adopted as a description of the ideal life toward which he believed mankind was slowly moving through history is a secularized version of the Sermon on the Mount. The real subject of *Jude the Obscure* is the story of the way this doctrine gradually developed in Jude's mind; Hardy calls him "a species of Dick Whittington, whose spirit was touched to finer issues than a mere material gain." Insofar as this doctrine is a description of imaginable conditions of life Hardy believed realizable somewhere, somehow, it gives Jude's death meaning. Insofar as it is a description of imaginable conditions he could not believe realizable anywhere or any time, Jude is a little mad and his death is meaningless: this second implication was obviously no part of Hardy's intention. But Hardy could not suspend even for a moment his disbelief in a place outside time where these possibilities would be realized. Consequently he was forced to think they would be realized, however slowly, in this world — forced, that is, to assert that earth's ingrained conditions are not ingrained. If it is difficult to imagine that the temporal life of man is evil and that an eternity exists where life is not evil, it is even more difficult to imagine that the ingrained evil of temporal life will, in due time, evaporate.

Hardy's best novels are powerfully moving despite his inability to escape this difficulty; and that is a great tribute to the purity and depth of his feelings about human experience. In this sense the power of his novels is striking evidence of the integrity of his imagination; the continuity of feeling throughout both the novels and the poems shows how deep his feeling of the horror of human life really was, and it is remarkable how that feeling comes through in his work despite his failure to organize his stories in a way that would allow them to realize what he called "his personal impressions."

About the idea around which *Jude* is organized he was quite explicit. *Jude* was "to show the contrast between the ideal life a man wished to lead, and the squalid real life he was fated to lead. . . . [This] idea was meant to run all through the novel." The phrasing of this idea is revealing; the novel does not deal with "the ideal life men wish to lead" but with "the ideal life *a man wished* to lead." The novel does not, that is, show us an individual but representative man caught between the permanent and unavoidable demands of the life he is living and the possibilities of a life without these limitations that he might live. No life without these limitations exists for Hardy; it is only the daydream of Jude, a particular man who lived at a specific time in history, whose experience is presented with all the scientific and historical accuracy — all the "Truth," that is — Hardy can give it; Jude's life is in fact closely modeled on Hardy's own. "There is something [in this] the world ought to be shown," he said in his journal of his plan for *Jude*, "and I am the man to show it them — though I was not altogether hindered going, at least to Cambridge, and could have gone up easily at five-and-twenty." The fundamental conception of re-

ality in the novel, then, is historical; and in the history of his
times Hardy found no realization of the ideal life, either in this
world or in any other. The only existence that life can have
in the novel, therefore, is as a daydream of Jude's.

But because a vision of the ideal life is crucial to Hardy's conception of experience, he must put the weight of his authority
behind Jude's dream. He can do so only by identifying himself
as author with his central character, by dreaming, as Jude does,
that in due time the ideal life will be realized in this world.
Hardy's feelings are not represented by the action of *Jude the
Obscure* as a whole; they are represented by Jude. At the
same time, Hardy's sense of the conflict between the possibilities of life and its actualities was so powerful that he was constantly reaching out for means to express it in the action of the
novel. He found it impossible to stay within the limits set for
his story by historical truth even while he persisted in making historical truth the criterion of probability for it. The difficulty about the much discussed coincidences of Hardy's novels
is not that coincidence is in itself a fault; in fact, in certain
kinds of fictions something very like coincidence — that is, a
persistent patness of event — is an almost necessary virtue. The
difficulty with Hardy's coincidences is that such persistent patness of event is glaringly inconsistent with the kind of probability scientific history knows. The same objection holds against
Hardy's carefully planned symbolic contrasts. "Of course the
book is all contrasts . . ." he said, "*e.g.*, Sue and her heathen
gods set against Jude's reading the Greek testament; Christminster academical, Christminster in the slums; Jude the saint,
Jude the sinner; Sue the Pagan, Sue the saint; marriage, no marriage; &., &." These contrasts, for all Hardy's attention to
them, are superficial; they are not manifestations of a contrast
that is fundamental, because at bottom Hardy's novel is committed to a monolithic truth.

The nearest Hardy came to ignoring this truth was in his

treatment of the life of his Wessex peasants, which he sometimes came close to representing as a pastoral idyll. He was
clearly tempted to see their life as what he called "a type of
Paradise"; "it is the on-going — *i.e.*, the 'becoming' — of the
world that produces its sadness," he observed. "If the world
stood still at a felicitous moment there would be no sadness in
it. The sun and the moon standing still on Ajalon was not a
catastrophe for Israel, but a type of Paradise." The life of his
Wessex peasants in the old days seemed to him a felicitous moment, and he was greatly tempted to think that life was somehow exempt from time and would exist forever, to believe that
"this will go onward the same/ Though Dynasties pass."

But he was too honest a man to allow himself to think so for
long; the doctrine to which he was committed told him the
on-going of the world affected everything that existed, including Wessex. The life of the Wessex peasants can be for him
only a charming but essentially irrelevant anachronism, an example of the simpler and easier life of the past, preserved for
his day by an eddy in time. For the same reasons the comments of these peasants on the novel's main action, though
Hardy uses them chorally and seems to suggest they are expressing some unchanging wisdom, can be only the expression
of attitudes perhaps practical a long time ago but wholly imprac-
tical in Hardy's day. When Mrs. Edlin says of Sue's marriage,
"In my time we took it more careless, and I don't know that we
was any the worse for it," or when she is heard "honestly saying the Lord's Prayer in a loud voice, as the Rubric directed,"
she is only showing us how much more felicitous life was before man had developed with the on-going of the world to his
present high state of nervous and emotional organization. However much Hardy may wish to do so, he cannot honestly make
Mrs. Edlin a voice from some pastoral world, an Arden to which
Jude may flee from the squalid world of Duke Frederick's
court; if Mrs. Edlin and the rest of Hardy's Wessex peasants are

actual at all, then they exist in the same world as Jude and their life is subject, whether they know it or not, to the same historical changes as Jude's.

The moments of happiness that come in most of Hardy's novels just before the catastrophes constitute a similar problem. Grace and Giles in Sherton Abbey while they still believe the divorce possible, Tess and Angel between the murder of Alex and the arrest at Stonehenge, Jude and Sue at the Wessex Agricultural Show — these are felicitous moments when the characters believe they are living in "a type of Paradise," a kindly country world where the pure in heart may live as their hearts desire. Only what is, in Hardy's historically probable world, great naïveté on their part or the introduction of a staggering amount of coincidence by Hardy can produce such delusive moments. Moreover, because Hardy was an honest man, he felt obliged to show us that these moments were a fool's paradise — except, of course, as they might constitute a foreshadowing of the life of a reformed humanity sometime in the remote future, that larger hope Hardy so very faintly trusted.

The only place Hardy's conception of reality provided for a type of paradise was the remote future. It seems likely that he did not believe very strongly in the possibility of its existence even there; in any event, he does not describe in any detail in his novels what the world will be like after men have been gradually ennobled and the weary weight of all the unintelligible present has been lightened. To have done so would have been to suggest openly that the horror of human life is only temporary, that Earth's conditions are not so deeply ingrained as he felt them to be. Had the contradiction inherent in his work been made that obvious, he might well have seen it himself and been wholly baffled. Yet however faintly Hardy represents the ameliorated future, he has to make it at least implicit in his account of Jude's life; otherwise Jude's dream of the ideal life, to which Hardy as author of the book has committed all his hope, is pure delusion.

Insofar as Hardy's novels do rest, however uncertainly, on a belief in a felicitous moment in the remote future that, once attained, will become permanent, their meaning is the meaning of sentimental pastoral. They are what *As You Like It* would be without Jaques to put us and the Senior Duke in mind that "the penalty of Adam" was not merely "the season's difference" but the inescapable knowledge of good and evil, without Touchstone to convince us that the homely everyday necessities of life, such as his weariness of legs and physical desire for Audrey, are as eternal and, in their way, as significant as the spiritual necessities, such as Rosalind's weariness of spirits and her love of Orlando — to say nothing of Silvius' love of Phoebe.

If Hardy could have seen the world of *The Woodlanders* as a refuge and trusted Grace's natural wisdom and refinement of sensibility without worrying over her lack of formal education (after all, only urban society's artificial substitute for natural wisdom and refinement, in Hardy's view) he would have had a world for

> the innocent,
> The mild, the fragile, the obscure content
> Among the myriads of thy family.
> Those, too, who live the true, the excellent,
> And make their daily moves a melody.

The advantage would have been twofold: he could have presented the life of the pure in heart as an actuality (I suppose it would have looked something like the life of Wordsworth's Michael); and he would have been able to free his representation of ordinary life from the intolerable burden of blame he heaps on it for not being suitable to the pure in heart. As it is, Hardy is unable to do the life of ordinary men anything like the justice it deserves. Jude must live in the ordinary world because there is no other, and Hardy, concerned with the hopeless inadequacy of that world to Jude's dreams, is too preoccupied with showing us how wickedly it ignores Jude's purposes to show us what its own purposes are or what justification there is for them.

It is as if Shakespeare had first made Hamlet believe that the evil of the world is curable (as Jude and Hardy suppose it is) and had then shown us Claudius only as Hamlet sees him (as Hardy shows us Arabella only as Jude sees her). Hardy's Claudiuses are not mighty opposites; they are wholly inexplicable villains. At most, Hardy can give Arabella credit for being well adjusted to the world as it is at the moment, and the only irony he can direct against Jude is to suggest the lack of worldly wisdom Jude displays because, in his preoccupation with the values that will emerge in the future, he is badly maladjusted to the present world. There is no permanent justification for Arabella, because the world she belongs to is, however horrible, a temporary one that will only be kept in existence longer than it otherwise would be by the satisfaction people like Arabella take in it. There is no permanent defect in Jude's attitude because it is exactly the attitude required for the world that will in due course emerge — unless the temporal life of humanity is meaningless in a sense *Jude the Obscure* never considers.

The "vital problem that has not been . . . even posed" in *Jude the Obscure*, because Hardy's doctrine would not permit it to be posed, is the problem raised by the very real if limited wisdom of the Arabellas and the Claudiuses of this world:

> For what we know must be, and is as common
> As any the most vulgar thing to sense,
> Why should we in our peevish opposition
> Take it to heart? Fie! 'tis a fault to heaven,
> A fault against the dead, a fault to nature,
> To reason most absurd. . . .

Nor could Hardy recognize in *Jude* the real, if terrible, absurdity of Hamlet's "Go to, I'll no more on't; it hath made me mad. I say, we will have no more marriages. . . ."

Because Hardy's feelings are identical with Jude's, Arabella is shown to us in the novel only as Jude sees her; her conduct thus remains for us what it is for Jude, the consequence of an inexplicable and brutal stupidity rather than that of a different kind of wisdom from Jude's. This is a terrible price to pay for the preservation of a doctrine. Nobody understood better than Hardy did the point of view of those men and women for whom "the defense and salvation of the body by daily bread is . . . a study, a religion, and a desire," but his doctrine did not allow him to recognize the wisdom of this point of view; the word I have omitted from this quotation is "still" — "is *still* a study, a religion, and a desire"; clearly this attitude seemed to Hardy an anachronism, an inexplicable clinging to a way of feeling outmoded by the "nobler instincts" in man that pointed to a reformed world due to be realized by "progress."

That was one price Hardy paid in *Jude* for his meliorism. Another was his inability to conceive the possibility that a woman like Sue might, not in weakness but in strength, deny the validity of Jude's humanitarian idealism. It is one thing for Jude to preach to Sue the horror — for his idealistic point of view — of her final surrender to Phillotson and conventional conduct, or for Hamlet to preach to his mother the horror of letting "the bloat king tempt you again to bed." So far, we have only the limited and explicable attitude of a character — and, in the case of Hamlet, a character whose exaggerated revulsion from ordinary human love is clear in every phrase he uses. It is another thing for Hardy, who does, or for Shakespeare, who does not, to commit himself as author to this sermon and thus make it the attitude, not of a character within the fiction, but of reality itself.

At the same time that Hardy is representing people like Arabella as inexplicably cruel, however, he is also implying — inso-

far as he does imply that the world will in due course become
the place Jude dreams it will — that they will become noble
and kind. Thus Hardy's doctrine forces him to treat ordinary
men and women at once unjustly and sentimentally. Since he
can accept only a single reality, that of history, he must make
the human beings who constitute it appear brutal and cruel in
order to realize his horror of ordinary life, and also potentially
good, in order to make his meliorism plausible.

Jude the Obscure is, then, the history of a worthy man's education, of " a species of Dick Whittington, whose spirit was
touched to finer issues than a mere material gain." Part One of
the novel deals with Jude's youth, up to the moment he departs
for Christminster in search of learning. From the very beginning, however, both Jude himself and the world in which he
lives are presented as they appear to one who has accepted the
view of life that will be the end product of Jude's education.
Insofar as Jude already shares this view of life, he is not dram-
atized; he is the author. Insofar as, in his innocence, he is ig-
norant of truths he will later come to understand, he is drama-
tized, subject, that is, to Hardy's irony.

So long as Jude's education is incomplete, then — and to some
extent it is incomplete even when he dies — Hardy uses him to
demonstrate the consequences of innocent ignorance of "Nature's logic." In Part One of the novel, this is largely a matter
of sex. Nature entangles Jude with Arabella, who turns out
to be something his idealism is not prepared for. Hardy gives
this demonstration a complicated poetic elaboration that may
make the reader suppose he is pitting against one another two
different conceptions of experience, each in its own way valid.
That he is not, however, is clear from the fact that he takes advantage of every opportunity to support Jude's view of sexual
relations and to condemn Arabella's.

The poetic elaboration of this episode is characteristic of the
procedure of the book as a whole, of how Hardy's feelings,

striving to find an adequate expression, are constantly breaking
through the limits of the historical form to which his doctrine has committed him. The meeting of Arabella and Jude is
brought about by Arabella's hitting Jude with a pig's pizzle,
which hangs on the bridge rail between them throughout this
first meeting. It is, potentially, a fine image for what brought
them together — an image capable of representing both Jude's
disgust of sex as mere sex and Arabella's country-bred recognition of its homely realities. The trouble with Hardy's use of
it is that he allows only one aspect of it to exist in the novel. To
Arabella, as we shall see later, pigs are domestic animals with a
certain practical value for those to whom "the defense and salvation of the body by daily bread is . . . a study, a religion,
and a desire." To Jude, however, they are "fellow mortals"
and to consider them as Arabella does is to both him and Hardy
as inexcusable as it is to think of sex as she does. It is illuminating to compare Hardy's treatment of this image with the
scene in Allen Tate's *The Fathers* in which George Posey is
represented as not only too refined but too uncivilized to be
able to bear the sight of a bull mounting a cow. (See pp. 282-83.)
In Mr. Tate's scene, we understand and share the feelings of
both George Posey and of Major Buchan, but in Hardy's scene,
we share only Jude's feelings.

   Jude's dream of an education that will take him through
Christminster to a career as a philanthropic bishop is associated
with a vision of Christminster as seen from the roof of the
old Brown House against the blaze of the setting sun, like the
heavenly Jerusalem, as the child Jude says solemnly to the tiler.
This dream is also associated with the New Testament. In its
strictly moral aspect, the New Testament is the textbook of
Hardy's humanitarian morality; in admiring the New Testament's moral teaching, Jude is therefore demonstrating what
Hardy thinks instinctive humanitarian feelings. But to Jude
the New Testament also represents religion and learning (it is

a Greek text); in valuing it on these counts, Jude is demonstrating what Hardy thinks illusions.

During Jude's wooing of Arabella there are sporadic recrudescences of these symbols. For example, Hardy frequently brings the two lovers back to the rise on which the old Brown House stands, from which Jude had once seen his vision of the heavenly Jerusalem and where, under the influence of an impulse rather awkwardly motivated, Jude had also once knelt and prayed to Apollo and Diana, the god and goddess of learning and chastity. Under the influence of Arabella, Jude "passed the spot where he had knelt to Diana and Phœbus without remembering that there were any such people in the mythology, or that the sun was anything else than a useful lamp for illuminating Arabella's face." When the lovers stop at a tavern, Hardy notes that a picture of Samson and Delilah hangs on the wall; they stop for tea but instead, partly at Arabella's suggestion, drink beer (Arabella had been a barmaid). Thus Hardy links Arabella to Jude's "two Arch Enemies . . . my weakness for women and my impulse to strong liquor."

Images of this kind are handled with a good deal of skill and subtlety in the novel: Hardy clearly had a natural tendency to see experience in terms of them. But they remained localized and sporadic because the narrative as a whole never becomes an image of life: it is simply a history, and all its major objects and events are wholly natural objects and historically probable events. For example, in the climactic scene of Part One, the pig-killing scene, the pig is simply a pig. Arabella's attitude toward it is consistent with the attitude she has maintained throughout; her concern is practical; she wants the pig killed in such a way as to produce the most salable meat. Even when the pig squeals and she urges Jude to kill it quickly, she does so only because she feels a conventional social fear that the neighbors may discover the Fawleys have sunk to killing their own pig. When Jude protests against the "inhumanity" of slowly bleeding the pig to death, she says quite simply, "Poor folks must live." Hardy's description of the incident altogether precludes our sympathizing with this attitude, though Hardy obviously *felt* that it is in its own way profoundly true.

In direct contrast to Arabella's practical view of this killing Hardy set Jude's idealistic view of it: "The white snow, stained with the blood of his fellow-mortal [that is, the pig], wore an illogical look to him as a lover of justice, not to say a Christian. . . ." There is irony here, of course, but it is directed solely to the point that Hardy "could not see how the matter was to be mended" at this stage in human history, not at all to the point that in one very real sense, the sense that Arabella understood, it could never be mended in this world, and conceivably ought not to be. In every other respect, Hardy is wholly committed to Jude's view of this incident, as is clear from what he himself writes about it; for example: "The dying animal's cry assumed its third and final tone, the shriek of agony; his glazing eyes rivetting themselves on Arabella with the eloquently keen reproach of a creature recognizing at last the treachery of those who had seemed his only friends."

By putting the full weight of his authority behind Jude's view of the pig-killing in this way, Hardy makes Arabella's view of it appear inextricably hard-hearted, however commonplace. He can see that Arabella's complete unconsciousness of Jude's attitude — and his — is grimly comic: " ' 'Od damn it all!' she cried, 'that ever I should say it! You've over-stuck un! And I telling you all the time —' " But he cannot see that she is in any sense right. As a result the scene as a whole becomes sentimental about pigs and brutally uncomprehending about Arabella. It is, in fact, difficult to avoid thinking of it as an unintentional parody of the murder of Duncan, with the pig cast as the king and Arabella as Lady Macbeth. The reader is expected to associate this scene with the earlier one in which Farmer Troutham whips Jude for allowing the rooks to eat his corn. Hardy

shares — and requires us to share — Jude's feelings about the
rooks; for him they "took upon them more and more the aspect
of gentle friends and pensioners. . . . A magic thread of
fellow-feeling united his own life with theirs. Puny and sorry
as those lives were, they much resembled his own."

This anthropomorphic view of animals is a commonplace
in pastoral fictions: Jacques habitually moralizes in a sentimental vein on the animals in the Forest of Arden and even the
Senior Duke deplores the necessity of killing the "native burgh-
ers of this desert city." But we are not in a pastoral forest in
Hardy's novels; we are in the ordinary world, and Hardy
means us to see his animals as quite literally "fellow-mortals,"
as is all too clear from his poem "Compassion: An Ode in Celebration of the Centenary of the Royal Society for the Preven-
tion of Cruelty to Animals." It is a little difficult not to wonder about the domestic economy of Hardy's ideal world if it is
going to have to provide as lovingly as Farmer Troutham is
apparently expected to for plagues of locusts, rooks, and other
small deer.

Part Two of *Jude the Obscure* (at Christminster) brings
Hardy's spiritual Dick Whittington to his London, where he is
taught that his desire for learning had been only "a social un-
rest which had no foundation in the nobler instincts; which
was purely an artificial product of civilization." At the very
beginning Jude catches a glimpse of what Hardy flatly asserts is
the truth: "For a moment there fell on Jude a true illumination; that here in the stone-yard was a centre of effort as
worthy as that dignified by the name of scholarly study within
the noblest of the colleges." Phillotson is used in this part of
the novel to foreshadow Jude's discovery of this truth and to
suggest what happens to a weak man when he makes this discovery. Arabella's temporary conversion after Catlett's death
has a similar formal relation to Sue's conversion, with the addi-
tional irony that Sue's conversion involves a return to the ac-

tive sexual life she hates and Arabella's a loss of it that she cannot stand.

After Jude has discovered that in this world learning is a fraud, he has only his belief in the nobility of the Church to sustain him. Hardy tells us directly that he will soon discover the Church is "as dead as a fern-leaf in a lump of coal." This comparison reminds us once more that Hardy believes social change, the "on-going" of history, is a part of the evolutionary process of nature and explains why he makes much of the tearing down of the "hump-backed, wood-turreted, and quaintly hipped" Marygreen church and the construction of a "tall new building of German-Gothic design" in its place.

Meanwhile Jude meets his cousin Sue. We always see Sue as Jude first saw her in the picture at Marygreen, "in a broad hat, with radiating folds under the brim like the rays of a halo." Sue never ceases to be, in Jude's eyes, a saint, and by a terrible irony, she becomes at the end of the novel something like what conventional Victorian opinion thought of as a saint, something Hardy deeply disapproved of. (As broadly as he dares to, Hardy hints that the "real" cause of Sue's final retreat to conventional Victorian saintliness is that she is undersexed.) Sue has twice Jude's quickness of wit and half his strength of character. She therefore sees from the beginning that the universe is governed by "Nature's law"; but because she lacks real moral depth, she thinks it is "Nature's . . . *raison d'être*, that we should be joyful in what instincts she afforded us. . . ." When she discovers that nature has no *raison d'être* and that paganism is as false as Christianity, she does not have the strength to face it and retreats into conventional wifehood and conventional Christianity.

All this, even the impermanence of Sue's paganism, is implicit in the episode of the images in Chapter II and in the recollections of Sue's childhood in Chapter IV. Hardy is, for example, careful to tell us that the figures of Venus and Apollo are plas-

ter and come off on Sue's gloves and jacket. By a fine piece
of irony — since Sue is, while her strength lasts, really a saint of
Hardy's humanitarian faith — Hardy has Jude focus not only
his sexual but his religious feelings on her and think of her as
an Anglican saint. Of this illusion Hardy makes much, and in
incident after incident he reemphasizes the irony of this love
between the pagan but undersexed Sue and the Christian but
passionate Jude. But with Sue's daring opinions to guide him,
Jude gradually learns from experience that "Nature's law" is
omnipotent and Christianity false.

In Part Three Jude, having now realized that learning is a
vanity, that only his "altruistic feeling" had any "foundation
in the nobler instincts," goes to Melchester, partly because it is
"a spot where worldly learning and intellectual smartness had
no establishment," partly because Sue is there. There follows
a series of episodes that represent the conflict between Sue's
daring humanitarian faith and her weak conventional conduct,
on the one hand, and Jude's "Tractarian" faith and his coura-
geously honest conduct, on the other. In the end, of course,
Hardy arranges events so that they demonstrate the wicked
power of "the artificial system of things, under which the
normal sex-impulses are turned into devilish domestic gins and
springes to noose and hold back those who want to progress."
This metaphor of trapped animals suggests that the social aspect of marriage is almost as wicked as Farmer Troutham's
provisions for protecting his corn.

In Part Four Jude's education is almost lost sight of in the
welter of historical details. Occasionally, however, its progress
is indicated, as when Sue asks whether she ought to continue to
live with Phillotson and Jude replies: "Speaking as an order-
loving man — which I hope I am, though I fear I am not — I
should say yes. Speaking from experienced and unbiassed nature, I should say no." Though Sue and Jude make up their
minds to sacrifice their love to right conduct, their meeting at

Marygreen, when their aunt dies, finally forces Jude to recognize that the Church's marriage system is evil and Sue to see that she must leave Phillotson for Jude. At first Sue tries to avoid marriage or an active sexual life, but when Arabella returns, Sue has to yield to Jude in order to hold him. In a letter reproduced in *The Later Years* this point is made more clearly than Hardy dared to make it in the novel itself: "[Sue] fears it would be breaking faith with Jude to withhold herself at pleasure, or altogether, after [marriage]; though while uncontracted she feels at liberty to yield herself as seldom as she chooses. This has tended to keep his passions as hot at the end as at the beginning, and helps to break his heart. He has never really possessed her as freely as he desired." The delicacy of public statement in the period prevented Hardy from making this point in a novel as clearly as he wished to, made it impossible for him to show, for example, that Jude's spending the night with Arabella when they met unexpectedly in Melchester was a demonstration of how powerfully sheer physical desire was fighting against suppression in him.

Part Five begins with a period when "the twain were happy — between their times of sadness. . . ." We see them as devoted lovers at the Great Wessex Agricultural Show, where they are carefully contrasted with Arabella and Catlett, the conventional married couple (Chapter V). But the conventional world's disapproval of them as unmarried lovers forces them down and down, until Jude, "still haunted by his dream," brings Sue and the children to a "depressing purlieu" of Christminster. Here Jude makes a speech that is Hardy's version of a speech from the cross to the Roman soldiers; in it Jude sums up the result of his education: "I perceive there is something wrong somewhere in our social formulas: what it is can only be discovered by men or women with greater insight than mine — if, indeed, they ever discover it — at least, in our time." The stutter of qualifying phrases at the end of this sentence is a measure of Hardy's own scepticism about the meliorism he and Jude rely on.

It is here, too, that Hardy makes his most extravagant symbolic gesture with the character he calls Father Time. Father Time produces an effect of sensational sentimentality that was obviously far from Hardy's intention. But since Hardy is committed by his doctrine to a true history, he is forced to try to do what is ludicrously impossible, namely to make Father Time a historically probable character. He tries by having Jude say, "The doctor says there are such boys springing up amongst us — boys of a sort unknown in the last generation — the outcome of new views of life. . . . He says it is the beginning of the coming universal wish not to live." This is social Darwinism with a vengeance. All through Part Five, Father Time's gloomy presence is used to remind us that Sue and Jude's moderate happiness is a snare and a delusion. Then, influenced by what is, realistically speaking, his perfectly arbitrary melancholy, Father Time misinterprets something Sue says and kills all the children, including himself. Hardy has made Father Time the son of Jude and Arabella and had him brought up by Jude and Sue in order that he may say:

> On that little shape had converged all the inauspiciousness and shadow which had darkened the first union of Jude, and all the accidents, mistakes, fears, errors of the last. He was their nodal point, their focus, their expression in a single term. For the rashness of those parents he had groaned, for their ill-assortment he had quaked, and for the misfortunes of these he had died.

The effect of this incident on Jude and Sue is to place each of them in the position from which the other had started at the beginning of the book:

> One thing troubled [Jude] more than any other, that Sue and himself had mentally travelled in opposite directions since the

tragedy: events which had enlarged his own views of life, laws, customs, and dogmas, had not operated in the same manner on Sue's. She was no longer the same as in the independent days, when her intellect played like lambent lightning over conventions and formalities which he had at that time respected, though he did not now.

As a consequence of this change, Sue returns to Phillotson and to conventional Christianity; and Jude, partly out of stunned indifference (he takes to drink), partly as a result of Arabella's predatory sexuality, returns to his first wife. Hardy makes it perfectly apparent that he thinks Sue has done an unforgivably inhuman thing to save a perfectly imaginary soul. "Do not do an immoral thing for moral reasons!" Jude says to her. "You have been my social salvation. Stay with me for humanity's sake! You know what a weak fellow I am. My two Arch Enemies you know — my weakness for women and my impulse to strong liquor. Don't abandon me to them, Sue, to save your own soul only. . . ."

Hardy is willing to suggest a conflict in Sue between her affection for Jude and her religious belief, but he leaves us in no doubt that Sue's religious belief is a delusion of weakness that makes her act inhumanly. Thus, when Jude departs from their last meeting, to which he has gone knowing that in his condition he will probably be killed by the trip, "[Sue,] in a last instinct of human affection, even now unsubdued by her fetters, sprang up as if to go and succor him. But she knelt down again, and stopped her ears with her hands till all possible sound of him had passed away." On his way home Jude feels "the chilly fog from the meadows of Cardinal [College] as if death-claws were grabbing me through and through." College, the Church, social convention — the very things Jude had in the beginning believed were the embodiments of his ideal — have killed him, either by betraying him directly or by teaching Sue to betray him.

When Hardy comes to Jude's death, he presents Arabella with a choice, too, the choice of staying with the dying Jude or going to the Remembrance games. Once more, Arabella appears melodramatically implausible here because Hardy refuses to grant that she is human, however imperfect her conduct. There is no conflict in Arabella's mind over what she should do. She goes off to the games without hesitation, flirts with the quack physician Vilbert, and is disturbed only by the thought that "if Jude were discovered to have died alone an inquest might be deemed necessary." As in the pig-killing scene, Arabella is allowed to feel only brute passion and fear of convention: she is the villainess of melodrama.

The immediate pathos of Jude's death derives from Arabella's callous neglect of him; but, like the cheers of the Remembrance-day crowd which are counterpointed against Jude's quotation from *Job,* this neglect illustrates only the complete indifference of society to the ideal life Jude has dreamed of. We are also meant to feel the pathos of Jude's uncertainty as to why he had been born at all. But this pathos is not quite genuine, unless *Jude the Obscure* is altogether meaningless; for unless the novel has no point, Jude's life has been meaningful; it has been the life of a man who sought to lead the ideal life several generations before the world was sufficiently reformed to allow him to. His life has not demonstrated that "Nature's law" is absolutely set against mankind's "nobler instincts"; it has only demonstrated that the temporarily squalid life of Jude's time is, for the moment, too much for such instincts. This is, at least, the logic of Hardy's meliorism.

In fact this ending suggests again what is evident enough in other ways, that the conditions of Jude's life were, for Hardy's deepest feelings, Earth's ingrained conditions. But *Jude the Obscure* cannot make this point about the world, because Hardy's doctrine required him to believe that the world could be reformed into a type of Paradise and to make *Jude the Obscure* a true history of how an obscure but worthy man, living a life that Hardy conceived to be representative, learned gradually that, at the moment, "the social moulds civilization fits us into have no more relation to our actual shapes than the conventional shapes of the constellations have to the real star-patterns" (another revealing comparison). Jude learned, that is, what the true morality of "unbiassed nature" is, and learned at the same time that society was a long way from recognizing it and a longer way from living by it.

Thus, insofar as Hardy gave Jude hope that in time society would recognize and live by this true morality, he denied the most persistent and powerful feeling in his work, the feeling that is struggling for realization in the conclusion of *Jude the Obscure*, the feeling that earth's conditions are ingrained. Insofar as this feeling dominates the conclusion of the novel, however, Hardy has made Jude's meliorism an illusion and his life in the service of idealism essentially pointless.

In the preface to *Jude the Obscure* Hardy says that the novel "is simply an endeavor to give shape and coherence to a series of seemings, or personal impressions, the question of their consistency or their discordance . . . being regarded as not of the first moment." To the extent that the presented life of the novel has a powerful coherence of feeling, this is a justified defense of it. But it is precisely the consistency with his doctrine Hardy imposed on his narrative that prevents his deepest feeling about life from realizing itself fully and ends by making the novel as a whole incoherent.

Jude the Obscure is a striking example — all the more impressive because it is in many ways a novel of great poetic intensity — of how a powerful imagination can be frustrated when the form of the novel it is committed to is determined, not by the imagination's sense of life, but by some doctrine about life the author believes in so deeply that he feels an overriding social obligation to express only so much of his sense of life as is consistent with it.

IV

THE NOVEL AND NATURE IN THE TWENTIETH

CENTURY: ANTHONY POWELL AND

JAMES GOULD COZZENS

IT is not easy to find twentieth-century novelists with imaginations so fine that they have never been frustrated like Hardy's by a doctrinal commitment. Perhaps the best examples are James Gould Cozzens in America and Anthony Powell in England, though Cozzens has certainly had his moments of peril when some one of those immediate opinions that are a part of the surface life of the realistic novel comes close to being the whole purpose of a scene. Cozzens has, for instance, strong views on the Catholic Church. They serve him well in scenes like the one Arthur Winner describes to Julius Penrose in *By Love Possessed*, in which Father Albright, Brocton's priest, tells Arthur Winner that the local high school must not show sex-education films because the Catholic Church does not permit Catholic children to go to them; even Catholics can, I assume, be legitimately amused by this comic consequence of Catholic provincialism. But in the long scene in which Mrs. Pratt complacently explains to Arthur Winner, with a series of theological observations of the most commonplace kind, how far beyond Arthur Winner's comprehension she — a Catholic — is, Cozzens' views come perilously close to dictating the action.

Like Cozzens, Powell has had to wait a long time for recognition and even now is not so widely read as he deserves to be. Though his first novel was published over thirty years ago, no one has seemed to know quite how to place him. He has

The Sense of Life

never had the kind of reputation that literary political parties
give their candidates because he has never belonged to any party
and has never been touted by any gang — unless Evelyn Waugh
may be counted one. Despite Powell's inexhaustible interest in
the highly competitive literary and artistic life of London, he
has never shown the slightest desire to gain power for himself, a characteristic that helps explain the strange, almost an-
thropological interest with which he examines those men — of
whom the power-hungry are the most obvious example —
whose public image of themselves is so important to them that
they subdue their whole natures to it.

With this insight into the folkways of men of will, Powell
gives us an understanding of a fundamental distinction of character in twentieth-century life. His sense of its refinement is remarkable.

> Quiggins — he will observe — controlled [aesthetic] instincts in
> himself according to his particular personal policy at any given
> moment. Widmerpool would genuinely possess no opinion as
> to whether the view from the cottage window was good or bad.
> The matter would not have the slightest interest for him. He
> would be concerned only with the matter of who owned the
> land. Perhaps that was not entirely true, for Widmerpool
> would have enjoyed boasting of a fine view owned by himself.
> Quiggins, on the other hand, was perfectly aware that there
> might be something to be admired in the contours of the coun-
> try, but to admit admiration would be to surrender material
> about himself that might with more value be kept secret. His
> rôle, like Widmerpool's was that of a man of the will, a rôle
> which adjudged that even here, in giving an opinion on the land-
> scape, the will must be exercised.

Powell is specially fascinated by the comic predicament of
men of will who, though wholly engrossed by personal policy,
are pitifully incapable of effective action, as is Erridge, the
eldest brother of Nicholas Jenkins' wife Isobel, the head of the

immensely complicated Toland family, "the Red Earl," who is "one of those egotists unable . . . to organize to good effect his own egotism, to make public profit out of it." In *The Kindly Ones* Hugh Morland comments on the desperate poverty of emotion among people who commit *crimes passionnels.* "Underneath," he says, "is an abject egotism and lack of imagination," and he raises the whole question of how men of will may be taken in by "the tyranny of action." Jenkins observes that marriage is, "if not a *sine qua non* of action," a "testing experience, surely," as it certainly is throughout *The Music of Time.* "What was it Foch said?" General Conyers remarks in *At Lady Molly's,* "War not an exact science, but a terrible and passionate drama? Something like that. Fact is, marriage is something like that too." And in *The Kindly Ones* Jenkins goes on to observe that "the baronet's wife's subsequent married life with the gamekeeper opens up more interesting possibilities than any of their adulterous frolics."

But Erridge, having snatched Mona from the hands of his companion in Communist causes, Quiggins, and taken her on an inconclusive trip to China for the Communist revolution there, promptly loses her. He is shortly off to Spain, ostensibly again the bold man of action, but as Quiggins (who has now lost St. John Clarke's money as well as Mona to Erridge) says, "He appears to have treated POUM, FAI, CNT, and UGT, as if they were all the same left-wing extension of the Labour Party. . . . If you can't tell the difference between a Trotskyite-Communist, an Anarcho-Syndicalist, and a properly paid-up Party Member, you had better keep away from the barricades" — where only properly paid-up Party Members are presumably allowed to become heroes. After thus getting in trouble with the Communist authorities in Spain, Erridge comes home with dysentery and establishes himself in a nursing home, where his efforts to set up as a little tyrant of the sickroom are defeated by his own bad-tempered ineffectuality and the success of his younger brother Hugo's "rival *salon*" (unluckily for Erridge, Hugo has recently broken a leg in an automobile accident).

In his attitude toward these men of will, successful or unsuccessful, Powell is not unlike the John Aubrey of whom, in 1949, he wrote a study. Aubrey was a man of profound common sense whose profession, if he can be said to have had one, was antiquities and whose passion was the nature of his fellow men. Incapable of sustained personal resentments, completely without ideological passions, he was, as he said himself, "like Almansor in the Play, that spare neither friend nor Foe, but a religious John Tell-troth." The value of Aubrey's *Brief Lives* is their remarkable combination of a feeling for the characteristic life of a time and place and a feeling for the individual life and its private oddnesses. He had a wholly humanized sense of experience.

Powell's first novel, *Afternoon Men*, appeared in 1931, and he has published ten since. The last six belong to an unfinished series called *The Music of Time*, which has so far covered the period from the childhood of its hero, Nicholas Jenkins, at the outbreak of the First World War to his induction into the army at the outbreak of the Second World War. The first novel in the series, *A Question of Upbringing* (1951), covers the six years from 1921 to 1926 when Jenkins is at Eton and Oxford. *A Buyer's Market* (1952) begins in the spring of 1928 and covers about eighteen months, ending in October 1929, a period during which Jenkins is working in London for a publisher of art books and going about to dances and on country weekends, watching his friends fall in love and start careers. *The Acceptance World* (1955) begins in the autumn of 1931 and ends in the late summer of 1932; during this period Jenkins begins to write novels and is much involved in the London literary world.

At Lady Molly's (1957) covers a period of a few months in

1935 when the people Jenkins has known throughout these books are becoming fixed in character and Jenkins becomes involved with the Toland family and, eventually, engaged to Isobel Toland. With *At Lady Molly's* something like the second act of *The Music of Time* begins, for in it Jenkins is committed to a course of life. This process is completed in the next two novels, *Casanova's Chinese Restaurant* (1960) and *The Kindly Ones* (1962), which carry us to the edge of war. *Casanova's Chinese Restaurant* deals, in a less chronologically straightforward way than the earlier novels, with the years 1936 and 1937. It is a series of brilliant variations — it is much preoccupied with music — on the theme of marriage: Morland and Matilda, Maclintock and Audrey, Carlos and Matilda, Audrey and Carlos, Moreland and Priscilla, Donners and Matilda, Stringham and Audrey, Mrs. Foxe and Norman Chandler, Miss Wheedon and Stringham, Jenkins and Isobel — but, as in all these novels, the dance is too complicated to be diagrammed. *The Kindly Ones* deals with that strange pause that preceded the outbreak of the Second World War. But it begins with an account of the similar period that preceded the First World War, when Jenkins was seven. Both periods are curiously haunted, as if some divinities more terrible than those known to the novel's theosophical crank, Trelawney, were at work — the Eumenides, The Kindly Ones. It is no accident that General Conyers, the best military mind so far to appear in *The Music of Time*, should be interested in the occult and an old acquaintance of the egregious Trelawney, for whom, however, he never quite finds time. ("Then I shall expect to hear from you, General, when you wish to free yourself from the bonds of Time and Space." "You will, Trelawney, you will. Off you go now — at the double.") General Conyers' interest in the occult has been evident since *At Lady Molly's*, in which he unexpectedly offers a psychoanalytical explanation of Widmerpool.

It is possible to work out the chronology of *The Music of Time*, but there are astonishingly few dates in it. It is the human sense of time rather than chronology that interests Powell, the shape of the feelings at a particular age, the characteristic tone of a period. He fixes our attention on "that feeling of anxiety . . . that haunts youth so much more than maturity," or the "sense of guilt in relation to [marriage that] makes itself increasingly felt" as one approaches thirty; and he is always observing that some act was "a piece of recklessness that well illustrates the mixture of self-assurance and *ennui* which together contributed so much to form the state of mind of people like St. John Clarke at that time [the early thirties]," or noting "that odd sense of intellectual emancipation that belonged, or, at least, seemed, perhaps rather spuriously, to belong, to the art of that epoch [immediately after the first war]: its excitement and its melancholy mingling with kaleidoscopic impressions of a first sight of Paris."

This representation of the shifts and changes in our consciousness of reality as both we and society change with the passage of time is made possible by the scope of *The Music of Time* and by the controlled variety of circumstances through which the dancers to this music move. But these conditions only make the effect possible; the effect itself has to be realized in the action of the novel or in Jenkins' comments on the action, and it may be that Powell's comparative lack of popularity is a consequence of the quietness with which Jenkins presents the action and comments on it. He never stops to point out to the reader the comic significance of such things as General Conyers' remark to the theosophist Trelawney, with his solemn superiority to Time and Space, "Off you go now — at the double," or to explain to him what he is to deduce from the many marriages of *Casanova's Chinese Restaurant*. He clearly has an instinctive dislike of what Henry James called "the platitude of statement," and it is only when the significant action is an event in Nicholas Jenkins' consciousness that something of what Powell is driving at becomes overt.

When, after an interval of ten years, Jenkins finds himself once more at Sir Magnus Donners' castle, Stourwater, he thinks, "I was far less impressed than formerly. . . . Memory, imagination, time, all building up on that brief visit [of ten years before], had left a magician's castle (brought into being by some loftier Trelawney), weird and prodigious, peopled by beings impossible to relate to everyday life." That loftier Dr. Trelawney is the personification of perfectly explicable forces — "memory, imagination, time" — that are no less mysteriously powerful for being explicable, forces not unlike the explicable but uncontrollable forces that dominate men's lives in Cozzens' novels. In Nathaniel Hicks's meditation at Sellers Field, in *Guard of Honor*, Cozzens compares these forces to a storm: "The dark forces gathered, not by any means at random or reasonlessly, but according to a plan in the nature of things, like the forces of a storm; which, as long as heat expanded air and cold contracted it, would have to proceed." But in the epigraph of *Guard of Honor* he compares them to Ariel and his fellows, much as Powell compares his forces to some Prospero.

About the relation of these forces to the human will, Powell and Cozzens differ in a way typical of the difference between British and American writers, and possibly between British and American culture. Powell is a man for whom "in human life, the individual ultimately dominates every situation, however disordered, sometimes for better, sometimes for worse," and constitutes the operative center of energy and value in society, however complex the organization and immediately irresistible the conventions of society may be. Powell's awareness of society's power is very acute, but he never fails to suggest that it is both energized and used by the egos of individuals. He is in this sense, as are most British writers, an individualist. Cozzens, on the other hand, as his storm image suggests, has the American feeling that social patterns are almost natural forces of a violent and uncontrollable sort; "When the tempest reached its hurricane violence, uprooting, overturning, blowing away, you must make the best of its million freaks," Nathaniel Hicks thinks.

Cozzens' characters have egos as energetic as Powell's characters have, but though these egos constitute the heat and cold that expand and contract the air and make the storm of events, his characters are free only to make the best of them and are almost never able to use them. They are like the paratrooper General Nichols describes to Colonel Ross who, hanging from his chute, sees bad trouble below; "What's his right course?" General Nichols asks. "Why, unless the man's a bloody fool, he climbs back into the plane and tries somewhere else." This joke is fundamental to Cozzens' conception of experience; he repeats it in another form in *By Love Possessed*, when Alfred Revere, who has just discovered he has an incurable heart disorder, is reminded of the anecdote about the man who, falling from a building, shouts to the people in a window he passes, "Don't worry! All right so far!" For Cozzens' people are, as Colonel Ross puts it to himself, like "a chess player who had in his head no moves beyond the one it was now his turn to make. He would be dumbfounded when, after he had made four or five such moves (each sensible enough in itself) sudden catastrophe, from an unexpected direction by an unexpected means, fell on him, and he was mated." Insofar as his characters insist on some continuity between their wills and events, as do both the egregious Edsell and the innocent Andrews, they are, like Colonel Ross's chess player, dumbfounded by what happens. The best of them foresee and accept their inevitable confounding without ceasing to struggle. "What I hate, that I do!" as Amanda Turck says of herself, but she never stops trying not to. In the end they are far lonelier people than Powell's characters, for what they are is never in any important way reflected by what they succeed in doing. Cozzens is in this sense, as are most American writers, an individualist.

Beneath this difference that characteristically divides British fiction from American, however, Powell and Cozzens resemble each other in an important way. Both recognize that men can express their natures at all only by means of a guard of honor or some other conventional form of behavior, firmly established in their society, that will make men appear to be what they wish to be and sometimes even help them to become so; both recognize that, though men are all possessed by love of one kind or another, they exist by virtue of the manners dictated to them by these shared conventions. Both recognize, too, that society is constituted of individuals, that it possesses no other power than that generated by its individual members, who are trying to realize their own natures. Both are therefore fascinated by the elaborate rituals of society and by the way individual men deal with them, because they understand that men are most completely themselves when they are performing these rituals, well or badly.

Powell, an expert on the rituals of British upper-middle-class life, is fascinated by the essential independence of those who sustain these rituals with such skillful concern for their own egos. Cozzens is equally expert on the rituals of those American sub-societies that are as highly organized as Powell's world — the law, the army, the American small town — and is fascinated by the persistence with which their members assert their egos in an endless and unsuccessful attempt to control these rituals and dominate their societies. Thus, for both writers, Prospero and his agents are the perfect image for the forces that govern men's sense of reality and their conduct.

For Powell the joke is that Prospero transforms Sir Magnus Donners' ill-conceived castle — "Nobody warned me it was made of cardboard," says Isobel; "I told you it was Wagnerian," says Moreland — into the cloud-capped towers and gorgeous palaces of his revels, a trifling vanity of his art. He even provides a masque — not exactly of Hymen, though not unrelated to it either — when the guests agree to act out The Seven Deadly Sins in order to allow Sir Magnus to enjoy his latest hobby, photography. (The camera never lies, but no one ever knows what truth it is talking about.) Upon this pleasant scene Widmerpool erupts, like some self-important Caliban, dressed in the uniform of his Territorial regiment. "You look very military, my dear fellow," says Sir Magnus, to Widmerpool's visible gratification. But the effect is really of some one who has stolen a costume from the trees outside the cave, for as Jenkins observes, Widmerpool does not look "innately military. On the contrary, he had almost the air of being about to perform a music-hall turn, sing a patriotic song or burlesque, with 'patter', an army officer."

For Cozzens the joke is that Prospero has set in train the storm of war in which everyone — from Lieutenant Edsell yearning to pin back the ears of all officers of field grade to Don Andrews with his innocent belief that men reap as they sow — is shown how little power over the storm authority — royal, military, or even just moral — gives a man, how wrong he has got things. Cozzens' Prospero transforms the scruffy little Florida town of Ocanara into a magic island: it too has its cloud-capped towers, in the form of the Oleander Towers hotel "with its absurd domes and minarets." This is the setting for the military pageant that comes to its spectacular climax with Pop's celebration for General Beal's forty-first birthday and the mass descent of the parachute troops, like gods in machines; the machines do not, of course, function successfully, despite the elaborate military ritual for assuring their smooth operation.

We end with Generals Beal and Nichols standing at sunset by the lake where the paratroopers have drowned. "Around [them] a circle of officers had gathered, posed in concern. In this sad, gold light their grouping made a composition like that found in old-fashioned narrative paintings of classical incidents or historical occasions. . . ." General Beal has tears in his eyes. It is a scene not unlike the one depicted in the painting that hangs in the Union League Club of Brocton in *By Love Possessed*, "in the genre tradition — after Meissonier or perhaps Julian Scott. In detail scrupulously realistic, the Eighth Pennsylvania Cavalry waited at Hazel Grove in the spring dusk of Chancellorsville woods" for the charge that was supposed by all right-thinking people in Brocton to have saved the Army of the Potomac that day. It was not, of course, historically true, as Judge Lowe has discovered, but a manifestation of "man's incurable willful wish to believe what he preferred to believe. . . . If rumor, whispering idiots in the ear, told a story he liked, he was stubborn in crediting it." It reminds us of Powell's Mr. Deacon, with his interest in classical incidents and his "huge pictures that might have been illustrations to [children's] lessons about the gods of Olympus."

Or perhaps we end with Sal Beal saying to Benny Carricker, that "honey of a flyer," "her chin up, surveying him for a triumphant instant," "Benny! . . . You just go to hell!" Or perhaps we end with the stoic but not discouraged wisdom of General Beal reviewing in a later mood the disastrous three days they have just, at best, muddled through; his "thin strong fingers, nervous but steadily controlled, pressing" Colonel Ross's arm, he says: "I'll do the best I can, Judge; and you do the best you can; and who's going to do it better?" But of course we end with all these implications in *Guard of Honor*, just as we do in *The Music of Time*.

Of all the characters in *The Music of Time* Nicholas Jenkins is the most subtly and fully developed, but he is no more significant than a number of others. The most important of these are perhaps Charles Stringham, the brilliant and melancholy hero of Jenkins' young manhood, and Kenneth Widmerpool, the

formidable school fool — "at once absurd and threatening," as
Jenkins observes of him much later in their lives. By the end of
The Acceptance World a significant contrast between these
two is becoming evident. Stringham, the man of imagination
with his heightened sensitivity to the promises of life and his
objectless passion, is on the verge of disintegration; Widmerpool, the self-absorbed man of will, is on his way to success in
the City. Stringham, with his immense charm, has almost deliberately cut himself off from those who love him; Widmerpool,
with his purely mechanical sense of human relations, is about to
be involved in a disastrous attempt at marriage.

Near the end of *The Acceptance World*, after the Old Boys'
Dinner at the Ritz, Stringham collapses from drink against the
railings of the Green Park and Widmerpool gets him home and
into bed. When Stringham comes to and tries to get up again,
Widmerpool holds him in bed, and in the end Stringham laughs
helplessly and accepts the position. "That boy," Stringham
had said of Widmerpool at school, "will be the death of me"
— if not that boy, then the world he and his kind have manufactured. A major contrast of twentieth-century natures is
implied here, but it is dangerous to analyze Powell's work this
way, so completely is it dedicated to the observation of life, so
little to abstract classification.

Powell's sense of character is like his sense of time. Even
Jenkins is almost always revealed to us by implication, as he is
in his response to Sir Magnus Donners' castle or when he remarks, after hearing of a favorable comment on his novel by
St. John Clarke, "I found myself looking for excuses to cover
what still seemed to me his own shortcomings as a novelist."
When Jean Templer tells him of her affair with Jimmy Strip-
ling, he first notices in himself that "a desire to separate myself physically from her and the place we were in was linked
with an overwhelming sensation that, more than ever, I wanted
her for myself."

Thus Jenkins' thoughts — and he is a thoughtful man — always effective and often brilliant as comments on experience in general, are always dramatic revelations of character. There is a marvelous moment in *A Buyer's Market* when Widmerpool suddenly materializes like Guido da Montefeltro, "sanza tema d'infamia ti rispondo." Jenkins discovers him peering through a barred window above the stairs leading to the cellarage of Sir Magnus' castle and looking like a prisoner "in an underground cell, from which only a small grating gave access to the outer world" — as indeed he is. From this point of vantage he explains to Jenkins his relations to Gypsy Jones, whose abortion he has paid for, though he had nothing to do with making it necessary. Jenkins thinks:

> A crisis of this kind appeared to me so foreign to Widmerpool's nature — indeed, to what might almost be called his station in life — that there was something distinctly shocking, almost personally worrying, in finding him entangled with a woman in such circumstances. . . . Having regarded him, before hearing of his feelings for Barbara [Goring], as existing almost in a vacuum so far as the emotion of love was concerned, an effort on my own part was required to accept the fact that he had been engaged upon so improbable, indeed, so sinister, a liaison. If I had been annoyed to find, a month or two earlier, that he was in a position to regard himself as possessing claims of at least some tenuous sort on Barbara, I was also, I suppose, more than a trifle put out to discover that Widmerpool, so generally regarded by his contemporaries as a dull dog, had been, in fact, however much he might now regret it, in this way, at a moment's notice, prepared to live comparatively dangerously.

What this meditation reveals about Jenkins is perhaps less immediately evident but certainly no less important than what it tells us about Widmerpool. If Widmerpool, explaining in these fantastic circumstances and with all his unconscious self-regard how he came to pay, without recompense, for Gypsy Jones's abortion, is ludicrous, so is Jenkins, filled with dismay at finding Widmerpool so much more dashing a fellow than he. Mental events of this kind always have their causes and their consequences, often strikingly incongruous, in the external action of the fiction. This one, for instance, has a good deal to do with Jenkins' later making love to Gypsy Jones — as does too, Jenkins' earlier contemplation of Widmerpool's claims on Barbara Goring, with whom Jenkins then fancied himself in love, and Mr. Deacon's painting, "The Boyhood of Cyrus," and the fact that Gypsy lives with Mr. Deacon, and a great many other subjects of Jenkins' contemplation whose delicate tracery on his consciousness it is hopeless to try to reproduce. The point to be observed is that in Powell's novels passages of speculation are always dramatic displays of the speculating character's motives for action as well as acute general comments on the life about him.

There are seventy or seventy-five major characters in what we so far have of *The Music of Time* and perhaps as many more who make frequent occasional appearances, or are going to later — for example, Sonny Farebrother, who appears briefly in *A Question of Upbringing* and then, as Jenkins says, "passed out of my life for some twenty years." Powell's conception of these characters and of their immensely complex interrelations has been clear since the opening pages of *A Question of Upbringing*, where, in a timeless prologue that may well describe the actual genesis of *The Music of Time*, Jenkins is reminded, by a London street scene, of the Poussin in the Wallace Collection called "A Dance to the Music of Time"

> in which the Seasons, hand in hand and facing outward, tread in rhythm to the notes of the lyre that the winged and naked grey-beard plays. The image of Time brought thoughts of mortality: of human beings, facing outward like the Seasons, moving hand in hand in intricate measure: stepping slowly, methodically, sometimes a trifle awkwardly, in evolutions that take recognizable shape: or breaking into seemingly meaningless gy-

rations, while partners disappear only to reappear again, once more giving pattern to the spectacle: unable to control the melody, unable, perhaps, to control the steps of the dance.

This beautifully disciplined comparison really tells us all we need to know about the design of *The Music of Time*. It proposes that we contemplate the interaction of these brief lives as constituting a loosely woven pattern within which parallels, contrasts, repetitions will occasionally occur, sometimes planned by the characters, sometimes unexpected by them. Its emphasis is on the relations of the dancers to the dance, and what it finds important is not what abstract meanings may be ascribed to the dance or to the melody by which the winged and naked greybeard guides it, but what response of the order evoked by Poussin it arouses.

The allusion to Poussin is not accidental. Powell's imagination is intensely visual and his deepest responses express themselves as images. It is characteristic of him to see loiterers outside a nightclub as "two Shakespearean murderers, minor thugs from one of the doubtfully ascribed plays"; or to compare the conduct of a character to that of "some savage creature, anxious to keep up appearances before members of a more highly civilized species, although at the same time keenly aware of her own superiority in cunning"; or to describe one as "a dissipated cherub, a less aggressive, more intellectual version of Folly in Bronzino's picture, rubicund and mischievous, as he threatens with a fusillade of rose petals the embrace of Venus and Cupid; while Time in the background, whiskered like the Emperor Franz-Joseph, looms behind a blue curtain as if evasively vacating the bathroom." It is when, as here, such images are specifically drawn from the fine arts that we can be sure the controlling attitudes of Powell's imagination are asserting themselves.

In *A Question of Upbringing*, for example, Charles Stringham "looked a little like one of those stiff, sad young men in ruffs, whose long legs take up so much room in sixteenth-century portraits." In *A Buyer's Market*, Mr. Deacon's carefully described painting of "The Boyhood of Cyrus" is the key psychological particular in the representation of Jenkins' passion for Barbara Goring, an affair that begins and ends by the Albert Memorial's statue of Asia, "where, beside the kneeling elephant, the Bedouin forever rests on his haunches in hopeless contemplation of Kensington Gardens' trees and thickets, the blackened sockets of his eyes ranging endlessly over the rich foliage of these oases of the mirage." Walking up Grosvenor Place from the Huntercombes' dance, where he has suffered the double shock of discovering that Widmerpool loves Barbara Goring and that he no longer does, Jenkins notices how, "like a vast paper-weight or capital ornament of an Empire clock, the Quadriga's horses, against a sky of indigo and silver, careered desperately towards the abyss." When he finally arrives at his flat in Shepherd's Market in the early dawn — "touched almost mystically, like another Stonehenge, by the first rays of the morning sun, the spot seemed one of those clusters of tumble-down dwellings depicted by Canaletto or Piranesi, habitations from amongst which arches, obelisks and viaducts, ruined and overgrown with ivy, arise from the mean houses huddled together below them."

Images like these dominate *The Music of Time*, establishing and defining the pattern of feelings for the action. They make us feel — even as Charles Stringham leans over his school-room fire toasting a piece of bread on the end of a paperknife — the splendid but tragic melancholy that will ultimately destroy him. They give us a glimpse of Powell's deep, quiet sense of the twentieth century as a wrecked civilization grubbing along in the shadow of its greatness's ruins, a world nearly transformed by the Widmerpools though still haunted by the Stringhams. "Though ominous," as Jenkins puts it, "things still had their enchantment." This is the tone everywhere in *The Music of Time*

— for example, in Jenkins' description of a bombed London pub that had figured largely in his past:

> In the midst of this sombre grotto five or six fractured steps had withstood the explosion and formed a projecting island of masonry on the summit of which rose the door. Walls on both sides were shrunk away, but along its lintel, in niggling copybook handwriting, could still be distinguished the word *Ladies*. Beyond, on the far side of the twin pillars and crossbar, nothing whatever remained of that promised retreat, the threshold falling steeply to an abyss of rubble; a triumphal arch erected laboriously by dwarfs, or the gateway to some unknown, forbidden domain, the lair of sorcerers.

The pictorial metaphors associated with Jenkins' passion for Barbara Goring mark the crucial stages in the affair. That passion is as inexperienced and as sincere as Mr. Deacon's "The Boyhood of Cyrus"; when it ends, Jenkins is in a state to feel that the Quadriga's horses are careering toward the abyss — if only of Hyde Park Corner, if only with the somewhat fictitious dash of an Empire ornament. Jenkins' passion for Barbara has been immaturely romantic and unintentionally incongruous in the smoky air of the contemporary world, but it has nonetheless had its genuine idealism. The rest of one's life one is likely to remember such an occasion, with all its frustrated longing for the oases of a mirage, with feelings of consciously indulged sentiment not unlike the feelings with which the twentieth century contemplates the conception of Asia — so appropriate to the Victorian Age — on the Albert Memorial.

It is the continuous triumph of *The Music of Time* to show us, in these ways, without resort to extravagance of representation or distortion of perspective, that "all human beings, driven as they are at different speeds by the same Furies, are at close range equally extraordinary" and that human affairs are therefore both absurd and sad. The title of Powell's first novel,

Afternoon Men, comes from Burton's *Anatomy of Melancholy:*
". . . as if they had all . . . landed in the mad haven in the
Euxine sea of Daphne Insana, which had a secret quality to
dementate; they are a company of giddy-heads, afternoon men,
it is Midsummer moon still, & the Dog-days last all the year
long, they are all mad." Like Burton, Powell assumes without argument that, despite some superficial appearances to the
contrary created by social convention, men, seen close up, re-
veal themselves to be dementated, driven by invisible but
powerful spirits to behave in extraordinary ways. He is fully
aware of the horror this is. What could be sadder than the life
of Charles Stringham, about whom, by the time of *Casanova's
Chinese Restaurant,* when Charles makes his truly terrifying appearance at Mrs. Foxe's party for Hugh Moreland, Jenkins has
"begun to learn . . . that . . . there is really no answer"?
What could be more frightening than the single-minded, unre-
lenting, inhuman drive for power of men like Widmerpool,
the destructive anarchy of Audrey Maclintock's nature and of
the scores of other characters like them in their self-regard if in
nothing else?

Yet, however terrifying, these people are also ridiculous, "to
reason most absurd," an endless source of comic enchantment.
What could be more so than Stringham and Audrey Maclintock
deeply absorbed in recounting to one another their experiences
of marriage? What more so than St. John Clarke, the once-
famous, third-rate novelist who has turned Marxist to keep up
with the times but still sounds hopelessly like some Edwardian
stylist such as Yeats at his worst? — "To tell the truth, Lady War-
minster, I get more pleasure from watching the confabulation
of sparrows in their parliament on the roof-tops opposite my
study window, or from seeing the clouds scudding over the
Serpentine in windy weather, than I do from covering sheets
of foolscap with spidery script that only a few sympathetic
souls, some now passed on to the Great Unknown, would even

care to read." St. John Clarke, a great advocate of revolution
and "upheaval for its own sake," is in fact a passionate climber
in the established social order and would be quite lost without
it. In moments of despair he bitterly sums up the defeat he
thinks his life has been by saying, "One week-end at Dogdene
twenty years ago. Forced to play croquet with Lord Lonsdale.
. . . Two dinners at the Huntercombes', both times asked the
same night as Sir Horrocks Rusby. . . ." At the end of his
life he basks in the reflected glory of Thrubworth, where he
is welcomed — a rare event — by Erridge because of his Marxist enthusiasm, and so deep is his respect for an earl that it
reaches out beyond the grave: he leaves all his money to Erridge.

No doubt the hopeful generalization to be deduced from
these observations of life would be some conviction of the temporary decline of our culture and the need for energetic re-
form, as the unhopeful generalization would be one of the more
or less gloomy cyclical theories of history. But feelings in
Powell never ossify into doctrine, which is associated in his
mind with egotism and inhumanity; all his doctrinaires are men
so egotistical as to be incapable of enough human experience
to engage their feelings, who must substitute doctrine for understanding. It is characteristic of him to have remarked of Aubrey that he "lacked the egoism and self-pity required for carrying his romanticism to . . . the extravagant stage [where]
ruins, spectres, and lonely places [become] the baleful symbols
of the Soul's dark journey."

Like his sense of the absurdities of the human imagination —
willful or not — Powell's sense of its sadness asserts itself as
implication, a shadow behind the character's immediate responses and conscious intentions. Thus Jenkins, riding late one
snowy night out the Great West Road, falls deeply in love
with Jean Templer just after noticing that he is in a kind of
hell:

On either side of the highway, grotesque buildings, which in daytime resembled the temples of some shoddy, utterly unsympathetic Atlantis, now assumed the appearance of an Arctic city's frontier forts. Veiled in snow, these hideous monuments of a lost city bordered a broad river of black, foaming slush, across the surface of which the car skimmed and jolted with a harsh crackling sound, as if the liquid beneath were scalding hot.

This conjunction of feelings is pervasive in *The Music of Time;* it even appears with characters like Peter Templer, whose life consists mostly of the pursuit of women — at least until his second marriage. Templer is to all appearances what Stringham implies when he says to him, "If you're not careful you will suffer the awful fate of the man who always knows the right clothes to wear and the right shop to buy them at." Yet Templer has a gift for self-analysis comparatively rare for men of his taste that makes all the more terrible the fury "not far away from Templer that generated a sense of horror," as Nick senses when he runs into Templer again at Stourwater after a long break in their relations. Even as early as *The Acceptance World,* Templer had a trick of gazing "thoughtfully round [the lounge of the Ritz], as if contemplating the deterioration of a landscape, known from youth, once famed for its natural beauty, now ruined beyond recall." Even more remarkably, this sadness is evoked by the great comic egotists of *The Music of Time,* the J. G. Quigginses, the Uncle Gileses, the Widmerpools. It is a faint but persistent aftertaste of the comedy of their marvelous, unremitting self-absorption. In the end, despite their outrageous selfishness, one always sees the sadness of the defeat they have, from their own point of view so unjustly, suffered.

The heart of Powell's work is these brief lives, these beautifully realized characters, all moving within the pattern of Time's dance, but all moving in their own ways, and, as they suppose, at the dictates of their own desires, more or less ludicrous according to the extent to which their sense of reality

has been distorted by the willful assertion of their public images
of themselves, but — ludicrous or not — always a little sad.
Every one of them is both a period piece and himself, and it is
not easy to forget even the minor ones like Sillery, the Oxford don, with his coy vanity — "There is some nonsense about
the College wanting a pitcher o' me old mug"; or Dicky Um-
fraville, the unrepentant man of the twenties who says of the
thirties, "What an extraordinary world we live in. All one's
friends marching about in the park"; or the singer, Max Pilgrim, whose naughty songs have become merely silly and sad:
"Di Di, in her collar and tie,/ Quizzes the girls with a mono-
cled eye,/ Sipping her hock in a black satin stock,/ Or shooting
her cuffs over *pernod* or *bock*."

The most fully realized of these defiant anachronisms is Uncle Giles, who has been an anachronism all his life. "It was one
of Uncle Giles' chief complaints that he had been 'put' into the
army . . . instead of entering some unspecified profession in
which his gifts would have been properly valued." Possibly as
a result, his gifts asserted themselves early in his career, when
he was stationed in Egypt and got into trouble over both a
woman and money and had to send in his papers. On the way
home he stopped off in South Africa, where he planned to settle
in Port Elizabeth, but an unfortunate affair connected with
the marketing of diamonds made it necessary for him to move
on again. From then until he chose a thoroughly inconvenient
moment during the summer after Munich in which to die, he
circulated restlessly about the Home Counties, occasionally
turning up at the Ufford in Bayswater, a hotel where "the passages seemed catacombs of a hell assigned to the subdued regret
of those who had lacked in life the incomes to which they felt
themselves entitled." Uncle Giles dislikes London, where "your
hand is never out of your pocket," and repeatedly suspects
"though exact proof was always lacking — that the pieces [of
luggage he leaves at the Ufford] . . . had actually been reduced in number by at least one canvas valise, leather hat-box,

or uniform-case in black tin." During the first war he had worn a uniform, "though not one of an easily recognized service," and was known as Captain Jenkins, "probably a more or less honorary rank, gazetted by himself."

"It was an article of faith with him that all material advancement in the world was the result of influence, a mysterious attribute with which he invested, to a greater or less degree, every human being on earth except himself." The rich and well-born of course had influence; and, in the new egalitarian world, those beneath him in the social scale did too. So indeed, did the members of his own class, "because [they] possessed, almost without exception, either powerful relations who helped them on in an underhand way, or business associations, often formed through less affluent relatives, which enabled them — or so he suspected — to buy things cheap. Any mention of the City, or, worse still, the Stock Exchange, drove him to hard words. Moreover, the circumstances of people of this kind were often declared by him to be such that they did not have to 'keep up the same standards' in the community as those that tradition imposed on Uncle Giles himself." This attitude Uncle Giles describes as "being a bit of a radical."

All this is fully realized in Uncle Giles's conduct and conversation.

"Aylmer Conyers had a flair for getting on," he used to say, "No harm in that, I suppose. Somebody has got to give the orders. Personally I never cared for the limelight. Plenty of others to push themselves forward. Inclined to think a good deal of himself, Conyers was. Fine figure of a man, people used to say, a bit too fond of dressing himself up to the nines. Not entirely friendless in high places either. Quite the contrary. Peacetime or war, Conyers always knew the right people."

It is a wonderfully ludicrous life, and it would be easy to be so amused by Uncle Giles as to miss his underlying pathos, for his is not a despicable life; it is an "aimless, uncomfortable, but in a sense dedicated life. . . . Dedicated, perhaps, to his own egotism; his determination to be — without adequate moral or intellectual equipment — absolutely different from everybody else . . . propelled along from pillar to post by some force that seemed stronger than a mere instinct to keep himself alive." It is in this way that Powell makes his great egotists, for all their absurdity, something not essentially different from the rest of us; even Widmerpool, the most extravagant of them all, is not. However sublimely ridiculous he becomes, he continues to remind us, not so much, perhaps, of what we have done, as of what we have, in our time, known we might do.

Thus, when Widmerpool has become engaged to Mildred Haycock, a rather rackety woman of unimpeachable antecedents, he asks Jenkins to lunch, and it turns out he is worrying over whether Mildred will not expect him to make love to her during their engagement.

"In fact my fiancée — Mildred, that is — might even expect such a suggestion?"
"Well, yes, from what you say."
"Might even regard it as *usage du monde?*"
"Quite possible."

"I had the impression," Jenkins observes, "that the question of how he should behave worried him more on account of the figure he cut in the eyes of Mrs. Haycock than because his passion could not be curbed" — and, alas, it turns out that, when Widmerpool does finally nerve himself to invade Mildred's easily accessible bed on their weekend at Dogdene, he fails utterly. This disaster is the revealing climax of all the triumphs of prestige Widmerpool has won at the cost of failing as a human being.

Nevertheless, when we see him at his luncheon with Jenkins fuming with all the transparency of the wholly self-absorbed man over where to go on a clandestine weekend and what *name* to use ("As my name is an uncommon one, I take it I should be called upon to provide myself with a sobriquet"), our hearts must go out to him in pity. The whole matter is so intimately involved with his public image of himself and its importance — "I do not like doing irregular things. But this time, I think I should be behaving rightly in allowing a lapse of this kind. It is expected of me." How easy it is to imagine him working it out that Dogdene, which has been in Lord Sleaford's family since the days of Pepys, was the perfect place for the socially satisfying if somewhat irregular consummation of his union with the daughter of a lord. That he should be betrayed in these happy expectations by the — to him — utterly trivial fact that the achievement of physical passion is not wholly at the command of the will is, however ridiculous when viewed reasonably, pathetic when seen from Widmerpool's own point of view.

The effect of *The Music of Time* is a very remarkable one for the mid-twentieth century. It is as if we had come suddenly on an enormously intelligent but completely undogmatic mind with a vision of experience that is deeply penetrating and yet wholly recognizable, beautifully subtle in ordination and yet quite unostentatious in technique, and in every respect undistorted by doctrine. Great as the achievement of many twentieth-century novelists has been, they have been, almost to a man, novelists of ideas, in whose work experience is observed from the point of view of some more or less rationally conceived "philosophy" and functions essentially as illustration, and the writer's passion manifests itself as rhetoric rather than poetry. This is equally true, in different ways, of the great American metaphysical romances like *Light in August*, and of the best British novels, with their deep concern for the inadequacies of Midlands culture to the needs of their sensitive heroes, or their preoccupation with the theological inadequacies of modern civilization for Catholic converts and worshippers of Quetzalcoatl.

However powerful such novels may be — and most of the great novelists of our time have written such novels — there is something more immediately human and satisfying about an equally great novelist whose imagination apprehends all the dogmas of our time and the uses men make of them without itself being at the mercy of any of them. Such an imagination has the profound common sense, the unshakable awareness of other people, that has always given the great comic writer his sense of the discrepancies between motive and theory and allowed him to see human affairs, not as an illustration of some social or philosophical generalization, but as some kind of dance to the music of Time.

THE AMERICAN NOVEL AND NATURE

IN THE NINETEENTH CENTURY

MATTHEW ARNOLD was much distressed when he discovered that there were people going about in the United States with the notion that there was an American literature. In one sense he was obviously right. American books, like the books of other speakers of what the Oxford Dictionary calls "extra-British" English, are a part of English literature, not only because they are in some sort of English but because the literary culture of America is still to a considerable extent British. In another sense, however, Arnold's attitude was a version of what might be called the Sydney Smith syndrome ("In the four quarters of the globe, who reads an American book?"), which is still widespread in Britain today, at least in academic circles. There is of course that little awkwardness about Henry James, but it can be got around by pretending that James is British. It is, to be sure, not easy to be certain exactly what James meant when he told Hamlin Garland that "the mixture of Europe and America which you see in me has proved disastrous . . . . I have lost touch with my own people, and live here alone." But whatever his precise meaning, it was not that he was British.

Yet, in spite of this firm stand on the part of Arnold's countrymen, Americans go on asserting that there is what they like to call "a native tradition" in American literature. Mr. Marius Bewley's *The Eccentric Design* offers a recent manifestation of

this assertiveness, which first displayed itself frankly in the late
F. O. Matthiessen's *The American Renaissance* (1941), a book
Matthiessen originally intended boldy to call — in a phrase of
Whitman's — *Man in the Open Air.* There has been formidable
support for Matthiessen's central assumption — for instance, Al-
exander Cowie's *The Rise of the American Novel* (1951),
Marius Bewley's *The Complex Fate* (1952), Charles Feidelson's
Symbolism and American Literature (1953), R. B. W. Lewis's
The American Adam (1955), Richard Chase's *The American
Novel and Its Tradition* (1957), Harry Levin's *The Power of
Blackness* (1958), Leslie Fiedler's *Love and Death in the Ameri-
can Novel* (1960). What is most trying about these writers is
that they are all, like Dogberry's prisoners, in a tale.

What do they think they have to make a fuss about? Mr.
Bewley puts it very directly in *The Eccentric Design:* "The
American novel has had to find a new experience and discover
how to put that experience into art." These critics all agree that
there is something distinctive about the American perception
of experience, and that this perception manifests itself in what
Mr. Bewley calls "the eccentric design" of American fiction.
Mr. Bewley, for example, says that

> because the American tradition provided its artists with abstrac-
> tions and ideas rather than with manners, we have no great
> characters, but great symbolic personifications and mythic em-
> bodiments that go under the names of Natty Bumppo, Jay
> Gatsby, Huckleberry Finn, Ahab, Ishmael — all of whom are
> strangely unrelated to the world of ordinary passions and long-
> ings, for the democrat is at last the loneliest man in the universe.

Mr. Chase says that the form of the American novel

> is suitable to writers who do not have a firm sense of living in a
> culture. The American novelists tend to ideology and psychol-
> ogy, they are adept at depicting the largest public abstractions
> and the smallest and most elusive turn of the inner mind.

And Mr. Levin says that "in his anxiety over the self-isolated individual, and in his curiosity to read the cosmic scheme of things, Hawthorne is truly the founding patriarch of our fiction." It is what Henry James once called "the American passion" — "primordial — antecedent to experience. Experience comes and only shows us something we have dreamed of."

The first American figure in this tradition is James Fenimore Cooper. Cooper was in some ways a comic figure — "a gentleman," as D. H. Lawrence said, "in the worst sense." Cooper liked to declare that "it takes a first-class aristocrat to make a first-class Democrat" and made a habit of provincial gracelessness. Sir Walter Scott observed that he had "a good deal of the manner, or want of manner, of his countrymen" (Cooper, incidentally, thought the same of Scott), and it seldom failed him: the Thames, he noted on his first visit to London, is "a stream of trivial expanse." But it is none the less true, as Mr. Chase puts it, "that crotchety as Cooper's thinking was, he exemplified a dilemma, and explored some of the aesthetic uses to which it might be put, that was not peculiar to him but was at the heart of American culture." Of this dilemma and its aesthetic uses Mr. Bewley makes a fascinating analysis in *The Eccentric Design*.

He begins by trying to show that the moral feelings that clash so dramatically in American fiction have had their effect in American political thought from the beginning. There is certainly something to be said for the idea that Cooper's dilemma was a consequence of the historical developments John Adams watched with anticipatory distress. But one would almost suppose, to hear Mr. Bewley tell it, that Alexander Hamilton, by supernaturally cunning machinations, committed the United States to a conflict between the culture of a brutalized plutocracy and the culture of a promptly defeated but gracious landed aristocracy, and that this conflict has continued unchanged to the present.

John Adams is a figure of peculiar charm for intellectuals (as Ezra Pound discovered when he made Adams one of the epic heroes of the *Cantos*), and it is easy to sympathize with Adams' feeling that American society needed a responsible class independent of the popular will and to be distressed by Hamilton's ruthless genteelness. It is equally easy to understand that in his day Adams could hardly have conceived his responsible class as anything but a landed aristocracy. It is quite another thing to hold, as Mr. Bewley apparently does, that a landed aristocracy is still the only possible source of the kind of influence in society that Adams was seeking and that all wealth not vested in land operates in American society in our time as Adams and Cooper thought it did in theirs, producing nothing but insensitive and irresponsible people like Scott Fitzgerald's Tom Buchanan. Nevertheless, this notion pops up in the social thinking of America at regular intervals, particularly in the South, especially among literary people. It leads Mr. Bewley to think that Cooper's particular version of the American dilemma is more permanently significant than it is, and that Fitzgerald's work is a demonstration of the causes of American "decadence." This is to make American history into a symbolic romance, a dramatic clash of mythic characters called Adams, Jefferson, and Hamilton instead of Pathfinder, Chingachgook, and Lieutenant Muir.

It is, of course, theoretically possible that the only way to have a ruling class with a properly developed sense of responsibility to its society is to establish a landed aristocracy, but it is necessary to hope there is some other way, since the landed aristocracy that Adams and Cooper dreamed of has been a practical impossibility in America for nearly a hundred years. Even if the establishment of a landed aristocracy were a practical political expedient in our time, the question of Cooper as a novelist cannot be settled by proving that the doctrine at which he arrived as a result of his political analysis of American so-

ciety is extensively present in his novels. Social doctrine, however admirable, does not in itself make a novel good. To
argue that it does is to apply the doctrinal reduction of literature with a vengeance.

It is possible to feel great if often exacerbated respect for
Cooper as a social observer, but the critical question about his
novels is a question of the quality of the felt life in them and
the degree to which that life really embodies feelings that are
congruous with the social opinions he so often and so stub-
bornly expressed in his essays — and novels. The fact that
Cooper wrote romances does not free him of the need to consider that "nutritive or suggestive truth . . . of the perfect dependence of the 'moral' sense of a work of art on the amount
of felt life concerned in producing it." There have been a
number of negative reports on this aspect of Cooper's work,
though perhaps it is only fair to say that both the unnecessary
denigration of adventure stories and the hapless awkwardness of
Cooper's personality have encouraged an excessively scornful
attitude toward his work. Trollope was certainly right about
adventure stories. "No novel is anything," he said in his downright way, ". . . unless the reader can sympathize with the
characters. . . . If there be such truth, I do not know that a
novel can be too sensational."

Mr. Bewley's discussion of Cooper does, I believe, impute a
certain amount of unearned literary grace to him on purely
doctrinal grounds: "Cooper," he says, "has been consistently
underestimated as an artist. He ranks with Hawthorne, James
and Melville. . . ." On the other hand, Mr. Bewley's admiration of Cooper's social views allows him to see something
that is — to what extent it remains to determine — certainly
alive in Cooper's work, to show what seriousness is given Cooper's mythic characters and brilliantly deployed actions by the
conflict of convictions about American experience that is sometimes embodied in the scenes of *The Deerslayer* and *The Prai-*

rie. It also helps him to see a great deal of what matters in Hawthorne's work, even though Hawthorne's dilemma may have been less immediately political than he suggests.

What oddly enough emerges from this fresh analysis of American literature is the special force in American culture of "that inebriated *sense of self* that the American still cherishes." "We are asked by these novelists," as Mr. Chase puts it, "to judge characters, not by measuring them against socially derived values, but by their adherence to an idea of conduct which is personal, intuitive, and stoic." Though Mr. Chase is thinking of the nineteenth-century American novel when he says this, he might equally have been thinking of all of Hemingway's heroes, many of Faulkner's, and a number of Fitzgerald's in the twentieth-century American novel.

They are, these characters, in an even more extreme form than Lord Jim, "romantic" in the sense Stein had in mind when he described Jim. The only kind of human relation possible for such heroic exemplars of the American temper as these novelists characteristically deal with is an idyllic imaginary one or a hopelessly unstable actual one — in either instance one for which it is almost impossible to imagine any social support. From Deerslayer and Chingachgook or Ishmael and Queequeg to Nick Adams and Bill or Zack Edmonds and Lucas Beauchamp, human solidarity in American fiction has been idyllic, and Melville's attempt to realize with Hawthorne a friendship that would manifest as personal affection what he supposed to be ideological compatibility is only an extreme case of a failure — at once absurd and pathetic — that is familiar enough in American experience.

Hawthorne himself is a striking case of a man unable to come to terms with his society and unhappy that he could not. He felt a real horror of what "Ethan Brand" calls the Unpardonable Sin, the invasion without human warmth and affection of another personality, that seemed to him habitual with people

like Hollingworth, who were, he thought, made "spectral monsters" by their passion for ideological abstractions and for re-
form. Yet he was never sure that the scorn directed at him by
his Puritan ancestors in "The Custom House" was not justified,
never sure — such were the tortured subtleties of his mind —
that the worst of all unpardonable sinners was not Nathaniel
Hawthorne with his habit of invading the most remote and
private recesses of the personalities he contemplated, for no better reason than that he was a novelist. "But never again will we
desire more light than all the world can share with us," says
Matthew to Hannah in "The Great Carbuncle." "No," says
Hannah, "for how could we live by day, or sleep by night, in
this awful blaze of the Great Carbuncle!" The sleepless soli-
tude of Captain Ahab and — it is hard not to believe — of
James's Strethers and Maggie Ververs, after all their triumphs
of insight have been achieved, is evidence enough of the suffering such illumination can cause. But perhaps only an American writer like Hawthorne could suppose it really possible to
stop seeing the Great Carbuncle by merely desiring not to, by
an act of the will.

Like so many of their descendants, Hawthorne's novels are
all what he once planned to call a group of his stories, "Alle-
gories of the Heart." As Mr. Bewley puts it, perhaps a little
too solemnly,

> What Hawthorne leaves us with is not a sense of living char-
> acters whom he has endowed with deep psychological com-
> plexities, but a set of exploratory symbols which vibrate with
> a peculiar intensity in a moral ambience that is objectively
> grounded in Hawthorne's society.

The subtle and beautiful balance of moral feelings represented
in *The Scarlet Letter* is an impressive demonstration of this
point. It has been said, doubtless with some justice, that
Hawthorne was frightened of the full, passionate life and pre-

ferred women like Priscilla (and Sophia Peabody) to women
like Zenobia. But Zenobia is his own creation, and it would be
difficult to imagine a richer dramatization of all the relevant
feelings about the passionate woman than the scene in the
dark, uncultivated forest where Hester Prynne plans a fresh
start, far from organized Puritan society, for herself and
Dimmesdale. It is a touching and terrible moment, almost the
equal of some of Ahab's, and most of its greatness will be
missed unless one reads it as a fiction designed in the characteristic manner of the classical American novel.

What is true of *The Scarlet Letter* is equally true of the
greatest American fiction, *Moby Dick*. Far more than Hawthorne, Melville had a passion for fact, sharing that pedantry
of the particular that recurs in the American imagination, in
and out of literature, from the time of Whitman to the time
of Hemingway. What is odd about Melville's imagination is
the way it related facts to ideas and feelings; but this is an odd-
ness Melville shares with most American writers. They are all,
in this sense, transcendentalists for whom scenes and characters are symbols and actions "images of the mind," linked analogies, as Melville himself called them.

Moby Dick is a book about the alienation of a mind from
life to some realm of metaphysical abstraction, an alienation
produced by excessive self-dependence. Captain Ahab (though
not Ishmael) is the victim of an obsessive need to control the
universe, to make it conform to his private vision, and ultimately, though not in *Moby Dick*, Melville appears to have
been too. Finally he could see the actual world only as a betrayal of a metaphysical opinion of it — unless Billy Budd, with
the noose around his neck crying "God bless Captain Vere," is
evidence of a different vision. For Melville in his way (as for
Hardy in his) there were "a world of abstract ideas and ideals,
and a world of bitter fact, but no society or tradition or or-
thodoxy in which the two worlds could interact and qualify
each other."

Henry James modified the attitude and complicated the form of this tradition. He put the idealistic hero (in fact it is usually a heroine in James's novels) with his concentration on the limitless possibilities he can imagine, his heightened — not to say exacerbated — sensitivity to the promises of life, into the realistic novel with its consciousness of the limitations society sets for the realization of imaginable possibilities. It is somewhat misleading to speak of these novels as having an International Theme. James's theme is really all that he came to understand about the life of the idealizing individual in a highly developed society, and the most remarkable thing about his handling of this theme is not simply the subtlety and range of his expressed understanding of it but the way he avoids the comparative simple-mindedness of sentimentality or cynicism: James's "International" novels neither glorify the idealizing individual by making society villainously stupid nor make society heroic by showing the individual as an irresponsible and destructive egotist. But in his ruefully amused, self-aware way, James fully recognized the way his interest always returned to the imagination of the hero: "The matter comes back again, I fear, but to the author's irrepressible and insatiable, his extravagant and immoral, interest in the personal character and in the 'nature' of a mind. . . ."

It is not, of course, insignificant that James, with his intimate knowledge of both America and Europe, *found* this theme by contemplating the American trying to realize his ideal life in European society. This fact shows us how much James was an American, with the characteristic American preoccupation with the idealizing hero; it also gives us a conviction of the authenticity of James's observation, for there is overwhelming evidence in both the lives and the works of other American novelists that the American at his best and most serious was the kind of individual James makes him, and that European society was, if not in fact, at least in the eyes of Americans, what James makes it, as — to an extent often ignored — both still are.

What James represented, though he can hardly be said to have caused it, was a change in the American novel that has continued into the present. American novelists are still writing novels that are in many respects metaphysical romances of the traditional kind: Faulkner's novels, despite their adaptation of certain technical devices of Joyce's and James's (or at least Conrad's), are of this kind, and much the same thing can be said of Saul Bellow's *Adventures of Augie March* and, more obviously, *Henderson the Rain King*. Both these writers have had a host of imitators. But since James's time American novelists have also written another kind of novel which, if it is not exactly the European realistic novel, has certainly been strongly influenced by it in much the way James's work was. The prestige of Flaubert, very high — at least until quite recently — among contemporary American writers is evidence of this influence, the nature of which shows clearly in Allen Tate's "Techniques of Fiction."

However powerful the influence of the old American preoccupation in such novels as *The Sun Also Rises, Tender Is the Night,* or *All the King's Men* — and that influence is powerful, in different ways, in all of them — there is in them also a sense of the intrinsic significance of a reality independent of the writer's understanding of it, a sense that "the way it was," in Hemingway's phrase, includes something more than the way it was for the author's or the hero's theory about it. Willie Stark may, as he is dying, urge Jack Burden to believe that "it might have been all different" had he had just a little more time to put it right, but he is essentially a man like Kutuzov who goes — with extraordinary shrewdness if not wisdom — where events lead him, and in Warren's novel events have a reality of their own, are something observed in all their recalcitrant integrity, rather than something set down only after the author has found for them a meaning that fits into his explanation of things and has thus transmuted them into symbols of his view of life.

Nevertheless the extent to which the American metaphysical temper is still at work in these writers is quite clear in James's work itself, most obviously perhaps in the resemblance of that work to Hawthorne's — in the resemblance of *The Bostonians* to *The Blithedale Romance*, of *The Golden Bowl* to *The Marble Faun*. *The Portrait of a Lady* is particularly interesting in this respect. (How loaded with the ironies of James's peculiar combination of European and American attitudes that *"Lady"* is.) Isabel Archer is an embodiment of the American "inebriated sense of self"; she thinks of herself as something wholly independent of circumstances: "Nothing that belongs to me is any measure of me; everything's on the contrary a limit, and a perfectly arbitrary one." "The fitful events," as Whitman said. "These come to me days and nights and go from me again. But they are not the Me myself." Isabel's self is everything, and she judges the world by the conception of things that self generates as the arena in which it can be realized. "I never saw a person judge things on such theoretic grounds," as Lord Warburton says of her. It is Isabel's devotion to the ideal this self conceives that carries her, heroically, to disaster, precisely as it is Jay Gatsby's "Platonic conception of himself" that leads him, heroically, to disaster.

"It's a complex fate," James said, "being an American, and one of the responsibilities it entails is fighting against a superstitious valuation of Europe." Another is fighting against a superstitious valuation of America. James was beautifully ironic about Isabel Archer's sense of self, but he is not so ironic about Milly Theale, who is more like the Hilda of Hawthorne's *Marble Faun* than she should be, as perhaps Maggie Verver is more like Chillingworth than James meant her to be.

The tradition of the American novel that was established in the nineteenth century, then, is a tradition that locates reality in the individual consciousness but does not conceive that consciousness as, in the ordinary sense, merely self-regarding; on the contrary, it makes itself responsible for nothing less than the

universe and does so with a dependence on its own capacity
for dealing with the problem that is extreme — perhaps desperate, for where is a man with this attitude to turn if his own
wisdom fails him? Thus, though reality is nearly exclusively
personal for this tradition, it is not merely a visionary reality
that takes lightly "the world of ordinary passions and longings."
On the contrary, it is much preoccupied with this ordinary
world. It conceives the capacity of the individual to do what
he sets out to do on his own to be limitless, and it supposes that
what he sets out to do is to justify the ways of God to everyman.

To satisfy the demands of a temper like this, a fiction must
fulfill three major requirements. It must present an action that
carries with it an implication of universal significance at every
stage. Events may sometimes be presented with painstaking
descriptive accuracy, but they never exist for themselves, as
observed occurrences in a world independent of the author;
they are always moralized, made symbolic of some aspect of the
author's explanation of the universe, and usually this purpose
dominates the presentation of the events and constitutes their
main interest. In the second place, the symbolic action of the
fiction must take place on the stage of the author's mind and, if
the relation between author and hero is close, as it frequently
is, on the stage of the hero's mind. This action does not,
however, symbolize some traditional explanation of the universe, as does the action of a morality play, for example; it sym-
bolizes the passionately felt personal understanding of the nature of things that the author has worked out in the privacy
of his own mind in order to satisfy the irresistible demands of
his own passionate self. Thus, neither physically nor meta-
physically can the world be allowed to take on an independent
and recalcitrant life of its own and become to some degree
absolutely resistant to the requirements of the author's feelings about it, unless the book is to show the meaninglessness

of the universe and to end in confusion and despair, because reality is what the author feels, never, even in part, what the world is. Or, to put this another way, the world in these novels is ultimately what the author finds it necessary to believe the world is in order that life may be bearable.

The strain of this necessity is all the greater because the American author is peculiarly concerned with the world; the drama that is to take place on the stage of his mind is anything but a private one, is indeed, characteristically a drama in which the hero seeks, in Scott Fitzgerald's words, "to dominate life." In the third place, therefore, such a drama requires the hero to elaborate an account of the world that is both inclusive and detailed, and yet at the same time governed at every point by the author's private conception of a meaningful universe.

The characteristic result of these three requirements is a novel that deploys a fairly elaborate metaphysical explanation of the world, an explanation that is charged with the impassioned feelings of an author and often a hero wholly involved in it, and at the same time a novel that includes a maximum number of concrete particulars of the world, since the success of the metaphysical explanation of the world depends even more on how completely it can shape to its own understanding the familiar world than it does on its internal coherence. This symbolic action will then be set before the reader as the impassioned personal "thought" of the author, usually through a narrator who may also be the hero. When it is presented in the third person, its style will be such as to bring the mind of the author vividly before the reader and thus make him feel that the action he is observing takes place, not in the everyday world, but in a reconstruction of that world in the author's mind. Faulkner's use of traditional Southern rhetoric in third-person narratives is a striking example of this method.

Thus the characteristic American novel of the tradition is one in which the particulars of the world are presented in great, even exhausting detail, but are presented, not as final realities, but as the analogical manifestations of a metaphysical explanation of the universe that constitutes for the author the final reality of experience.

VI

THE AMERICAN NOVEL AND NATURE

IN THE TWENTIETH CENTURY

SOMETIME during the early 1920's Gertrude Stein, addressing one of her interminable monologues to Ernest Hemingway in her flat at 27 rue de Fleurus, is supposed to have remarked that Hemingway and his contemporaries were "all a lost generation." (Hemingway later told Carlos Baker that in fact she said it, in French, "to a garage-keeper in the Midi," about his young mechanics.) She thus gave a name to that group of writers who appeared on the American scene during the two decades following the First World War and whose achievement still dominates American fiction, as is indicated by a bare list of names like Hemingway, Faulkner, Fitzgerald, Dos Passos, Lewis, and Cozzens.

There is a popular generalization about these writers that runs something like this: After the first war there was a rebellion by the Younger Generation against established American customs and manners. Out of this generation's disillusion with the stodgy world of prewar America came the novel of the twenties: it was full of drinking, sex, and wild living, usually in foreign parts. Then, almost exactly at the mid-point between the two wars, there was a depression. Money ran out and the expatriates had to come home. Once back in America they were led by depression conditions to an interest in radical ideas. There followed, therefore, the proletarian novel of the thirties: it was full of class conflict, heroic workers, and dialectical morality.

As a social history of the intellectuals, this generalization has some truth in it, and the value of novels — particularly second-rate novels — as evidence of that history is very considerable; you can learn more about the feel of American society in the twenties from a chapter of Percy Marks's *The Plastic Age* (1924) than you can from the whole of Mark Sullivan, and a small shelf of popular novels like Benét's *The Beginning of Wisdom* (1921), Dorothy Speare's *Dancers in the Dark* (1922), Samuel Hopkins Adams' *Flaming Youth* (1923), and Cyril Hume's *The Wife of the Centaur* (1924) is a revelation. There were also in fact many expatriates during the decade and there were novels about them like Charles Brackett's *American Colony* (1929), John Monk Saunders' *Single Lady* (1930), and David Burnham's *After This Our Exile* (1931).

Many of these expatriates did return to America in the early thirties to express a renewed interest in the peculiar country they belonged to; as Archibald MacLeish put it in 1929, writing to Gerald Murphy, the dedicatee of Fitzgerald's *Tender Is the Night* and Philip Barry's *Hotel Universe* and nearly every American expatriate's Bayard:

> This is our race, we that have none, that have had
> Neither the old walls nor the voices around us,
> This is our land, this is our ancient ground —
> The raw earth, the mixed bloods and the strangers,
> The different eyes, the wind, and the heart's change.

There is a hint here of a commitment to James's complex fate, a commitment central to the achievement of the best American novelists of the next two decades. But for several years this commitment was obscured by a widespread excitement among opinion-makers over Marxist ideas and a much publicized longing — an ideological need not unlike an earlier age's need for remote Bermooths and Noble Savages — for the imagined natural sincerities of working-class life and proletarian heroes. For

a few years there was a great hullabaloo over various proletarian writers and in 1935 *The New Masses* gave a prize to a
novel called *Marching! Marching!* by an otherwise unmem-
orable proletarian writer with the delightful name of Clara
Weatherwax.

In both the twenties and the thirties novels of the second order fitted very neatly into the patterns worked out for the period by columnists and reviewers. Among people influenced by
these patterns there was, in the early twenties, a great flurry
when Fitzgerald's *This Side of Paradise* (1920) was reported
— quite falsely — to have told all about the sex life of the
Younger Generation; it was a time when the New York papers
could solemnly consider whether *The Waste Land* was not a
hoax (it had, after all, been written by an expatriate, in *Switzer-
land* or some such implausible place), and when the expatriate
Hemingway was exposed as an anti-intellectual tough guy.
Similarly it was an Occasion for the thirties when Edmund Wilson produced a two-part article for *The New Republic* on "The
Literary Class War" and settled the question of literature as
propaganda. This was a time when it became of the first importance to decide whether Michael Gold was right in condemning Thornton Wilder's work as frivolous, or Comrade Levy
right in condemning Michael Gold's *Jews Without Money* —
in *The New Masses* itself — as individualistic; when it was important to know what one thought of John Strachey's *Literature and Dialectical Materialism* and to have a position on the
Southern Agrarians with their Confederate flags and their
Southern Review, published by Huey Long's university.

Good novels are, of course, not good because they provide
material for social history — though they do — or because they
are occasions for journalism — though they are — but because
they have a significant sense of life. It is ludicrous to think of
The Sun Also Rises (1926) as an exposé of wild-living expatriates or *Tender Is the Night* (1934) as a revelation of capital-

ist exploitation; Faulkner's work in the twenties is not "jazz-age," not even *Soldiers' Pay* (1926), nor are the fine novels of the thirties — *As I Lay Dying* (1930), *The Last Adam* (1933), *The Late George Apley* (1937), *The Pilgrim Hawk* (1940), and the like — proletarian.

Nor does Gertrude Stein's name for this generation of writ-ers give us a very satisfactory sense of them — at least, it does not unless we understand it in a way it is usually not applied. It does suggest well enough the generation's own feeling that there was almost nothing in the attitudes they inherited, noth-ing in the conventional moral and political assumptions current in America in their time, that they could accept. They felt that they had to start over again from the beginning to work out a conception of experience and a code of conduct they could live by, and to construct a conception of American so-ciety they could respect. "All I wanted to know," says the hero of Hemingway's *The Sun Also Rises*, "was how to live in [the world]. Maybe if you found out how to live in it you learned from that what is was all about." In this sense, then — the sense that all maps were useless and that they had to explore a new-found land for themselves — this generation was lost.

It was, however, anything but lost in the sense that it felt despair at this situation. On the contrary, though it was fash-ionable to talk about being disillusioned, these writers were filled with a typical American energy and optimism. Their scorn of what seemed to them the provincialism of American manners and the crass hypocrisy of American public life in their time is the scorn of people confident in their idealism. Sinclair Lewis' attack on Main Street is only partly successful, but not because Lewis doubted that Main Street's stupid pro-vincialism could be defeated. What limited Lewis' success was his inability to imagine with any effectiveness a cultivated com-munity with which to replace Main Street; he had an inadequate sense of life.

Nearly all the writers of The Lost Generation attacked the provincialism of American life in their time. But the best of them also sought to rediscover what Henry James called "the great good place" they were all sure existed, like some El Dorado, in the American sensibility; and since few Americans willingly admit that what exists in the imagination cannot be made to exist in the world, they tried to conduct their lives in such a way as to make their part of the world that great good place. In a significant sense all the important American novels since the first war — from Fitzgerald's *This Side of Paradise* in 1920 to Cozzens' *By Love Possessed* in 1957 — are pilgrims' progresses to this Celestial City. Fitzgerald said of the hero of his finest novel, *The Great Gatsby*, that he had "a heightened sensitivity to the promises of life," and there could hardly be a better phrase to describe the attitude of the writers of this generation. If they were lost, they were lost as explorers are, not as the damned are — though it should perhaps be added that in their best novels, as in *The Great Gatsby* and *By Love Possessed*, the heroes fail to reach the Celestial City of their imaginations, and that in their lives most of the writers did, too.

It is now possible to see that the First World War did a good deal to make possible the achievement of this generation of writers. Perhaps it is true that America had been a world power for some time, but it was the shock of the war that forced Americans to recognize that their country was a responsible part of Western culture. The immediate — and much advertised — effect of this discovery was to make most alert Americans dissatisfied with the inadequacies of American civilization, to the point where they preferred to live elsewhere. As early as 1921 Harold Stearns performed the symbolic act of the decade. Having edited a symposium called *Civilization in the United States* which demonstrated that there was very little, he moved to Paris. A considerable number of writers of the period did the same thing. But the significance of Harold Stearns's act was not that he sat through the decade at the Dome in Paris; it was his editing *Civilization in the United States.* For all these writers Europe was a means to an end, something that would help them to discover the possibilities in themselves as Americans.

As long as America had remained, for its own imagination, a provincial backwater, it had been difficult for gifted Americans to take it quite seriously, for reasons that James, in a famous passage in his book on Hawthorne, described with considerable accuracy if, perhaps, a somewhat limited range of illustration. The great American writers of the nineteenth century were all — however reluctantly — alienated from their society, whether they went literally into exile, as James did, or only metaphorically, as Hawthorne and Melville did. But the writers of the 1920's went to Europe to discover the American consciousness, not only of private but of social experience. It might well be argued that their greatest achievement was to add to their nineteenth-century predecessors' understanding of the American soul an imaginative grasp of American society and of the relation of the individual soul to it. By doing so, they acclimatized James's "International Novel" in America.

There is a historically significant irony in the fact that, in an age — the twenties — when a certain doubt about the absolute success of the American social experiment was beginning to creep into the minds of ordinary Americans, writers should have begun to think American life a possible subject for great literature, whereas in the late nineteenth century, when both Americans and Europeans were dazzled by the apparent success of the American social experiment and The New Man it was presumed to be creating, the best American writers found American life an impossible subject for literature.

William James, a good example of how deeply committed to the American social experiment a fine nineteenth-century mind could be, always resented his brother's refusal to write about American life: Henry's ironies about The New Man in the Eu-

ropean context — from Newman of *The American* to Adam
Verver of *The Golden Bowl* — were not at all what William
was looking for. He seems always to have hoped that Henry
would feel the inspiration of American life and he was always
looking eagerly for signs that Henry was beginning to appreciate it properly, as when, during one of Henry's visits to New
Hampshire, he asked him if he had seen anything interesting on
an afternoon's walk. Henry, obviously aware of William's motive, observed that he had indeed seen "a peasant gathering fag-
gots." The joke was not fair, even to Henry himself, who in
his way understood the Wentworths (in *The Europeans*) and
their kind at least as well as William did. But the point of the
joke, that no good writer can turn himself into a socialist-
realist propagandist for a doctrine, explains why American
writers of the nineteenth century were all exiles. It was in fact
only when doubts about the experiment had arisen and the
conception of man ceased to be inextricable from the official
New Man that American society became a possible subject for
serious fiction. So long as the idealized image of the American
was a Van Bibber or a Dink Stover there was little a serious
writer could do with him. It was indeed only by giving his
American heroes and heroines — from Caroline Spencer and
Gertrude Wentworth to Lambert Strether and Ralph Pendrel
— an un-American, an almost European, range of sensibility
very disturbing to conventional Americans like Waymarsh or
the Newsomes that James was able to deal with them seriously.

    The fundamental situation of the hero of the American novel
has not changed in the twentieth century. Indeed, he can,
without any great refinement of ingenuity, be traced all the
way back to Cooper; there is an evident resemblance between
Jay Gatsby standing in a formal pose of farewell before the
house that only his colossal illusion has made into his ancestral
home and Natty Bumppo — that image of "a perpetual possibility of perfection to the American imagination" as Marius

Bewley has called him — outlined on the crest of a hill against "the fiery light" of the setting sun, a "colossal" figure, "musing and melancholy," whose "just proportions and true character . . . it was impossible to distinguish." By the time of *The Prairie* Natty had "lighted out for the Territory," but he had not escaped the mundane Americans who were making the perpetual possibility he stood for impossible to realize. He ends his life somewhat as James Gatz ends his, a man for whom the actual American world was no longer "commensurate to his capacity for wonder" but had become "material without being real" — thanks to the Tom Buchanans, for whom the world had never been anything else.

The range and variety of the forms this hero could take in the novels of the American twentieth century are evident if we remind ourselves of the mute inglorious Gatsbys like Flem Snopes. Flem too has a Platonic conception of himself. It includes founding a dynasty by marrying Eula, who does not love him, as Gatsby plans to marry Daisy, who does not love him either; it includes acquiring a daughter — an unfortunate substitute, to be sure, for a son, but since Flem is impotent and Linda the daughter of Hank McCarron anyway, this defect in his realization of his dream is the least of Flem's troubles; it includes the acquisition of an ancestral mansion like Gatsby's, the remodeled de Spain house with "colyums across the front now, I mean the extry big ones so even a feller that never seen colyums before wouldn't have no doubt a-tall what they was, like in the photographs where the Confedrit sweetheart in a hoop skirt and a magnolia is saying good-bye to her Confedrit beau jest before he rides off to finish tending to General Grant." As Eula says of Flem, "He knew exactly what he wanted. No, that's wrong. He didn't know yet. He only knew he wanted, had to have." Like Gatsby, Flem is convinced that you can repeat the past, in order to make it what it ought to have been, and that what people do that is "only personal"

— not, that is, an act of the properly Platonic conception of the Self — is insignificant.

The important difference between the American novelists who appeared after the First World War and their predecessors of the nineteenth century is not a matter of what they saw when they looked at America or even of the main outlines of the fable they constructed about the relation of the American hero to his community. It is rather a matter of how they felt about that community, of their sensing the richness of American society as a subject for fiction, and their consequent feeling that it was possible to write directly out of the whole range of American experience, individual and social, and produce major novels. When Scott Fitzgerald was an undergraduate at Princeton, in 1916, he said to his fellow undergraduate Edmund Wilson, "I want to be one of the greatest writers that ever lived, don't you?" If this remark is comically brash, it was also quite serious, as is evident from Fitzgerald's persistent, perhaps even heroic, efforts throughout the rest of his life to write great novels. He clearly believed it was possible for him as an American to be a great writer, and this feeling had hardly existed in America before his time, in spite of — indeed, largely because of — the widespread ideological conviction that American democracy was a radically new and in many ways highly successful social experiment.

In the early 1920's young men with Fitzgerald's feeling for the possibilities of American experience suddenly began to emerge from nearly every region and every social class in the United States. Fitzgerald himself was a second-generation Irish-Catholic boy from St. Paul, Minnesota; James Gould Cozzens came of an old and well-to-do Staten Island family; John Dos Passos was the son of a successful New York father and the grandson of a Portuguese immigrant; Ernest Hemingway was the son of a doctor in a middle-class suburb of Chicago; William Faulkner came from a backwoods county seat in northern

Mississippi, where his family had lived for over a hundred years. There was John O'Hara, the Irish doctor's son who ate his heart out because he did not belong to what passed for society in the hard-coal region of Pennsylvania, and Sinclair Lewis, the amazingly ugly Minnesota redhead who said to his Yale classmates at a reunion, "When I was in college, you fellows didn't give a damn about me, and I'm here to say that now I don't give a damn about you." (If so, what was he doing at that reunion telling them so?) There was John Marquand, a Bostonian in feeling and a Harvard man in fact, who, because he did not go to a preparatory school, never could forget what it must feel like to be a Dartmouth man. This list could be extended, but wherever these writers came from, they were all convinced of the special significance of the common American experience and were sure that, by discarding their parents' provincial conception of it, they had become free to tell the truth, the complex, fascinating, inner truth, about it.

This common belief made their books similar in some unexpected ways, however different their different temperaments may have also made them. They shared a set of values and a sense of social experience that are easy to recognize. They were all acutely aware of the typical American social institutions of their times and of the manners imposed by these institutions; unlike their predecessors, they thought such things important and interesting. They had a strong sense of the kind of American history that — for better as well as for worse — lay behind these institutions. It is a misconception imposed on literary history by the public-relations talents of Southerners that only the American South has an awareness of its past. This kind of awareness is alive in the imaginations of most regions of the United States, even in California, as books like John Steinbeck's *The Pastures of Heaven* and *East of Eden* clearly show.

These feelings are common to the novels of all of them. For example:

Her family had been in Gibbsville a lot longer than the great majority of the people who lived on Lantenengo Street. She was a Doane, and Grandfather Doane had been a drummer boy in the Mexican War and had a Congressional Medal of Honor from the Civil War. Grandfather Doane had been a member of the School Board for close to thirty years, before he died, and he was the only man in this part of the State who had the Congressional Medal of Honor.

This happens to be O'Hara, but it might be almost any other novelist of the period; only the queer feeling about the insignia is, I think, special to O'Hara (and Scott Fitzgerald felt something very like it, too). Faulkner has a similar feeling for local family history and its moral and social importance, and so have Marquand and Cozzens; Fitzgerald has a similar awareness of the fine social shadings marked by the streets of the "residential" sections of old American towns; and this paragraph's curious artful-naïve return upon itself in the repeated reference to Grandfather Doane's Congressional Medal of Honor is pure Hemingway: the very first paragraph of *The Sun Also Rises* uses such a return in almost exactly the same way (see p. 132).

The set of attitudes common to these writers is, at least in outline, a sense of experience; it consists of the major consequences of that heightened sensitivity to the promises of life that they took to be a special product of American life. Because they were convinced that what they were trying to realize was peculiarly a product of American experience, they set out to express it in the terms of American experience. As a result their novels are filled with the minutiae of daily American life, not infrequently in a way that appears more thorough than illuminating (the novels of James T. Farrell and of Raymond Chandler, to take two quite different types, seem to fail in about the same degree in this respect).

It is not surprising that they do not always make a success of this device; it is not an easy one to bring off, least of all in

America. Ever since the seventeenth century imposed on Western culture what is sometimes called the Descartian Dualism, the West has had to live in a world where there was a serious gap between thought and nature, between the inner life of the consciousness and the outer life of the physical and social world. American society may almost be said to have been invented by seventeenth-century theorists, and one of the results is that the discontinuity between the inner life of the consciousness and the outer life of society is even greater here than elsewhere in Western culture. If the thing that made American life rich with dramatic conflict for these writers was the way it realized in its daily activities the clash between the possibilities and the all too commonplace probabilities of life, the difficulties of representing their understanding of this clash constituted their main technical problem. This was the problem, discussed in the next chapter of this book, of bridging the gap between their heroes' heightened sense of the promises of their life and the actualities of the society which, though it had taught them these promises, resisted their realization with a peculiar recalcitrance.

The simplest solution to this technical problem was to make the gap itself a part of one's subject, to exploit with romantic irony what was called in the cliché of the time, "the alienation of the artist from his society." This is the effect of the technique Dos Passos designed. His "Newsreels" are montages of slogans, newspaper headlines, snatches of popular songs, that represent the average, public awareness of society, a sort of crude folklore of industrialized society. For example:

TO THE GLORY OF FRANCE ETERNAL

Oh a German officer crossed the Rhine
  Parleyvoo

Germans Beaten at Riga Grateful Parisians Cheer
Marshals of France

> *Oh a German officer crossed the Rhine*
> *He liked the women and loved the wine*
> *Hankypanky parleyvoo*

PITEOUS PLAINT OF WIFE TELLS OF
RIVAL'S WILES
Wilson's arrival in Washington starts trouble. . . .

In immediate and ironic juxtaposition with the "Newsreel" Dos Passos characteristically places "The Camera Eye," the expression of an intense, subjective perception of the personal life — for example, of waking up in the morning:

> daylight enlarges out of ruddy quiet very faintly throbbing
> wanes into my sweet darkness broadens red through the warm
> blood weighting the lids warmsweetly then snaps on
> enormously blue yellow pink

Between these formal extremes, Dos Passos puts his dry, neutral narrative.

Though other novelists of the twenties did not make a formal principle out of the discontinuities of their consciousnesses, as Dos Passos did, they had to confront them. There is, for instance, a gap between the passages of Hemingway's *For Whom the Bell Tolls* that express his deepest private feelings and the passages the first-rate journalist in Hemingway wrote about the history of the Spanish Civil War. Robert Jordan's death is a magnificent image of Hemingway's deep personal feeling for "grace under pressure." But it is almost completely unrelated to the public feelings Robert Jordan has about the values at stake in the Spanish Civil War.

Hemingway is much more successful when he limits himself to the consciousness of his hero and does not attempt a direct account of the historically important social and political circumstances of his times. For instance, Jake Barnes in *The Sun Also Rises* does in fact learn a great deal about what the everyday world is like by slowly discovering what he calls "how to live in it," what attitudes he must take if he is to retain his self-respect, and Hemingway is thus able to show us, indirectly, a great deal about that world. The very first sentences of the book illustrate beautifully how Hemingway, starting from the private consciousness of Jake Barnes, can work his way outward to the powerful realities of the society around him.

> Robert Cohn was once middleweight boxing champion of Princeton. Do not think that I am very much impressed by that as a boxing title, but it meant a lot to Cohn. He cared nothing for boxing, in fact he disliked it, but he learned it painfully and thoroughly to counteract the feeling of inferiority and shyness he had felt on being treated as a Jew at Princeton. . . . He was Spider Kelly's star pupil. Spider Kelly taught all his young gentlemen to box like featherweights, no matter whether they weighed one hundred and five or two hundred and five pounds. But it seemed to fit Cohn. He was really very fast. He was so good that Spider promptly overmatched him and got his nose permanently flattened. This increased Cohn's distaste for boxing, but it gave him a certain satisfaction of some strange sort, and it certainly improved his nose. In his last year at Princeton he read too much and took to wearing spectacles. I never met any one of his class who remembered him. They did not even remember that he was middleweight boxing champion.

Among other things, this paragraph contains the materials for a whole history of the Jews in America and of the helpless attitude of non-Jewish Americans in the face of it ("it certainly improved his nose"). Hemingway's understanding of the Jew's feeling at Eastern universities in the twenties, a "feeling of shyness and inferiority," is admirably precise. He understands perfectly the place such universities — with their pseudo-British "young gentlemen" and their privileged but nonetheless servile "Spider" Kellys — had in the American social hierarchy and can measure exactly how devastating it is that no one "of his class [at Princeton] remembered" Cohn. Like any American, he wishes to be known as an informed amateur of sports, but he recognizes the absurdity of our solemn concern for sports: "They did not even remember that he was middleweight boxing champion"; if not even this athletic distinction is remembered about you by your Princeton classmates, you were not so much obscure as systematically ignored. Finally there is the fact, so characteristic of the novelists of this period, that Spider Kelly is, in his modest Princeton way, a historical character and may lead us to inquire about the claims to historicity of the other characters in the book, like Cohn, whose claims are easy to determine now that Harold Loeb has published *The Way It Was*. Thus, in a remarkable variety of ways, *The Sun Also Rises* moves outward from the private consciousness of its hero to the political, social, and historical realities of its world.

This way of dealing with the gap between the private consciousness and the public world has, however successfully executed it may be, its intrinsic limitations, and it is easy to understand why Hemingway may, on purely literary grounds, have decided to try something different in *To Have and Have Not* and *For Whom the Bell Tolls*. Social and political realities that emerge only by implication offer a writer no opportunity for a systematic account of these matters or what reviewers call a "hard-hitting" expression of opinion about them. These things are sacrificed in order that such social judgments as are implied may be continuous with the book's other reality, the hero's personal sense of experience. In *The Great Gatsby* Fitzgerald tried to extend the limits of this form and came close to overextending them.

He begins by making his hero much more idealistic than Jake Barnes about the possibilities of the personal life, so idealistic that he has no capacity for irony about himself at all. Gatsby lives a Platonic conception of himself with deadly seriousness;

he is a man who has committed himself without qualification to
his vision of an ideal self; when that vision is destroyed he dies.
Fitzgerald has thus maximized the American hero's idealism;
Gatsby lives, like Isabel Archer, on the assumption that "Nothing that belongs to me is any measure of me; everything's on
the contrary a limit, and a perfectly arbitrary one." It would
be impossible to present such a hero directly: he would appear
absurd or mad, as Hemingway's heroes (and even Hemingway himself, who sometimes seems to have imagined himself
one of them) occasionally did. Fitzgerald sought to get
around this difficulty by presenting his hero indirectly,
through a narrator, and by having the narrator provide the
irony. He does it brilliantly, but in the end we recognize that
he means us to be wholly on the side of his hero, to believe
that without Gatsby's extreme idealism life is simply unlivable.
When Gatsby's dream has at last been shattered, we are told,
he "must have looked up at an unfamiliar sky through frightening leaves and shivered as he found what a grotesque thing a
rose is and how raw the sunlight was upon the scarcely
created grass. A new world, material without being real. . . ."

Moreover, Fitzgerald tried to identify Gatsby's personal
idealism explicitly with the social idealism that had been the
origin — and was to him still the only endurable purpose —
of American society. He ends the book with the narrator sitting
on the beach back of Gatsby's deserted house, looking out over
Long Island Sound and thinking of what it had been like there
when the Dutch sailors first caught sight of it three hundred
years before.

> . . . for a transitory enchanted moment — Nick thinks — man
> must have held his breath in the presence of this continent, com-
> pelled into an aesthetic contemplation he neither understood nor
> desired, face to face for the last time in history with something
> commensurate to his capacity for wonder.
>
> And as I sat there brooding on the old, unknown world, I
> thought of Gatsby's wonder. . . .

This is a daring, and eloquent, attempt to bridge the gap between the private sense of the possibilities of American life and the public sense of what it is; but the cost is considerable. For all *The Great Gatsby*'s brilliant surface realism, it remains a romance, almost a fairy story, in which not only the hero but mankind becomes the unappreciated younger son, the male cinderella, whose essential fineness is destroyed by an impersonal and indifferent world.

The novels of Dos Passos, Hemingway, and Fitzgerald are the most characteristic of the period. They are tragic novels in the sense that their heroes are defeated by a society that has not — or at least has not yet — fulfilled the optimistic eighteenth-century vision of perfection, whose truths had then seemed a part of the course of nature, to which these novelists are all, in their different ways, committed. None of these heroes ever seriously doubts what Nick calls in Gatsby's case his Platonic conception of himself, his idealized vision of the personal life. Rather than compromise this ideal, they either die — as do Gatsby and Harry Morgan and Robert Jordan — or fade from the world — as does the hero of Fitzgerald's *Tender Is the Night*, who will wander forever about the Finger Lakes country of upstate New York ("he is almost certainly in that section of the country, in one town or another") or the hero of Hemingway's *A Farewell to Arms*, who "went out and left the hospital and walked back to the hotel in the rain." For all their practical unsuccess, these heroes, though broken, are what Hemingway once called another of his, The Undefeated. But they are also the completely isolated. Like Frederic Henry of *A Farewell to Arms* they have had to make "a separate peace," to resign from society, in order to preserve the integrity of their visions of themselves.

Despite the fact that Faulkner's novels are all concerned with what he calls The Unvanquished, his heroes do not all resign from their society. Faulkner's "Unvanquished" is not an individual living by the dictates of his private dream of himself, as is Hemingway's Undefeated. Faulkner's Unvanquished is a community, the community of those Southerners who, defeated physically in the American Civil War a hundred years ago, have refused to surrender spiritually. But Faulkner presents this community with all the romantic idealism and sense of greatness that his contemporaries give to their individual heroes. When Faulkner is dealing with the relations between his romanticized Southern community and the rest of the United States, his resemblance to his contemporaries is evident: in Faulkner's novels The South is always broken but unvanquished, exactly as are the individual heroes of Hemingway and Fitzgerald. But when he is dealing with an individual hero within his Southern community, he is a different kind of novelist, because his heroes — especially, perhaps, the Ike McCaslin of *Go Down, Moses* — confront within their communities the difficulties Faulkner otherwise shows the Southern community itself facing in its relations with the country as a whole; their problems are not unlike those of the speaker in Allen Tate's "Ode to the Confederate Dead."

The heroes of James Gould Cozzens' novels also exist primarily as members of a living community; even Cozzens' rebel heroes, like Dr. Bull of *The Last Adam*, really represent the resistance of an older strain in the life of the community itself to new manifestations of that life. The observation of typical American communities in the half dozen novels from *The Last Adam* to *By Love Possessed* is remarkable, but its success may conceal the reason Cozzens makes it, what is finally most remarkable about his work. This is his compassionate but wholly responsible commitment to reason, to the necessary limitations on individual achievement. In Cozzens' world, as in the world of Allen Tate's *The Fathers*, the man who commits himself without restraint to a personal dream of life is, however great his talents and charm, a private self-deceiver and a public menace.

Cozzens' heroes are men of reason who have, by an effort of the intelligence and the will, disciplined their own natures to the possibilities of their society. Their triumph is to learn how to sacrifice their most cherished vanity, as does Arthur Winner in *By Love Possessed* when he sacrifices his image of himself as a man wholly beyond reproach in order that the *modus vivendi* of the community he lives in and loves — a *modus vivendi* by no means strictly legal or even morally defensible — may continue to exist. The conclusion of *By Love Possessed* is the climax of all Cozzens' novels, for what Arthur Winner sacrifices is his private — and indeed even secret — image of himself as a man of absolute public virtue. We are made to see that sacrifice as the surrender of the final delusion of the romantic individualist, and that surrender is the conclusion toward which the lives of all Cozzens' heroes since Francis Ellery have been leading.

This Lost Generation of novelists, then, constitutes the first coherent group of novelists in the history of American literature. They were not a school, for they only occasionally influenced each other directly and consciously, though their personal relations were, for American writers, close. Each had a distinctive voice of his own and his own special preoccupations. But they shared a common belief in the usableness of American experience and, consequently, a common point of view and conception of the novel's form that are new in America. This similarity of intention is all the more striking because it was arrived at spontaneously and independently.

Americans have, of course, been discovering Europe and Western culture, in one way or another, since the days of Franklin and Jefferson. But the Lost Generation's much advertised expatriation was a discovery of American experience as a distinctly different if still recognizable version of the experience of the West as a whole, something that could be accepted without apology or self-consciousness as the material of a great act of the imagination. None of the novelists of the Lost Generation was as gifted as the great and lonely giants of nineteenth-century American fiction. But taken together — as the impulse common to their generation requires that we should take them — they constitute the finest group of novelists America has produced, one that suggests American fiction can, without ceasing to understand the American's apparently ineradicable commitment to the promises of life, still recognize with justice the actualities of the world in which those promises have to be realized.

VII

THE DILEMMA OF THE AMERICAN NOVELIST

HOWEVER gifted were American novelists of the period following the First World War and however fortunate, in certain
ways, their circumstances, it can hardly be expected that they
would have escaped the difficulties created for them by the circumstances of the American culture of which they were a part.
During this period the effort of American criticism (perhaps
battle would be a better word, considering the violence of the
debate) to resolve the conflict between the novel of inner consciousness and the novel of public action reached a new
intensity. It was, as criticism often is, the reflection of a struggle that was going on in the novelists themselves, a struggle that
had begun in the minds of English writers at least as early as
Matthew Arnold with his anxiety about the gap between the
buried life and the life of the world:

> Alas! is even love too weak
> To unlock the heart, and let it speak?
> Are even lovers powerless to reveal
> To one another what indeed they feel?
> I knew the mass of men conceal
> Their thoughts, for fear that if revealed
> They would by other men be met
> With blank indifference, or with blame reproved;
> I knew they lived and moved
> Tricked in disguises, alien to the rest
> Of men. . . .

As Scott Fitzgerald put it for his time, "It is in the thirties that we want friends. In the forties we know they won't save us any more than love did." Tennyson struggled to suppress, along with poems like "The Mystic," a similar anxiety, and something like it is present in all the great romantics and in the Gothic novelists. Exacerbated by the assumption of American society that no such gap need exist in the properly run world, the conflict between the two kinds of novels became intense in this period.

At the beginning of the period between the two wars, the novel participated vigorously in the life of American society; it was very much a party to the new and shocking ideas about war and politics and The American Way of Life. The novelists were representing experience as men ordinarily knew it and implying the immediate judgments and attitudes which that experience called for. However inadequate the evaluation of experience and however wooden the prose which expresses it in Joseph Hergesheimer, for example, his novels were an attempt to represent what was, for the time, a significant part of experience for large numbers of people. Had his books not had this characteristic, it would be quite impossible to explain how novels at once so tediously earnest and so bad achieved such success. There could hardly be better evidence of how the novels of the early twenties succeeded for their time in representing familiar experience than the way they were criticized. Those who disliked them did not say they were not life; they only said they were a much less widespread kind of life than their authors thought. Even Maxwell Perkins, one of the most sympathetic members of the older generation, thought that, though there may have been a few soldiers like Dos Passos' three, they were not representative; and Heywood Broun was sure *This Side of Paradise* was a case of not kissing but telling just the same.

But the pressures of the twenties and thirties were such that novels which had a representative sense of life had a harder and harder time surviving. For one thing they were under pressure from those deeply concerned with the techniques for rendering states of consciousness. Mr. Bennett's view of Mrs. Brown was discovered to be hopelessly old-fashioned and Joyce and Gertrude Stein and The Revolution of the Word began to be taken very seriously among all literary people who kept abreast of things. "My husband is finishing his first novel, you see," says Violet McKisco in *Tender is the Night.* "It's on the idea of Ulysses. Only instead of taking twenty-four hours my husband takes a hundred years. He takes a decayed old French aristocrat and puts him in contrast with the mechanical age —"

As time went on the novel was also under pressure from those who believed they had found a solution to what seemed to them the intolerable injustices of modern society, a solution that, in the thirties, took a more and more rigidly Marxist form. This drift carried a whole series of novelists into writing a kind of novel in which observed and imagined life could appear only to the extent that it illustrated doctrinaire social theories. Thus the novelists of the twenties and thirties were under considerable pressure to experiment with one or another unconventional and, for most of them, newly acquired sense of life. This was equally true of the home-keeping writers like Dreiser and of the "advanced" exile writers like Gertrude Stein.

These pressures encouraged, then, novels very different from the kind that had been written in the early twenties. In the early twenties, on the whole, novelists wrote Mr. Bennett's kind of novel; and, ill-defined though it is in her pamphlet, it was Mrs. Woolf's kind of novel Mrs. Woolf preferred, as it was preachment of the party line that *The New Masses* and the John Reed Clubs wanted. The period's romantic pleasure in a conviction of its own revolutionary character, together with a generous share of the characteristic scorn any age feels for its immediate predecessors, effectively concealed the fact that these pressures, together with the forms they seemed to dictate, triumphed as easily as they did because they were intensifications of the pressures that had been at work in the nineties and the Georgian period. (It is no wonder Virginia Woolf found herself severely at odds with her Victorian father, when her spiritual father was Walter Pater.) Nothing is more remarkable, as one reads over now the work of the twenties and thirties, than the extent to which the attitudes of the nineties survived into the later decades.

"No one," remarked Edmund Wilson later, "seems to have noticed that *Axel's Castle* and *To the Finland Station* are complementary books." It is quite true, and the complements are the two major preoccupations of the nineties; that is, the poetry of refined, inner experience, and the poetry of social awareness (one of the chapter titles of *To the Finland Station* is: "Karl Marx: Poet of Commodities. . . ."). There is a clear similarity between the values of Edmund Wilson and of the Thomas Parke D'Invilliers who set Amory Blaine to reading so energetically in Swinburne and Wilde and — the list is worth taking, name by name — "Shaw, Chesterton, Barrie, Pinero, Yeats, Synge, Ernest Dowson, Arthur Symons, Keats, Sudermann, Robert Hugh Benson, The Savoy Operas." Here — brought up to date — are the previous periods' two apparently discrepant lines of interest, the aesthetic assertion of the value of the individual consciousness and the socio-political assertion of the value of the community. Whether they are really complementary is the question.

The people who were in college when the first war broke out were still reading Swinburne almost as a contemporary; and even in the thirties, in one of the finest and most angry of the "Camera Eye" passages, Dos Passos was quoting from *Song in Time of Order* to support a revolutionary attitude. Like Swinburne himself, the writers who came of age in the period of the First World War committed themselves to both the aesthetic attitude and the social conscience without — at least at first — any sense of conflict. They were a generation that read Dowson and Wilde, Shaw and Wells indiscriminately. It is not easy now to understand how Wells could have seemed so important to them until you see how he appeared, for a moment, to have solved the problem inherent in this bifold tradition.

As technical innovations forced more and more into the open the discordance of the two strains in the tradition, writers were more and more forced to face the question of whether the passionate, sensitive inner life constitutes reality and so, represented in one form or another, is the business of the novel, or whether the world of the social and political theorists is reality and its representation the novel's business. Should the novel, that is, move toward the condition of the lyric with Virginia Woolf, or should it move toward the condition of the case history with Dreiser? Many young novelists in the early twenties were telling each other that the H. G. Wells of *Tono Bungay* and *The New Machiavelli* ("that queer confused novel," Wells called it twenty-five years later) was a great novelist because he seemed to have solved this problem. You can certainly see even today how Wells's political talk, for all its thinness, sounded exciting then. But what seemed to have struck these young novelists was the way Wells managed to make the political argument personal experience, to make a survey of contemporary history a part of the life of his hero so that the endless essay-writing of the political sections of *The New Machiavelli* appeared as human and personally significant as are the really fine accounts of Remington's childhood and of his affairs with Margaret and Isabel. "The glorious intoxicated efforts of H. G. Wells," Amory Blaine in *This Side of Paradise* called Wells's novels, "to fit the key of romantic symmetry into the elusive lock of truth." So he had seemed then.

Wells's solution was a picaresque novel of ideas. Compton Mackenzie, whose *Sinister Street* (1913) was, as Frances Newman said, "the apple of one's eye," wrote a similar kind of novel and had a similar appeal; *Youth's Encounter* is even referred to in *Manhattan Transfer*. Here then, in Wells and Mackenzie, for a moment anyway, appeared to be a solution to the problem of representing the intricate inner life of the individual and also doing a social history of the times. Therefore *This Side of Paradise* (1920) turned out, in Edmund Wilson's words, to be "an exquisite burlesque of Compton Mackenzie with a pastiche of H. G. Wells thrown in at the end." A number of other novels like Floyd Dell's *The Briary-Bush* (1921) followed suit and even Dos Passos' *Three Soldiers* (1921) showed the influence, though it made a significant change in the form.

It is ironic that Wells of all people should have had this effect, for though he certainly had a natural gift for "romantic symmetry," as Fitzgerald called it, he was himself belligerently opposed to any novelist's paying much attention to it. He believed the novel was primarily an instrument for setting forth social ideas and firmly distinguished himself from James and Conrad on exactly this point.

> I remember a dispute we had one day as we lay on the Sandgate beach and looked out at sea. How, [Conrad] demanded, would I describe how that boat out there, sat or rode or danced or quivered on the water? I said that in nineteen cases out of twenty I would just let the boat be there in the commonest phrase possible. . . . if I wanted to make it important then the phrase to use would depend on the angle at which the boat became significant. But it was all against Conrad's over-sensitized receptivity that a boat could ever be just a boat. He wanted to see it with a definite vividness of his own. But I wanted to see it only in relation to something else — a story, a thesis. (*Experiment in Autobiography*.)

There is a certain confusion in all this. Wells is probably right that Conrad sometimes indulged the fine shades of his awareness of particulars at the expense of the familiar whole and even, occasionally, took more interest in the evocative rhetoric of his thesis than its point; "essentially sentimental and melodramatic," Wells called his work, anticipating almost exactly Dos Passos' later judgment of Fitzgerald's. But if there is something in this judgment, Wells is himself either disingenuous or remarkably innocent about a boat's being just a boat — whatever that is. He talks as if there is an easily available objective boat which Conrad wants to clutter up with all sorts of decorative qualities, whereas Wells is content to present the boat itself, which Conrad knows as well as he does if he will only be sensible.

Yet Wells has a point; he wants to see things primarily "in relation to . . . a story." If it is a mistake to suppose that the shared world of the familiar conception of things is made up of boats which are "just boats," and that its realization does not involve a gift and a great deal of care and attention, it is also true that this is a world which it is perilous to omit from a fiction. Wells could have done with more of Conrad's regard for receptivity, but Conrad could certainly have done with more of Wells's interest in presenting and judging the world the everyday awareness receives. "My dear Wells," Conrad would say, apparently genuinely puzzled, "what is this *Love and Mr. Lewisham* ABOUT?" It is a fair question to ask about a novel that contains a h'penny worth of rendered life to an intolerable deal of doctrine about it. But it is easy to imagine Wells asking Conrad what *Lord Jim* is about, too, for in its preoccupation with rendering the obscure reaches of the romantic consciousness, *Lord Jim* sometimes gets a long way from any "natural" sense of life.

This is not to say that in his own way Conrad did not care as much about the fate of the world as Wells did, even though he never allowed that concern to break out in lectures and sermons in his novels but only to manifest itself in the rendered experience of his characters. No fair reader can doubt Conrad's conviction that the civilized world is preserved from chaos and savagery only by men's faith in the "sovereign power enthroned in a fixed standard of conduct," even though his sardonic awareness of the relativity of this standard and the inadequate conception of it in men's imaginations often led him into irony — "in truth, thanks to our unwearied efforts [the world] is as sunny an arrangement of small conveniences as the mind of man can conceive" — and sometimes drove him close to despair.

But if often desperately, he clung to a belief that chaos and savagery were to be held at bay, if at all, only by the white man's assuming to the full his burden of providing order and progress for the world. A part of his mind was always crying out that the burden was too great to bear. The very powers of imagination that make it possible for a man to visualize fully "the idea" that, as Marlow puts it in "Heart of Darkness," "redeems" "the conquest of the earth" also intensify for him the temptations of instinctive savagery and instinctive fear; it is on the cards that the most gifted men will be most tempted and fail, as Kurtz wholly failed, as Jim partly failed. A part of Conrad's mind also cried out that " 'giving your life up to them' (*them* meaning all of mankind with skins brown, yellow, or black in colour) 'was like selling your soul to a brute.' "

In spite of these corroding doubts, however, Conrad struggled to believe that the white man could and would bear his burden; he had to; there was no other way he could see to save the world. That is why his visit to the Congo of Leopold's brutal imperialistic exploitation seemed "like a weary pilgrimage amongst hints for nightmares"; it was the realization of his worst fears, a terrifying demonstration of what, in his moments of despair, he himself felt the only conceivable scheme for the salvation of the world became when you put it into practice — that is, "a flabby, pretending, weak-eyed devil of a rapacious and pitiless folly." Yet the Thames, where their yacht lies at anchor as Marlow tells this story of the Congo, "also [had once] been one of the dark places of the earth" and now is "spread out in the tranquil dignity of a waterway leading to the uttermost ends of the earth" on which for centuries men have gone out "bearing the sword, and often the torch, messengers of the might within the land, bearers of a spark from the sacred fire." Thus eloquently, if indirectly, Conrad realized in his work his desperate remedy for the world.

No doubt Conrad's tortured doubts seemed nonsense to the ebullient Wells, if he detected this aspect of Conrad's work at all. Certainly he would have been impatient with Conrad's insistence on letting his doctrine emerge only as it manifested itself in the rendered, private experience of consciousnesses so highly developed that you could make sense of them only with great effort, to say nothing of grasping the social doctrine incidentally revealed when you did wholly understand them.

Yet it is arguable that Conrad's way of realizing in his novels the public, historical aspect of our life is really the only way to do so, even though it seems to people deeply concerned with this aspect of life to blur, if not wholly conceal it. It is certainly a fact that Wells's almost instinctive though very considerable gift for rendering in his novels his personal sense of life was slowly stifled during the course of his career by his growing interest in social generalization. Almost simultaneously he and Mackenzie faded out, both as writers and as influences; by 1925, when the two generations met in the persons of Fitzgerald and Mackenzie, Fitzgerald was saying, "You get no sense from him that he feels his work has gone to pieces. . . . The war wrecked him as it did Wells and many of that generation." But it did not wreck Conrad for Fitzgerald and his generation; Fitzgerald had just finished *The Great Gatsby* when he wrote this remark about Mackenzie and Wells, and the influence of Conrad — whom Fitzgerald apparently read at Edmund Wilson's urging — is strong in that novel.

Meanwhile, the novel of inner experience was rapidly developing an elaborate and self-conscious form which made more and more delicate and lyrical accounts of that experience possible at the cost of excluding more and more of the world of our customary apprehension; and the novel of public experience was increasing its emphasis on social significance by excluding more and more of its characters' inner experience — and of its narrator's. The best of the novelists of the twenties were caught between the two, unable to bring them together. There is a dramatic display of this fact in a letter Dos Passos wrote Fitzgerald in 1936, when Fitzgerald published "The Crack-Up."

There has always been in Dos Passos, as there was not in Wells, a novelist fascinated by inner experience. This novelist turned up only slightly disguised as John Andrews in *Three Soldiers*, and made an appearance sounding like Joyce and E. E. Cummings in the "Camera Eye" passages of *U.S.A.*; the degree to which Dos Passos is capable in these passages of completely isolating himself in the small inner world of private responses is remarkable and, indeed, disturbing:

> The raindrops fell one by one out of the horsechestnut tree over the arbor onto the table in the abandoned beergarden and the puddly gravel and my clipped skull where my fingers move gently forward and backward over the fuzzy knobs and hollows . . . shyly tingling fingers feel out the limits of the hard immortal skull under the flesh . . . a deathshead and skeleton sits wearing glasses in the arbor under the lucid occasional raindrops inside the new khaki uniform inside my twentyoneyearold body that's been swimming in the Marne in red and whitestriped trunks in Chalons in the spring

Most of the time, however, Dos Passos is a social novelist and the social novelist is completely unacquainted with this thin-skinned and tingling-fingered death's-head in glasses. It is difficult not to feel that Dos Passos is a man who found himself confronted by two irreconcilable senses of life, the personal and the public, and resolved his difficulty by an act of the will, forcing his main attention onto a rigidly public sense of life and allowing his personal sense of it expression only on carefully limited occasions, in a form that carefully separates them from the central activity in his fiction, with the result that the expressions of his personal sense of life are exclusively and extravagantly personal and the expressions of his public sense of life seriously impoverished.

What nevertheless makes the main action of *U.S.A.*, with its predominately public sense of life, better than the similar actions in other social novels is the way his narrative does something more than present the interplay of typical social attitudes. Malcolm Cowley, in one of the best things that has ever been written about Dos Passos, observed that "we are likely to remember [*The Big Money*] as a furious and sombre poem, written in a mood of revulsion even more powerful than that which T. S. Eliot expressed in 'The Waste Land.'" The comparison is perhaps not very apt, but the point about Dos Passos is true. The effect of *U.S.A.* is the effect of a world in which no man wins, whether he "succeeds" as do Charlie Anderson and Richard Savage and Margo Dowling, or fails as do Mary French and Ben Compton and Eveline Hutchins; their defeat is in either case a defeat beyond political redress.

Yet on the whole Dos Passos' characters are the two-dimensional sort we expect in the Jonsonian tragedy of humors, and his events are thin and diagrammatic rather than full of the felt contingency of experience. *U.S.A.* has on a very large scale the architectural orderliness of the Jonsonian tragedy, but what it organizes is a set of notes for people and events, rather than a fully realized action. It is devastating, for example, to compare the scene where Daughter and Dick Savage decide not to have their baby with Hemingway's "Hills Like White Elephants." This is the significant part of Dos Passos' scene:

Dick was hoping she'd go, everything she did drove him crazy. There were tears in her eyes when she came up to him. "Give me a kiss, Dick . . . don't worry about me . . . I'll work things out somehow."

"I'm sure it's not too late for an operation," said Dick. "I'll find out an address tomorrow and drop you a line to the Continental . . . Anne Elizabeth . . . it's splendid of you to be so splendid about this."

She shook her head, whispered goodby and hurried out of the room.

"Well, that's that," said Dick aloud to himself. He felt terribly sorry about Anne Elizabeth.

What must be the deliberate and calculated thinness of this dialogue, its deliberate reduction of feelings to their bare idea, is clear enough if you put it beside an equal amount of Hemingway's dialogue, alive as it is in every phrase with the full quality of the characters' feelings and, ultimately, with Hemingway's feeling about the whole situation.

"It's really an awfully simple operation, Jig," the man said. "It's not really an operation at all."

The girl looked at the ground the table legs rested on.

"I know you wouldn't mind it, Jig. It's really not anything. It's just to let the air in."

The girl did not say anything.

"I'll go with you and I'll stay with you all the time. They just let the air in and then it's all perfectly natural."

"Then what will we do afterward?"

"We'll be fine afterward. Just like we were before.". . .

"And you think then we'll be all right and be happy."

"I know we will. You don't have to be afraid. I've known lots of people that have done it."

"So have I," said the girl. "And afterward they were all so happy."

The same thing happens if you put a passage of Dos Passos' narrative beside a passage of Fitzgerald's. This is Dos Passos' account of Dick's arrival at Harvard.

He sent his trunk and suitcase out by the transfer company from South Station and went out on the subway. He had on a new grey suit and a new grey felt hat and was afraid of losing the certified cheque he had in his pocket for deposit in the Cambridge bank. . . . Kendall Square . . . Central Square . . . Harvard Square. The train didn't go any further; he had to get out. Something about the sign on the turnstile *Out To The College Yard* sent a chill down his spine.

"He was afraid of losing the certified cheque. . . ." "Something about the sign . . . sent a chill down his spine." These are the merest notations of sentiments. Like Dos Passos' dialogue, they are deliberately deprived of immediacy, which has been isolated in the "Camera Eye" passages. This, in contrast, is one of Fitzgerald's schoolboys on his first weekend away from a school where he has been desperately and humiliatingly unpopular.

> . . . [Basil] went for luncheon to the Manhattan Hotel, near the station, where he ordered a club sandwich, French fried potatoes and a chocolate parfait. Out of the corner of his eye he watched the nonchalant, debonair, blasé New Yorkers at neighboring tables. . . . School had fallen from him like a burden; it was no more than an unheeded clamor, faint and faraway. He even delayed opening the letter from the morning's mail which he found in his pocket, because it was addressed to him at school.
>
> He wanted another chocolate parfait, but being reluctant to bother the busy waiter any more, he opened the letter and spread it before him instead. [This letter is from Basil's mother, suggesting a trip to Europe which will take him away from the school for the rest of the year.]
>
> Basil got up from his chair with a dim idea of walking over to the Waldorf and having himself locked up safely until his mother came. Then, impelled to some gesture, he raised his voice and in one of his first basso notes called boomingly and without reticence for the waiter. . . .

It required the din of Forty-second Street to sober his maudlin joy. With his hand in his purse to guard against the omnipresent pickpocket, he moved cautiously toward Broadway.

Fitzgerald is here dealing with a far simpler being than Dos Passos' Dick Savage, yet where Dos Passos is thin, Fitzgerald is richly concrete; moreover, every detail Fitzgerald introduces is there because it is a characteristic part of the awareness of young manhood and forces our minds to summon up and share Basil's feelings. We not only know in this way what Basil felt and assent to it; we also measure, with the guidance of Fitzgerald's irony, the distance between ourselves and boyhood, exactly how far we have come from club sandwiches and chocolate parfaits, from boyhood's habit of *finding* our morning mail in our pocket, from the fear of the busy waiter and the omnipresent pickpocket, from all the simple, intense suffering and joy of young manhood.

With Dos Passos we merely note the individual character's feelings and slide into a simple attitude toward him, but with Fitzgerald, as with Hemingway, we feel in imagination what he feels and grow gradually into an attitude toward all he is. This attitude is neither simple nor static because it has not, as in Dos Passos' work, been built up by details which have almost no purpose except to repeat the generalized idea of the paragraph as a whole. Our attitude toward what Hemingway and Fitzgerald tell us is complex and dramatic because each of the details which have contributed to creating it has had a considerable independent life of its own, and what they write provides us, in Coleridge's phrase, "such delight from the *whole*, as is compatible with a distinct gratification from each component *part*." In Dos Passos the component parts are, almost deliberately, given only the kind of interest they reflect from the whole.

Yet if Dos Passos' characters are two-dimensional and if

their experience is never more than outlined for us, the effect of the world of his narrative as a whole, unfashionable as some of its more superficial implications may be at the moment, is impressive. If you ignore the intrusive or undigested material like the "Camera Eye" passages and the biographies, then the pattern of successes and failures, with their common defeat, the controlled accumulation and variety of recognizable if only slightly realized people and experiences have a value which it is impossible to achieve without Dos Passos' largeness of subject and coherence of design. Because the basic evaluation of experience which develops is, at least through the latter half of *U.S.A.*, consistent and is in one way or another a part of the presentation of every person and event, it takes on a weight and meaning for us which the feeling in, for instance, *A Farewell to Arms*, with its comparatively small scope, cannot.

But the Dos Passos who wrote the narrative part of *U.S.A.* is, nonetheless, only part of Dos Passos, the public man and his public feelings. No doubt we, as citizens of the twentieth century, are bound to feel that a crucial part of our awareness of experience has been ignored by a novel that omits this public sense of the world; but we are equally bound to feel that something important has been omitted if the novel presents, as does Dos Passos' narrative in *U.S.A.*, only a public sense of the world. If anything, we probably feel, as Auden once put it, that

> Private faces in public places
> Are wiser and nicer
> Than public faces in private places.

The Fitzgerald whom Dos Passos was taking to task about "The Crack-Up" was a novelist who made a life work of being his personal self — of showing his private face in public — and of trying to understand what that self was. He understood in his way how much his private self was affected by the world

he lived in, but that understanding was not one that could be
represented by the techniques of the social novelist.

> Dos [he wrote Edmund Wilson in 1933] was here, & we had a
> nice evening — we never quite understand each other & perhaps
> that's the best basis for an enduring friendship. . . . He told me
> to my amazement that you had explained the fundamentals of
> Leninism, even Marxism the night before, and Dos tells me that
> it was only recently made plain thru the same agency to the
> *New Republic*. I little thought when I left politics to you &
> your gang in 1920 you would devote your time to cutting up
> Wilson's shroud into blinders! Back to Mallarmé!

No doubt Wilson — who, if he has never been able to recon-
cile them, has never ignored either Mallarmé or Lenin — was
similarly attacked by Dos Passos when he appeared to be sliding
back to Mallarmé.

As a novelist Fitzgerald works always with action, and action
typical of his community and familiar to us all; that is why even
his finest stories have something for the dullest readers and
could be sold to popular magazines. His lifelong desire to understand himself expressed itself largely as an avid curiosity
about the people around him, an effort to get at that part of
their experience that coincided, in kind, with his own. The
action in his novels is, like his account of Basil Duke Lee, a representation — in events, gestures, turns of thought — of the
movement of awareness in his characters or in himself as narrator. In his best work even the smallest detail of action, however realistic, has this purpose, as one can see clearly in a typical sentence: "She was asleep — he stood for a moment beside
her bed sorry for her, because she was asleep, and because she
had set her slippers beside her bed." This interest in the movement of awareness as it demonstrates itself in action is what Lionel Trilling has called an interest in "manners." "My manners,"
says Dick Diver in *Tender Is the Night*, "are a trick of the

heart"; and so are all the minutely observed manners, good or bad, kind- or hard-hearted, in Fitzgerald's novels. It was this kind of difference he had in mind when he said that "the very rich are different from you and me"; that is, in fact, the way Anson Hunter, "The Rich Boy" from whose story this remark derives, was different from you and me. "Almost for that remark alone," Mr. Trilling quite rightly says, "[Fitzgerald] has been received in Balzac's bosom in the heaven of novelists."

Fitzgerald's "Crack-Up" is an account of a major moral crisis in his life. To the task of understanding it he brought all his considerable resources, and because he was in so many ways a representative man, such an understanding has a good deal more than a merely biographical interest. But Dos Passos felt that Fitzgerald was fiddling while Rome burned, as in a way he was. Fitzgerald's account of his crisis — completely honest and fully imagined as it is — omits all that Dos Passos thought most real. Social forces, those more or less personified abstractions that have had, at whatever remove, their part in reducing him to the state he describes, hardly figure in his awareness of it.

Not that Fitzgerald has not a sense of history, just as Dos Passos has a sense of the personal life. History, in fact, fascinated Fitzgerald, and he fancied himself as an authority on the Civil War and Napoleon. But in his work history is never abstract forces; insofar as he is conscious of these forces, he knows them only as their consequences become evident in the personal moral experience of himself and the people he understands; the only history he could realize in his work was fully experienced history.

By 1927 [he could, for instance, write] a wide-spread neurosis began to be evident, faintly signalled, like a nervous beating of the feet, by the popularity of cross-word puzzles. I remember a fellow expatriate opening a letter from a mutual friend of ours, urging him to come home and be revitalized by the hardy, bracing qualities of the native soil. It was a strong

letter and it affected us both deeply, until we noticed that it was
headed from a nerve sanitarium in Pennsylvania.

This is Fitzgerald's way of knowing the forces of history, and
because he was a representative man, it was a knowledge that
many readers could share, even though they had not Fitzgerald's imaginative powers and could not have discovered it
for themselves.

Because Fitzgerald was unable to imagine history in any
other way than this, he was nearly impervious to theories.
About society and history he had no serious theory at all,
though in the middle thirties, when he was living at La Paix,
he liked to talk about being a Marxist. But as long as it does
not corrupt his imagination, a general conception of society is
surely something a writer cannot have too much of. As William Troy once put it, "Perhaps it is not well for the novelist to
encumber himself with too much knowledge, although one
cannot help recalling the vast cultural apparatus of a Tolstoi or
a Joyce, or the dialectical intrepidity of a Dostoievski or a
Mann. And recalling these Europeans, none of whom found-
ered on the way, one wonders whether a certain coyness toward the things of the mind is not one reason for the lack of development in most American writers."

Because Fitzgerald did not have a general conception of
society, he never quite reached the point in his novels where he
could construct a fable adequate to the full occasion of which
it is a particular instance. Something like this lack is the source
of our confusion about *Tender Is the Night*. Its brilliantly conceived parts, each charged with general implications that Fitzgerald obviously sensed, do not finally unite in a whole. They
have the nominal unity of all being events in the life of Dick
Diver, but they have the real incoherence that results from our
not knowing — and we suspect Fitzgerald did not either —
what meaning Dick Diver's life has. "Life," Fitzgerald con-

fessed to having thought when he was young, "was something you dominated if you were any good" — you made it whatever you were. Life, in an almost extravagantly brutal way, taught him that he could not dominate it, but the pathos of his personal history is that he seems never to have been able to recognize the extent to which it dominated him.

But if as a novelist Fitzgerald knew the life of the society around him only as it became the personal experience of himself or people close to him, Dos Passos, as the narrator of *U.S.A.*, knew the personal life he and those close to him led only as illustrations of social theory, as the generalized prejudices of groups and classes. He is so preoccupied with representing the clashes of these prejudices by newspaper headlines, historical figures, and — above all — type characters that he reduces the awareness within his characters to the simplified patterns we ascribe to the imaginary representatives of classes of people. You know his characters only as you know the journalist's average businessman, labor leader, or Vassar girl. Moreover, the "Camera Eye" passages are always there to remind you that the narrative omits a considerable part of Dos Passos' awareness of experience, by constantly confronting you with concentrated and stiflingly personal images of Dos Passos' private consciousness. The "Camera Eye" passages are Dos Passos' Mallarmé, as the narrative is his Lenin. The discontinuity between the two has always existed in Dos Passos' work. It is striking, for instance, in *Three Soldiers*, between Fuselli, a caricature whose consciousness consists, with improbable completeness, of the clichés of "the enterprise system," and John Andrews, who lives almost completely in an inner world of the imagination and is aware of the social world outside his imagination only as an unpleasant and sometimes intolerable intrusion.

Thus when Dos Passos, speaking as the narrator of *U.S.A.*, protests in his letter to Fitzgerald against "The Crack-Up's" disregard of the social and political life of his times, it is almost as if we were hearing the voice of H. G. Wells complaining that Conrad is much too concerned with his own feelings about boats or — speaking through Boon — that James's idea of unity "In practice . . . becomes just omission and nothing more. He omits everything that demands digressive treatment or collateral statement. For example, he omits opinions. In all his novels you will find no people with defined political opinions, no people with religious opinions, none with clear partisanships or with lusts or whims, none definitely up to any specific impersonal thing." Thus James's people, Boon complains, are all "denatured" and "The thing his novel is *about* is always there. It is like a church lit but without a congregation to distract you, with every light and line focused on the high altar. And on the altar, very reverently placed, intensely there, is a dead kitten, an egg-shell, a bit of string."

The circumstances of Dos Passos' complaint about Fitzgerald are, however, more revealing than the circumstances of Wells's complaints about Conrad and James. Dos Passos complains in a personal letter to an old friend — in circumstances, that is, that are highly personal. These circumstances underline the emotionally superficial and hollowly rhetorical character of the attitudes he is urging on Fitzgerald's attention; his letter sounds, as he knows himself, like a bad editorial.

> Why Scott — you poor miserable bastard [he wrote], it was damn handsome of you to write me. . . .
> I've been wanting to see you, naturally, to argue about your *Esquire* articles — Christ, man, how do you find time in the middle of the general conflagration to worry about all that stuff? . . . most of the time the course of world events seems so frightful that I feel absolutely paralysed. . . . We're living in one of the damndest tragic moments in history. . . . Forgive the locker room peptalk.

Locker room peptalk is just about right; this talk about "world events" is uncomfortably strained, like so much of our talk about the large-scale, impersonal events of history that we know ought to move us but do not, because we cannot imagine them fully and make them a part of our felt experience. However clearly we may recognize the need to, the achievement is not wholly within the powers of our wills. But unless we can do so, any talk of tragedy is, however unconsciously, fake. A moment in history is not tragic; only individual human beings are, and only when their experience is fully imagined. Forces that are more or less public, or at least not wholly personal, must produce the occasion in which the human being suffers; otherwise his story becomes sentimental and insignificant, as Dos Passos obviously feels Fitzgerald's has become. Yet the occasion, the moment in history, is not tragic; it only constitutes the circumstances in which the aware individual suffers the tragic experience of unavoidable moral choice. Thus, no matter what the scope or the violence of the occasion, the tragic rhetoric about it will sound like a locker room peptalk unless the circumstances of that occasion have been transmuted by the imagination into personal experience. As the subadar in Faulkner's "Ad Astra," faced with circumstances not entirely dissimilar to those Dos Passos is trying to face, observed, "we can do only within the heart while we see beyond the heart." Dos Passos' letter to Fitzgerald is filled with good, even necessary intentions, but it is an attempt to say as if from the heart something that exists for him almost entirely as something seen beyond the heart. This is the characteristic fault of his narratives, as the characteristic fault of Fitzgerald's is that he never saw beyond the heart in a conscious and controlled way at all.

The problem posed for novelists in the twentieth century is, then, the same problem that was posed for Wells and Conrad and James, the problem of how to absorb into the felt, personal awareness out of which genuine fiction comes the huge, impersonal world that otherwise exists for us only as journalism or social history. Yet the efforts of most talented writers of our time have gone into expressing the intense, personal apprehension of experience or the collective social apprehension of it. They have seldom been successfully devoted to combining the two.

No doubt the novel that is perfectly satisfactory in both these respects will not be written in our time. There are rigidities in both the "realities" the novelist must unite that can probably never be reduced. But the problem is fundamental, and a reasonable solution of its difficulties would benefit the novel very greatly. The possibility of such a solution is always present in writers like Faulkner and Hemingway and Fitzgerald, though none of these writers succeeded in producing a novel in which the eccentric and obsessive personal sense of life did not to some extent seriously distort or exclude a satisfactory account of the conditions that were its occasion. Hemingway's *For Whom the Bell Tolls* only seems to avoid this limitation; no other novel by these writers probably even seems to. In this sense, Dos Passos had a legitimate objection to the attitude Fitzgerald made clear in "The Crack-Up." Yet if a reasonably satisfactory solution to this problem is going to be discovered, it seems likely it will be found by a novelist like Fitzgerald rather than by one like Dos Passos. Fitzgerald's kind of novel starts with felt experience, even though it may not feel enough experience or all the experience we need it to. But Dos Passos' kind of novel rarely gets around to felt experience at all.

VIII

THE AMERICAN HERO AS GENTLEMAN:

GAVIN STEVENS

"A THIN, intelligent, unstable face, a rumpled linen suit from whose lapel a Phi Beta Kappa key dangled on a watch chain — Gavin Stevens, Phi Beta Kappa, Harvard, Ph.D., Heidelberg, whose office was his hobby, although it made his living for him, and whose serious vocation was a twenty-two-year-old unfinished translation of the Old Testament back into classic Greek." This is Faulkner's description of the hero of his short story "Go Down, Moses," and implicit in it is nearly every important aspect of the problem the novelist confronts when he sets out to imagine the hero — Aristotle's superior man — in American society. The description is particularly useful for a consideration of this problem because the characteristic passionate extravagance of Faulkner's style brings out sharply the elements of the problem and makes clear the ultimate ambiguity of our attitude toward it.

How much of this description is, with all its rhetorical extravagance, meant quite seriously? How much is the rhetorical extravagance meant to suggest an ironic qualification? Take that translation of the Old Testament back into classic Greek. Does Faulkner mean us to take this labor of love as a magnificent example of pure intellectual passion, refined to the point that Gavin, dissatisfied by the inferior late Greek versions of the scriptures, wishes to put them back into classic Greek? Is this assertion made, in short, in simple admiration? Or has Faulkner chosen this project, so remote from the needs or even the understanding of his society, as an example of the absurd extremes to which love may be driven by an overcultivation of the intellect?

This ambiguity hovers over nearly every phrase in Faulkner's description of his hero. The instability reflected in Gavin's face is not a practically admirable characteristic, but it is — at least for the romantic tradition — the established sign of the sensitivity that is almost the defining characteristic of the heroic man of feeling. That Phi Beta Kappa key from Harvard (which has been both an ideal and a joke in American society since the days of Channing) *dangles* with old-fashioned dignity and also with comic incongruity from the lapel of the rumpled linen suit that is clearly the dress of a gentleman in Jefferson, Mississippi. Perhaps the Heidelberg Ph.D. is an unintentional indication of Faulkner's own provincialism. At least, according to *Knight's Gambit* Gavin, now in his late forties, had completed his degree at Heidelberg in 1924, a time by which Heidelberg Ph.D.'s were pretty well out of fashion in the best American academic circles. But perhaps Faulkner knows that and is again suggesting, whether in earnest or in irony, Gavin's heroic loyalty to old attitudes. In any event, it is clear enough what Faulkner means by making Gavin a Ph.D.: sometimes Chick Mallison finds Gavin's voice "so garrulous and facile that . . . it was like listening not even to fiction but literature." What is not clear is whether Faulkner thinks that is absurd. Finally, the whole social aspect of the problem is implicit in Gavin's feeling that the office which gives him a living and, Faulkner might well have added, his place in the community, is a hobby and the translation of the Old Testament his vocation. This ambiguity is, I believe, ultimate; Faulkner can no more resolve it for himself or history than any American can.

Though this discussion is primarily concerned with the way this conflict gets into fiction, the way it gets into political, sociological, and even philosophical debate is so closely related that it is unavoidable. In some form or other, no doubt, it has concerned every society, but it is particularly exacerbating in a democratic society. American democracy is a society in which every man has certain unalienable rights in order that he may develop his own moral and intellectual capacities to the limit. Since the assumption is that every man, given the chance to do so, will leap at it, we anticipate no serious conflict between the values developed by those who exercise these unalienable democratic rights in full and the values of the society as a whole established by the opinion of the majority. But in fact, from the beginning the values of these two groups have been in conflict, and American society as a whole has always found particularly disturbing the special values which come out of fineness of intellect, sensibility, and conscience. Moreover, since the theory does not anticipate any distinctions of values among the members of the society, both parties to the conflict tend to think there is no excuse for their opponents and to treat them with a firm intolerance. Popular opinion in America can be tyrannical in its demands for conformity, and Adlai Stevenson was not merely joking when he said, "Eggheads of the world unite, you have nothing to lose but your yokes." By the same token, eccentricity of intellect or conscience can be abnormally extravagant and often wantonly destructive. In these circumstances the brilliant and the innocent must either attempt to ascribe their conception of the good life to the community, however desperate the attempt, and make themselves a part of the community by asserting that it in fact lives by the values they need to believe it does, or they must oppose, wholly or in part, the values to which the community has committed itself and be excluded from it. From at least the time of the Anglo-Saxon "Wanderer" men have understood the grief and loneliness of the excluded man, the out-law; his fate is nearly unendurable. The brilliant and innocent therefore struggle to retain both their vision of the good life and their place in their community.

It is precisely this struggle that Gavin Stevens goes through. He is determined to go on believing, as he does in *Intruder in the Dust*, that the community he is inextricably involved with is the just and honorable society that his highly developed consciousness requires. His special allies — they are, indeed, often ahead of him in seeing what this conception of the honorable life requires — are the young and the innocent, Chick Mallison and Miss Habersham in *Intruder in the Dust* (Miss Habersham is called Miss Worsham in "Go Down, Moses"). Great intellectual refinement finally reaches the wisdom unintellectual innocence knows from the start, what Faulkner calls "simple truth" such as a child or an old woman grasps best (those blest philosophers that shall lead us into heaven). Gavin needs desperately to believe that his native community lives by this truth — if not America as a whole, at least what he tries to believe is the homogeneous community of the South.

He needs to believe so out of the simple need of all men to belong to a community, and he clings to his special claims for the South because the sense of community in America as a whole, though strong and practically effective, is crude and superficial — possibly because only a crude and superficial one can be made to work over so vast and fluid a society. In America any deep-rooted sense of community almost has to be highly localized — though not necessarily in the rural, the suspiciously pastoral, geographical and economic circumstances people like the Agrarians have claimed it must be. Such a sense of community is also strong among people who spend their lives in a common pursuit with an inner discipline of its own (for instance, the priestly and to a lesser extent the academic and legal lives), and however little the fact has been advertised in literature, it flourishes in the middle-sized American industrial town as powerfully as in any market town, so long as the town is reasonably distant from a cosmopolitan center. Moreover, it can affect deeply not only those who are brought up in such towns but also people like Huck Finn, only partly — and then not very efficiently — brought up in St. Petersburg, or David Wilson, who moved to Dawson's Landing at the advanced age of twenty-five.

Gavin Stevens was, however, born and brought up in Jefferson, Mississippi, and he is as deeply attached to his home town as anyone can be. That is why he needs to believe that it, at least, is a just and honorable society. Like all of us, he has a hard time sustaining this belief in the face of the general attitude and conduct of his community, and in *Intruder in the Dust* he descends to a querulous attempt, altogether at odds with the implications of the novel's magnificent story, to blame all American democracy's bad qualities on what he calls "the coastal spew of Europe . . . quarantined unrootable into rootless ephemeral cities," in short on urban society, especially the urban society of the North and East. His main purpose is, of course, to make out that the attitude of the country folk of Yoknapatawpha County is, despite their occasional backsliding, identical with his high ideal. After watching Gavin's — and possibly Faulkner's — resort to vulgar rubbish about the coastal spew of Europe in this attempt to justify the claims he needs to make for his local community, we may well feel the heroic honesty of crusty old John Adams in asserting — over a hundred years ago, about O'Sullivan's *Democratic Review*, to which all the democratic writers of the age of Jackson contributed — that the intellectual values of literature are by nature aristocratic and a democratic review a contradiction in terms.

The resolution of the conflict between what Gavin wants Jefferson to be and what he sees it is is by no means a perfect one from Gavin's point of view, despite the fact that Faulkner idealizes the community considerably. Faulkner's account of Gavin's life in Jefferson is full of ironic demonstrations of the way Gavin's habitual, inherited sense of the "right" way of responding to a situation has been damaged, corrupted by his cosmopolitan cultivation. Nevertheless Gavin does manage, however awkwardly, to live as part of his community, performing — with the frequent help of hints from Mollie and Miss Worsham — the tasks it expects him to perform. But there is plenty of evidence in other stories about Gavin that Faulkner has doubts about the real possibility of even so partial a resolution of the conflict as the one he describes in "Go Down, Moses." It is difficult not to feel that this account of Gavin's life in Jefferson is as much an expression of Faulkner's desire to believe it possible as the expression of an actual belief. To this extent it is an assertion of faith in democracy that is more burdened with doubt than was characteristic a hundred years earlier in our history, when time, as Prospero says, went more upright in his carriage, less weighed down by the evidence of the last hundred years of our national experience.

Even then, however, there was much to trouble men's minds. The Transcendentalists were brave enough in their abstract commitments to the unalienable rights of the individual. "Whoso would be a man must be a nonconformist," says Emerson in "Self-Reliance," and in "Civil Disobedience" Thoreau says that "any man more right than his neighbors constitutes a majority of one already." No doubt every society founded on a revolution finds itself embarrassed by its own revolutionary propaganda, in which the possible desirable consequences to follow from the establishment of its principles have been much played up and the possible undesirable ones played down. When the revolution succeeds, it is difficult for men to cease to believe those revolutionary expressions of hope that have become for them through constant repetition descriptions of fact, however little they correspond to the actual facts: nothing is so embarrassing to such a society as its old revolutionaries.

That partly imaginary community of self-reliant and ceaselessly self-cultivating people that democratic society was established to serve had, even in Emerson's time, a trick of transforming itself into the worst of the supporters of Jackson, of whose political meetings Emerson himself — who voted democratic too — once remarked, "I doubt not the unmixed malignity, the withering selfishness, the impudent vulgarity, that mark these meetings would speedily cure me of my appetite for longevity." Like any loyal supporter of democracy, Emerson kept hoping that, given the opportunity, every man would seek what he called "that moment of adult health, the culmination of power . . . when, proceeding out of their brute youth, the perceptive powers reach their ripeness." Meanwhile, if he could not find what Whitman called "a large resolute breed" of such men, he felt it was at least the duty of every individual who was aware of the need and the opportunity to try to become what the great Humboldt — perhaps mistakenly — said George Bancroft was, one of "that noble breed of young Americans for whom the true happiness of man consists in the culture of the intelligence."

Yet, because the effort was not so widely made, or at least not so widely made successfully, as democratic theory assumed it would be, when it was made it isolated the individual from the common life of his society, where "the culture of the intelligence" was looked on with suspicion. Both Emerson and Thoreau paid a price of this kind which was in some ways only greater because Concord made it easy for them to pay by not harrying them about the bill. Emerson was not, in Concord, so smothered in Jacksonian political meetings that he could not rest easy in a general transcendentalist optimism, and there is something almost comic about the way the penalty for Thoreau's flourish of Civil Disobedience against the Commonwealth of Massachusetts is so quickly paid for that he comes out of jail after that one night to continue on his way to the shoemaker's to which he had been going when he was arrested.

It is difficult for anyone who cares for the intellectual life not to sympathize with Thoreau at that meeting between him and Whitman in 1856, about which Whitman observed afterwards that Thoreau had shown himself "a very aggravated case of superciliousness" and that he had an "inability to appreciate the average life." But Whitman is right that a man loses something vital when he does not remain a part of the life of his community, at whatever cost, even though it sometimes seems as if doing so did not cost Whitman as much as it should have. We are torn here as we are torn by the argument between Henry and William James about the usefulness of American experience for literature. Our immediate sympathies no doubt go out to Henry, yet William is right that Henry, for all his vast range of understanding, never quite faced the logical consequences of what he knew, perhaps because, like the rest of us, he did not know how to. For what one of Henry's American heroes is not the office that makes a living for him a hobby and some madcap and exiling project of the sensibility his vocation? Yet Henry would not — except as nightmares like "The Jolly Corner" — look at that office: from what did the Newsomes' money that supported the green-covered and undoubtedly undemocratic review that supported Lambert Strether come? How did Mr. Verver make the great fortune he used to buy Maggie a Prince and his American home town an art collection?

Emerson, Thoreau, Henry James, though far better men than most, could no more solve the problem than the rest of us, mostly still liberal democrats, mostly still horrified by Jacksonian demagogues. Their failure to do so perhaps helps explain the kind of doubt critics have always had about them as writers, doubts not unconnected with the ironic qualifications of Faulkner and a great many other twentieth-century writers about the unintended and perhaps even unavoidable "aggravated superciliousness" of the intellectuals in their novels.

The most interesting example of the writer personally in-

volved in this dilemma as a political and social being is of course
James Fenimore Cooper. With his genius for putting things in
their most unpalatable form, Cooper managed to describe the
duty of every American to devote himself to "the culture of the
intelligence" as the gentleman's democratic right to be exclusive.
Cooper inherited a good many eighteenth-century ideas about
the noble savage and the virtue-inducing powers of nature; he
also inherited Otsego Hall in a town named after his family. It
was only natural that he should begin, rather like Faulkner, by
thinking of democracy as founded on a stable land-holding class
and ascribing all the faults of America to the commercial middle classes. But beginning with his quarrel with the citizens of
Cooperstown over Three-Mile Point and continuing through
the anti-rent controversy and a long series of libel suits, Cooper
gradually convinced himself that no one in America except
Cooper had a grasp of the true democratic faith. By an excess
of Civil Obedience — for he relied on the courts and distrusted
popular opinion — Cooper was, in his crotchety way, also asserting that "any man more right than his neighbors constitutes a
majority of one" — and feeling bitterly his isolation from his
community. As his biographer, Mr. Grossman, has well pointed
out, "While he is discoursing on his country's faults and on
the distance to be kept between himself and his countrymen,
his aggrieved tone reveals his need for their affection."

Cooper was a difficult and violently independent man who
began by believing that a democracy depends for its success on
every man's desire to cultivate his taste and intelligence and
then discovered that — as he puts it himself — "in this part of
the world [that is, in Cooperstown], it is thought aristocratic
not to frequent taverns and lounge at corners, squirting tobacco
juice." He was made by his community to pay the full price
for his belligerent insistence on his democratic right to ex-
clusiveness, and perhaps the worst part of that price was his own
loss of faith in man's capacity for the democratic way of life,

so that he ended his life gloomily supporting the abstract rights of property, scornful of reforms of all kinds, and arguing for the merits of a little judicious flogging in the American Navy.

It is no doubt easy to be cynically amused by this complete reversal. But Cooper was a man torn between his honest belief in popular rule, a belief that was based on his conviction of the "superior innocence and virtue of a rural population," and what seemed to him the rural population's complete disregard for everything that made a civilized life possible. There can be nothing finally very amusing for Americans about this, whether they are Northerners who have, after a hundred years of the cultural instability of a commercial society, found no way to come to terms with it, or Southerners faced, as Gavin Stevens is in *Intruder in the Dust*, with the unendurable injustices of racial discrimination.

But the major consideration here is not the manifestations of this dilemma in our social and political life, but its importance to the life of our fiction. It turns up with great frequency and in astonishingly different forms there, and is often the occasion for a novel's most interesting complications of feelings. Perhaps the most obvious, though not necessarily the simplest, occasion for it occurs when a highly cultivated man lives in his small American home town because an irresistible part of him loves its life and has inherited its idea of virtue and he cannot survive without them. If he belongs to the middle classes of this town, its approval is the only real success he can know; if he belongs to the upper classes, he is held by some combination of paternal responsibility and guilt for the irredeemable past of less fortunate classes; and if he is a Southerner, he adds to these last two motives a feeling of special responsibility for the Negroes.

This is Gavin Stevens' situation in "Go Down, Moses." He is not merely involved in the responsibilities imposed on him by his home town; he is driven by them. When Mollie Beau-

champ takes it for granted without a moment's hesitation that
he will do what she — so much more instinctively a part of the
community than he is — assumes is right and will bring back
to Jefferson the body of her no-good grandson who has been
executed for murdering a policeman, he does not question her
right to do so. In fact he even finds, after he has done the mechanically necessary things and "had thought that he was going
home to his boarding house for the noon meal . . . that he was
not. *'Besides, I didn't lock my office door,'* he thought." The
intellectual's self-consciousness that makes him capable of seeing in this way his drivenness is of course what separates him
not only from Mollie but from Miss Worsham, whom he finds
sitting in his office.

Miss Worsham has no more uncertainty than Mollie about
what the proprieties of Jefferson require. Gavin explains to her
the sensible and practical course he plans to follow, a course
that, in any other context except the life of Jefferson, would
be absurdly extravagant in itself. But this "sensible" course
smashes against the solid rock of Miss Worsham's perfect assurance that the proper course is the even more absurd one
she has in mind. "He is the only child of her oldest daughter,
her own dead first child," she says. "He must come home."
" 'He must come home,' Stevens said as quietly. 'I'll attend to
it at once. I'll telephone at once.' " Miss Worsham then offers
to "defray," as she calls it, the expenses. Stevens looks her
straight in the eye and lies about the expenses, because he
knows she is very poor, and to add plausibility to his lie says,
"They will furnish a box and there will be only the transporta-
tion." " 'A box?' Again she was looking at him with that
expression curious and detached, as though he were a child.
'He is her grandson, Mr. Stevens. When she took him to raise,
she gave him my father's name — Samuel Worsham. Not
just a box, Mr. Stevens.' " So Stevens takes her twenty-five
dollars "in frayed bills and coins" and starts out around the

town to collect the remaining $225 he figures the job will really cost; and the rest of the town is as helplessly involved as he is.

> "And the hearse out there will be fifteen more, not counting the flowers —"
> "Flowers?" the editor cried.
> "Flowers," Stevens said. "Call the whole thing two hundred and twenty-five. And it will probably be mostly you and me. All right?"
> "No it aint all right," the editor said. "But it dont look like I can help myself."

Nor can he.

When it is all arranged, Stevens goes out to Miss Worsham's house to see Mollie and is met at the door by Mollie's brother, Hamp, who works for Miss Worsham, for Mollie and Hamp were children of Worsham slaves and Miss Worsham and Mollie grew up together, as she says, "as sisters would." "She expecting you," Hamp says to Stevens. "She say to kindly step up to the chamber." "Is that where Aunt Molly is?" Stevens asks, and Hamp says, "We all dar." And there, indeed, they all are, with Aunt Mollie sitting in the room's only rocking chair before the brick hearth "on which the ancient symbol of human coherence and solidarity smoldered." Aunt Mollie is swaying back and forth saying, "Done sold my Benjamin. Sold him in Egypt. . . . Roth Edmonds sold him. Sold my Benjamin." And Stevens, speaking out of his disciplined intelligence's concern for the immediately reasonable view, says, "No he didn't, Aunt Mollie. It wasn't Mr. Edmonds. Mr. Edmonds didn't —" "*But she cant hear me*, he thought. She was not even looking at him. She never had looked at him." And, his merely reasonable grasp of the situation again overwhelmed by the instinctive community wisdom that goes directly to the ultimate injustice he can do nothing about, he rushes from the room and almost runs toward what he calls "the breathing and simple dark" of the outdoors. *"Soon I will be outside,* he thought. *Then there will be air, space, breath."* Miss Worsham follows him and he apologizes for having rushed out so unceremoniously. "It's all right," Miss Worsham says. "It's our grief."

In due course the body arrives at the station in its gray-and-silver casket, and the brisk, horrible, commercial undertakers slide it into the hearse and fling the flowers over it and clap-to the door — these verbs are all Faulkner's — and the hearse "with an unctuous, an almost bishoplike purr" drives off through the town to take the body of the murderer home, "followed," as Faulkner says, "by the two cars containing the four people — the high-headed erect white woman, the old Negress, the designated paladin of justice and truth and right, the Heidelberg Ph.D. — in formal component complement to the Negro murderer's catafalque: the slain wolf."

"Go Down, Moses" is a beautifully concentrated illustration of the remarkable complexity of feelings generated in American fiction by the conflict between the cultivated private consciousness and the inherited customs of the community. It shows us the grandeur and the pathos, the innocence and the incongruity of the community solidarity that makes Miss Worsham speak quite unconsciously of the grief, primarily her Negro sister Mollie's, as "our grief"; it shows us the appalling bad taste of the casket and the flowers and the wonderfully incongruous, bishoplike purr of the hearse — and the essential irrelevance of this bad taste; it shows us the resolution of grief this small-town ritual brings Mollie and Miss Worsham — for at the end of the story Mollie asks the newspaper editor to put the whole thing, even her grandson's crime, in the paper, and Gavin thinks: "It doesn't matter to her now. . . . She just wanted him home, but she wanted him to come home right. She wanted that casket and those flowers and the hearse and she wanted to ride through town behind it in a car."

It shows us, too, how little this is a resolution for Gavin, because he is too cosmopolitan to enter with his whole nature into
the community's ritual, is too finicky to accept as irrelevant its
bad taste, is too frustratingly, intellectually conscious of the
irredeemable guilt in which they all participate ever to feel as
Miss Worsham does. It also shows us that Gavin is, for all his
intellectual's blundering among the assurances of those who live
wholly within the community's system of values, really its paladin, for the simple reason that he never ceases to recognize, in
full humility, what all Faulkner's tobacco-chewing rural saints
teach him: "the onus of any business is usually in the hasty
minds of those theoreticians who have no business of their
own," that is, mere intellectuals, especially, no doubt, reform-
ing intellectuals from the North.

Any community that contains Miss Worsham and Wilmoth,
the editor, and a Main Street willing to pay for Samuel Beauchamp Worsham's funeral, not to mention Gavin Stevens, is an
idealized one — though perhaps no more idealized than Sinclair
Lewis' is denigrated. Yet even in these idealized circumstances,
the man of cultivated intelligence and the democratic majority
do not get along very well, as is clear from Gavin's further adventures in Jefferson described in *Knight's Gambit* and *Intruder
in the Dust*. In spite of Faulkner's efforts to blame all the difficulties on the "outlanders" of "the North and East and West"
— those perennial outside agitators of the Southerner's self-
exculpation — most of the intellectual's familiar difficulties are
created for Gavin by the local community itself. Gavin is
caught between the sterile Hollywood crassness of the rich, like
the Harrisses, and the mechanical, inhuman violence of the de-
racinated poor (though by Faulkner's special dispensation, an
inversion of the proletarian novel's favorite trick, the rural
poor like Jackson Fentry behave well, and the city poor like
Buck Thorpe cause all the trouble). Gavin's major defeat is at
the hands of a cynical and intelligent but successful and power-

ful governor whom Faulkner describes as "a man without an-
cestry," a kind of homebred outlander.

On the other hand, Gavin finds himself at linguistic, cultural,
and moral ease with foreigners like Captain Gualdres, until, in
moments of despair, he is tempted to feel that "we in America
have debased ["the belief in more than the divinity of man"]
into a national religion of the entrails in which man owes no
duty to his soul because he has been absolved of soul to owe a
duty to and instead is static heir at birth to an inevictable
quit-claim on a wife a car a radio and an old-age pension." He
even has moments of feeling, with the typical intellectual's disgust at the complacent small-mindedness of his American peers,
that "what (if any) future Americans' claim not even to human
spirit but to simple civilization has, lies in Europe." But Gavin cannot ever forget that the American, however cultivated
his intellect, has been committed by his life to his home town,
"to the shabby purlieus themselves timeless and durable, familiar as his own voracious omnivorous insatiable heart or
his body and limbs or the growth of his hair and fingernails"
and to "the people [he has] lived with all his life."

Gavin is the county attorney. He puts at the service of his
community the trained intelligence of a man capable of discuss-
ing "Einstein with college professors," because, wanting like
Cooper to believe in the "superior innocence and virtue of a
rural population," he does not want to talk to college professors, but to spend "whole afternoons among the squatting men
against the walls of country stores, talking to them in their
own idiom." This image of the intellectual as lawyer-detective-
research student seeking to come to terms with his home town
is a stock character in contemporary American fiction, almost
its standard imaginative formulation of the dilemma of the
American hero. Abner Coates in *The Just and the Unjust*, the
aptly named Jack Burden of *All the King's Men*, Anson Page
of *The View from Pompey's Head* are other examples. In less

serious fiction the character is omnipresent; the answer to Edmund Wilson's question, "Who cares who killed Roger Ackroyd?" is, "Much the same kind of people who care who killed Vincent Gowrie."

Moreover, this character has been with American literature a long time, at least since Pudd'nhead Wilson. Judged by the standards of the well-made novel, *Pudd'nhead Wilson* is a crude and awkward fiction; it is wildly overplotted, careless of probability, marked by frequent overlaps of time and clumsy transitions, loaded with heavy-handed lectures that Twain puts in the mouths of the least likely characters. It is nonetheless a powerful image of the American hero's dilemma. Dawson's Landing is what Twain calls "a dull country town" with a "colorless history." Its leading citizens are provincial Virginia gentlemen very like Cooper, "men whose opinions were their own and not subject to revision or amendment, suggestion or criticism, by anybody, even their friends." Twain is amused by their provincial pride (it tends to fix on things like the local fire company), proud of their integrity, bitter that even the best of them are "fairly humane towards slaves and other animals," and distrustful of their addiction (so like his own) to financial speculation.

The ordinary citizens of Dawson's Landing are dull, honest, provincial people who are ludicrously dazzled by European culture in the persons of the Capello twins. These twins are impossibly high-minded and charming people. Nevertheless, at the first sign of trouble, Dawson's Landing turns on them as outlanders and accuses them of murder. At the end of the book they are absolved, but by that time they are, as Twain says, "weary of Western adventure and straightway [retire] to Europe." But for David Wilson, as for Mark Twain, Dawson's Landing is home and cannot be so easily retired from, "a snug little collection" of white-washed houses covered by "rose-vines, honeysuckles, and morning-glories," with gardens of old-fashioned flowers and a cat "stretched at full length, asleep and blissful," on each sunny window ledge.

At the start of his life in Dawson's Landing David ventures a modest metaphysical joke about wanting to own half a noisy dog so that he can kill his half. In a savagely satirical passage, Twain shows us the solemn, pompous, literal-minded citizens of Dawson's Landing deciding, on the strength of this impossible proposal, that David is a half-wit and naming him Pudd'nhead. Like many another intellectual, David has been landed in the soup by his irrepressible intelligence. "He was twenty-five years old, college-bred, and had finished a post-college course in an Eastern law school a couple of years before." He is interested in the latest advances in knowledge; Mark Twain's ideas of what such advances are — palmistry and finger-printing — are not much more improbable than Faulkner's apparently perfectly serious conviction that college professors are prepared at a moment's notice to discourse on Einstein. David uses his knowledge of these abstruse sciences to solve the novel's mystery and save his community from a gross miscarriage of justice. This demonstration that his knowledge has practical uses earns him the esteem of the community. But only the Negroes, the innocent ones, the heirs of "two centuries of unatoned insult and outrage," appreciate the intrinsic worth of David's disciplined intelligence. "My lan'," Roxy says, "dat man aint no mo fool den I is! He's de smartes' man in dis town. . . ." At the end, Twain shows the town manfully admitting its mistake about Pudd'nhead, treating him as a hero, and electing him mayor. But this is an arbitrary happy ending.

This story of the intellectual man who struggles to be at home in his native community is probably the commonest form in which fiction explores the dilemma of the American hero. But there are several others. There is, for instance, the one in which the small-town boy goes out into the big, urban world, becomes sophisticated if not cultivated, and then returns to his

home town. In many versions of this story, especially in popular fiction like the recent spate of "business" novels, the small-
town heritage modified by urban culture produces what we are
to think is — what perhaps really is — the good American like
Marquand's Charlie Gray. But in none of these stories, whether
we are asked to admire the hero or not, is the conflict between
his love of his native community and his commitment to the
urban world resolved. The hero of Marquand's *H. M. Pulham,
Esq.*, who chose one course, and the hero of his *Point of No
Return*, who chose the other — and in each case chose the girl
who went with the place — both remain in suspense between
these two worlds at the end, just as did their more famous pre-
cursor, Edith Wharton's Newland Archer. It is perhaps worth
noting that this version of the dilemma can be inverted, as it is
with all those heroines of Louis Auchincloss' novels, like Sybil
Rodman, who struggle to achieve their independence of soul
from the stifling world of urban upper-class life. Their pre-
cursor is Milly Theale or Charlotte Stant.

A third form has been used by some of our most important
writers. In this form it is not the sophisticated intellectual but
the innocent child — sometimes grown to manhood as in the
cases of James Gatz and Nick Adams — who is forced to struggle against the tyranny of institutionalized majority opinion,
to face the efforts of Aunt Sally, backed by all the forces of
the American community, to "civilize" Huck, or — though
neither Daisy nor Marjorie is exactly a widow — Jay Gatsby
or Nick Adams. Hemingway's remark that "all modern American literature comes from one book by Mark Twain called
Huckleberry Finn" is probably true in a number of ways (most
of which apply to Hemingway's kind of novel), but Twain's
wonderful, if possibly unconscious exploration of the American
hero's dilemma is certainly one of them. The innocent's story
is always essentially that of the individual who instinctively
conforms to the values of some prelapsarian, natural commu-

nity rather than to the one he is born into. In nineteenth-
century America, this story was always in serious danger of de-
clining into one of the clichés about noble savages. Huck's
story is saved from that danger, as Mr. Trilling has pointed out,
because his natural community is the river and the river in
Twain is not ethical and good; the ethical conflict is altogether
Huck's.

The life of the river allows Huck to see Faulkner's "simple
truth," about which Faulkner adds that "there didn't need to
be a great deal of it just to keep running something no bigger
than one earth and so anybody could know truth" — anyone,
that is, except a citizen of St. Petersburg or Dawson's Landing
or the whole of the United States except Yoknapatawpha
County. The community into which Huck naturally fits is the
one formed by him and Nigger Jim on a raft in the river. But
Huck is no more a merely natural creature than Chick Mallison
or Miss Habersham or Gavin Stevens; he is a man, with a
deep need for a community with his fellow men. He would like
to belong to the widow's world if he could, and when he finds
it too "dismal regular and decent" and lights out, that world
quickly invades his raft and involves him once more in social
responsibilities. There is very little he has not learned about
good and evil before he is through, for Huck is not stupid, only
innocent. If, by forgiving men, he can earn a place in their
community, he will succeed in coming home. Unfortunately he
cannot, so that in the end he has to light out for the Territory.

Huck's adventures are a sustained inner conflict between the
set of feelings that have been taught him by St. Petersburg and
that bind him to his fellow citizens and his own natural, innocent moral impulses. Everyone remembers the sad comedy of
Huck's struggle between the feelings he has learned from St.
Petersburg about runaway slaves and his "natural" impulse to
help Jim escape. It "most froze" him when Jim dared to go beyond thinking about escape and said "he would steal his chil-

dren [from their owner]," children, as Huck reminded himself, "that belonged to a man I didn't even know; a man that
hadn't ever done me no harm." But in the end evil triumphs in
Huck's soul and he sees that "it warn't no use for me to try to
learn to do right; a body that don't get *started* right when he's
little ain't got no show. . . ." Huck's natural goodness always
triumphs over the values he has acquired from his community
but he takes no pleasure in that triumph for it separates him
from the community forever. That first night, when he escapes
from Pap and drifts down the river toward Jackson's Island,
lying in the bottom of his canoe smoking his pipe and feeling
free, he listens to the foolish, dull talk of the men at the ferry-
landing with grief and longing. "After that the talk got further and further away, and I couldn't make out the words any
more; but I could hear the mumble, and now and then a laugh,
too, but it seemed a long ways off." It is always so for Huck,
with the Grangerfords, with Mary Jane, who "had more sand
in her than any girl I ever see," with Aunt Sally. Always Huck
has to choose between his own natural and superior conscience
and the conscience of the community to which everyone — including part of himself — is bent on his conforming. "Because
Aunt Sally she's going to adopt me and civilize me, and I can't
stand it. I been there before."

Nor can Nick Adams stand it up in Michigan. He cannot
endure the possibility of losing his freedom and getting what
Bill calls "this sort of fat married look" and taking on Marjorie's
mother and the rest of the town. But he cannot bear the loss of
them, either. His consolation is the pathetic delusion that he
can always return to them if he chooses: "He felt happy. Nothing was finished. Nothing was ever lost. He could go into
town on Saturday." Gatsby's case is even more desperate. By
the sheer energy of his faith he is going to impose his platonic
conception of himself and the good life on a community he
cannot afford to see is not the least bit interested. There he

stands, in his gorgeous pink rag of a suit with his ecstatic and understanding smile, on the front steps of the stage-set house that only the colossal vitality of his illusion can give even a momentary air of reality, his hand raised in a formal gesture of farewell over the mad confusion of crashed cars, wildly honking horns, and a drunken democratic citizenry on his front lawn. Like Huck, he fails to conceal the fact that he is corrupt according to the always nominal standards of the community (for who really believed in or practiced prohibition), because in the innocence of his heart he really does not know that what comes naturally to him is going to seem to conventional people wicked and in bad taste. Like Huck, he fails to show his incorruptible dream of goodness to anyone except Nick Carraway, who only gradually guesses it, because in the innocence of his heart he never suspects there is any special merit in living by it.

A conflict between the complex, delicate values of the developed private consciousness and the simple, sturdy values of the provincial community is not uniquely American; it is simply human and must arise in one form or another in every society. But for literature at least, if not for life itself too, the particular circumstances that create the dilemma and constitute our actual experience of it are nearly everything. Don Quixote in Yoknapatawpha County, up in Michigan, in West Egg, is an entirely different man from Don Quixote in La Mancha.

IX

THE AMERICAN HERO AS ENTREPRENEUR:

MONROE STAHR

THERE is a widespread tendency to think of Scott Fitzgerald as the "marvelous boy" of American literature, a writer who remained throughout a lifetime a little too long for this purpose the handsome, charming, talented young man of promise. One observer who went to pay his respects when Fitzgerald was laid out by the undertaker, in a parlor called "The Wordsworth Room," remarked that everything about him looked young except his hands, as if that were the fate of Dorian Gray in Hollywood. In the conduct of his life Fitzgerald provides so brilliant and representative a story of the American hero that his biography can hardly fail to enthrall us. As a result it is far from easy to disentangle our judgment of his work from our judgment of his life and opinions; we all have a strong inclination to see what he wrote as the typical work of the kind of man his life has persuaded us he is. Fitzgerald's life and the fascinating running commentary on it he provided cannot be wholly separated from his work and ought not to be; the connections are too intimate. But we ought to separate our judgments of the two, because if we do not we will end by having our judgment of his work largely determined by our judgment of his life. The result is about as unfortunate if we admire Fitzgerald personally as if we dislike him.

Because Fitzgerald's life is so striking and edifying an instance of the dilemma of the American hero, it brings into play some of our most powerful and confusing feelings, such as our feeling about youthfulness. As Glenway Wescott pointed out a long time ago, Fitzgerald was "our darling, our genius, our fool" in an age when the courage of our American conviction that nearly everything is well lost for youthfulness was at its height. With our special tendency to believe, whether with delight or resentment, that as we were young and easy we were living in a "type of Paradise," there will probably always be plenty of critics who see Fitzgerald's work as the life story of a prince of the apple towns. Even those who do not find it difficult to keep their judgments of what Fitzgerald wrote unaffected by their response to the life of a man who always seems to have appeared, even at his worst, with a glow about him, like an actor on a stage. Without perhaps exactly believing in his greatness as a writer, they are moved by the theatrical brilliance of this image — somewhat as they are by Byron and Wilde's — to make exaggerated claims for his work.

Thus we tend to deny that Fitzgerald ever matured as a writer and at the same time to exaggerate in a romantic way the value of his not having done so. Even in the very process of making this point about Fitzgerald, when he says that "except once [in Gatsby] Fitzgerald did not fully realize his powers and if we regard his work as a whole, it is to his pervasive personal quality that we respond rather than to a finally satisfactory literary achievement," Lionel Trilling cannot quite resist a certain extravagance about Fitzgerald's "heroic awareness" and his "exemplary role." The vulgar version of this feeling is Westbrook Pegler's assertion that the people of the twenties were a "group or cult of juvenile crying-drunks" living in an age when "Scott Fitzgerald's few were gnawing gin in silver slabs and sniffing about the sham and tinsel of it all."

This tendency to confuse Fitzgerald's work with his life is particularly strong in those for whom fiction is the process of fitting into a story ideas the writer has already formulated in expository terms, as abstract propositions about life. Ironically enough, no one saw more clearly than Fitzgerald himself that the natural mode of expression for his understanding was fiction, that his best work were embodied a perception he could never formulate abstractly. Characteristically, he expressed this insight itself as an observation of behavior rather than as an idea by noting his own habit of "sometimes reading my own books for advice. How much I know sometimes — how little at others."

At their worst critics of this kind demand of a writer that his books have not only an easily paraphrased moral but a moral that conforms to some doctrine of their own, as does the critic who remarks condescendingly that Fitzgerald "was fatally attracted by what he took to be the true romance of great wealth" and was not so interested as this critic requires writers to be in "what life somewhat nearer the center of the American economy was all about." At its best this kind of criticism is likely to stress the point that "*The Last Tycoon* is the best novel we have about Hollywood." Perhaps it is, but this sociological understanding of Hollywood is at most a minor aspect of *The Last Tycoon*. The same assumption is at work when *The Beautiful and Damned* is said to show that Fitzgerald had "discovered that there is another genre in favor: the kind which makes much of the tragedy and 'the meaninglessness of life,' " or when the significant thing about Fitzgerald's work is said to be its gradual shift from the technique of the novel of saturation to the technique of the novel of selection. Fitzgerald was not the kind of writer — if there are any — for whom understanding consisted primarily in the command of a technique. Judgments like these are far more intelligent than talk about "life . . . [near] the center of the American economy," but somewhere not very far back of them too is a notion that fiction is a theory to advantage dressed.

As a result of these distorting pressures we all tend to read the fully mature work of Fitzgerald's last period as if it were simply more of the same kind of work he produced during the early stages of his career, when he was, wholly or in part — as he was even when he wrote *The Great Gatsby* — immature. Two accidents help us to do so; the first is the neglect Fitzgerald's late work suffered when it was first published because of the decline in his reputation, a neglect from which it has never really recovered; the second is that anyone who approaches this late work on the assumption that it is merely a repetition of his early work will be encouraged by the fact that in one respect, in his perception of romantic love, Fitzgerald did mature early. The writer who could measure as precisely as Fitzgerald does in " 'The Sensible Thing' " the difference between first love and that same love deliberately renewed after a six months break is not in this respect an immature writer. " 'The Sensible Thing' " was written in 1924, when Fitzgerald was twenty-eight years old.

But the ending of " 'The Sensible Thing,' " where Fitzgerald attempts to place the story's acute insight into George O'Kelly's feelings in the context of an insight into experience as a whole, is vague and comparatively ineffective, a sort of bluff such as Fitzgerald disarmingly asserted he resorted to in *The Great Gatsby* when, as he said, he was unable to imagine the relations between Daisy and Gatsby from the time they were reunited at Nick's tea party to the time they were finally separated by the quarrel at the Plaza. "The lack [of any account of their relations]," he said, "is so astutely concealed by . . . blankets of excellent prose that no one has noticed it." In much the same way he alleges he covered this gap in the story of Daisy and Gatsby's romance, Fitzgerald resorts at the end of " 'The Sensible Thing' " to a seasonal metaphor that he develops with considerable rhetorical charm but that embodies only the vaguest perception of experience as a whole.

But for an instant as he kissed her he knew that though he searched through eternity he could never recapture those lost April hours. He might press her close now till the muscles knotted in his arms — she was something desirable and rare that he had fought for and made his own — but never again an intangible whisper in the dusk, or on the breeze of night. . . .

Well, let it pass, he thought; April is over, April is over.

The perception here is mature in one respect, and an important one, but in only one, and one we associate with youthfulness. The limitations of " 'The Sensible Thing' " are easy to see if we compare it with even an early example of Fitzgerald's late, mature work like "Outside the Cabinet-Maker's," written in 1928. "Outside the Cabinet-Maker's" begins as a wealthy man's wife goes into a cabinet-maker's shop to buy a very special doll's house for their daughter's Christmas, leaving the man and the daughter waiting in the car. "Listen," the man says to the little girl, "I love you." " 'I love you too,' said the little girl, smiling politely." Then, to keep the little girl entertained, the man begins to improvise a fairy tale around the commonplace events of the drab street — the casual passers-by, the pulling down of an apartment shade. One of the most striking characteristics of Fitzgerald's late work is the way it insists on the ordinariness, the homeliness, even the drabness of the actual events it deals with; Troilus has not accepted Hector's values, but he has stopped arguing with Hector about the source of value.

In the fairy story, the Princess is held prisoner behind the drawn shade of the apartment across the street; the King and Queen have been imprisoned by the Ogre thousands of miles inside the earth; the Prince is seeking the three stones that will set them all free. The little girl becomes so absorbed in this story that she even forgets her manners. When her father interrupts the story to say, "You're *my* good fairy," the little girl says with impatience, "Yes. Look, Daddy! What is that man?" "Outside the Cabinet-Maker's" has a fine comedy-of-manners ending, when the mother returns and the little girl suddenly takes the fairy story away from her father and gives it an ending of her own. But as she does so, something that has been implicit all along emerges clearly.

The father drops the fairy story with the remark that he is sorry they cannot stay to see the rescue of the King and Queen and the Princess.

> "But we did," the child cried. "They had the rescue in the next street. . . . The King and Queen and Prince were killed and now the Princess is queen."
> He had liked his King and Queen and felt they had been too summarily disposed of.
> "You had to have a heroine," he said rather impatiently.
> "She'll marry somebody and make him Prince."

The father "had liked his King and Queen," but in the interest of making the Princess all-powerful in the story, the little girl had killed them both without a qualm; and because she, as the Princess, plans to *make* a man a Prince in some dim future, she has killed off the Prince too.

The materials of "Outside the Cabinet-Maker's" are all very ordinary and domestic; its style is very quiet; it has no "symbolic" characters — at least it seems unlikely that even the most avid symbologist would turn the heroine into a little Pearl, though it is perhaps dangerous to assume anything about the limits of such criticism. Yet, despite the story's "realism," it is dominated by feelings of the pity and terror of things that the author nonetheless accepts so quietly that these big Aristotelian words seem quite incongruous. The ruthlessness in the story is not a product of violent passions or broken moral laws. Indeed, one can hardly say that the ruthlessness is in any personal sense even the little girl's; it is life's, and familiar every-day life's at that. Moreover, despite the ruthlessness with which the little girl destroys the mother and father of the fairy tale, she *is* her father's good fairy. At the height of his story, as his daughter stares intently at the drawn blinds that are for her the Princess's prison, "for a moment [the father] closed his eyes and tried to see with her but he couldn't see — those ragged blinds were drawn against him forever." All he can do is to buy her the doll's house that he cannot help knowing is only an expensive piece of cabinet-making and not a fairy castle and imagine for her fairy tales "whose luster and texture," as Fitzgerald puts it, "he could never see or touch any more himself." He can see and touch only through her: she is his good fairy.

At the same time he knows, without resentment, that this dependence gives him no right to her devotion. He is, half comically, annoyed by her summary disposal of the King and Queen, but he knows the story really belongs to her, and knows the ending she gives it is unavoidable. In the last sentence of the story Fitzgerald says that, as they drove away in silence, "the man thought how he had almost a million dollars," to spend, as it were, on doll's houses and fairy stories. It is not, I think, even irony, though possibly there is a certain amount of private irony about both wealth and talent in this detail of a story so close in all its details (but not in this one) to Fitzgerald's own life.

"Outside the Cabinet-Maker's" is, both in substance and technique, a wholly mature story. Only a writer who had seen that the significant values of experience exist in all experience could have said so much with material so magnificently homely and familiar; only a writer who had known and could remember what it felt like to see and had completely accepted the blindness of middle age could have presented that little girl's murderous innocence without romantic irony; only a writer with the most delicate sense of how meaning inheres in events could have kept his story so unpretentious; only a writer whose dramatic sense was a function of his understanding could have managed the ending of this story without leaving an impression of technical trickiness. "Outside the Cabinet-Maker's" is not the work of a man bemused by "the true romance" of great wealth, though the people in it are wealthy and charming. Nor is it a social analysis of Wilmington, where it takes place, or an allegorical fantasy. Its motive is an understanding — a lucid and wholly mature understanding — that exists as an action.

This is the character of Fitzgerald's best work from the late twenties on. So too is the kind of technical skill its expression requires. Fitzgerald's technical achievements are almost always direct products of expressive needs. He could learn from others, but only when he had an immediate need for what they could teach him, and then he could learn from almost anyone. In his letter to Kenneth Littauer about *The Last Tycoon* he refers to Conrad, but in his notes for the book, he refers to H. G. Wells, too. At one time or another he said he had learned a great deal from Owen Johnson, Booth Tarkington, and Compton Mackenzie, and when he wrote "Author's House" in 1936, when he was thinking hard about Hollywood (he was in the midst of making the arrangements that would take him there for the rest of his life), he was adapting a device of the movie magazines to his observation that in Hollywood writers are never thought of as quite human.

He begins "Author's House" with the remark that he has read frequently in movie magazines about the houses of Hollywood stars and seen photographs of them "explaining how on God's earth to make a Hollywood soufflé or open a can of soup without removing the appendix in the same motion," but that he never hears about authors' houses and wants to repair this oversight. He ends the essay by turning on himself the irony he had directed at Hollywood stars with his opening remark about opening a can of soup. "It's really just like all houses, isn't it" says the visitor he is showing around. "The author nodded. 'I didn't think it was when I built it, but in the end I suppose it's just like other houses after all.'" The best moment in "Author's House" occurs when the author takes his visitor up to the glassed-in cupola and throws open a couple of windows; "even as they stand there the wind increases until it is a gale whistling around the tower and blowing the birds past them."

> "I lived up here once," the author said after a moment.
> "Here? For a long time?"
> "No. For just a little while when I was young."
> "It must have been rather cramped."
> "I didn't notice it."
> "Would you like to try it again?"
> "No. And I couldn't if I wanted to."
> He shivered slightly and closed the windows.

We know a great deal of what it feels like to live up there when you are young because Basil Duke Lee does so. At the end of the series of stories Fitzgerald wrote about Basil in 1928 and 1929, when Basil finally accepts the loss of his fatal Cleopatra for whom, he decides, he will not gladly lose the world — that Cleopatra with the marvelous name of Minnie Bibble — he walks out on the veranda of the New Haven Lawn Club.

> There was a flurry of premature snow in the air and the stars looked cold. Staring up at them he saw that they were his stars as always — symbols of ambition, struggle and glory. The wind blew through them, trumpeting that high white note for which he always listened, and the thin-blown clouds, stripped for battle, passed in review. The scene was of an unparalleled brightness and magnificence, and only the practiced eye of the commander saw that one star was no longer there.

Writing nearly a decade later, the author of "Author's House" has not forgotten what it felt like to live up there with the conviction — as Fitzgerald put it, in "The Crack-Up," about his own youth — that you could dominate life if you were any good. But he knows that he not only does not but cannot live up there now. Here again we have the full acceptance of a loss, the magnitude of which is fully understood; here again, that is, we have the characteristic attitude of Fitzgerald's mature work, an acceptance of loss, not because a weakening of desire has made the loss seem less, but because there is a clear perception that "if all time is eternally present,/ All time is unredeemable." That perception is unusually difficult for people like Fitzgerald for whom the past is always intensely present; but it is, of course, precisely this difficulty that gives his achievement its value.

In the companion essay to "Author's House," called "Afternoon of an Author," Fitzgerald describes an afternoon's visit to the barber's by an author so worn out that the trip downtown is a major adventure; he describes the trip almost gaily, certainly quite impersonally. At the end, when the author arrives back at his apartment,

> He went through the dining room and turned into his study, struck blind for a moment with the glow of his two thousand books in the late sunshine. He was quite tired — he would lie down for ten minutes and then see if he could get started on an idea in the two hours before dinner.

Effects like this require the most delicate imaginable control. This is nothing so grossly palpable as a symbol; it is scarcely even an overtone of feeling. The integrity of the passage is the integrity of a direct perception of immediate experience. Nothing the author may see beyond the immediate experience itself is allowed to stretch or distort that perception. Yet we are made to feel that it is an image of a whole life and, ultimately, of an aspect of all lives. This is only a moment, a very ordinary moment, experienced, we recognize, as casually as most ordinary moments are, when we have the experience but miss the meaning. But that moment nonetheless becomes, as it is realized here, quite truly "a new and shocking/ Valuation of all we have been" — without in any way ceasing to be what it originally was.

I have been quoting T. S. Eliot deliberately because I think Fitzgerald's late work shows us, in a homely and unostentatious, even an amused way, what Mr. Eliot is describing in the "Quartets," at least insofar as the "Quartets" are concerned with how we know the truth. It is typical of Fitzgerald's late work that, on the first page of *The Last Tycoon*, Cecilia should say of her experience that "It can be understood, too, but only dimly and in flashes." "Ridiculous," she might have added, "the waste sad time/ Stretching before and after."

The resemblance, in fact, extends in part to the two writers' conceptions of reality. Fitzgerald's author is a man whose powers of responding to experience are intense, "as if he were related to one of those intricate machines that register earthquakes ten thousand miles away"; he can be struck blind by the glow of even the afternoon sunshine reflected from his books. At the same time he is a man so exhausted that he is, after a visit to his barber's, "quite tired"; he will have to rest before taking up once more what is his job, turning experience into words. There is something inescapably pitiable about this man. But the attitude of "Afternoon of an Author" is not pity. The essay moves as if its author were quite unconscious of his character's pitiableness — or rather, as if he were aware of it and had long since written it off as irrelevant. If "what might have been and what has been/ Point to one end, which is always present," then every end is like this end, this afternoon of an author, a new beginning.

One can trace this attitude and the delicacy of control that makes its expression possible in a good many of Fitzgerald's late stories, in " 'I Didn't Get Over,' " "The Long Way Out," "Design in Plaster," "The Lost Decade," "News of Paris." But the most interesting example to consider is Fitzgerald's last novel, *The Last Tycoon,* which illustrates on a large scale both the attitude and the style of his late work, even though it is unfinished, even though, as Fitzgerald's notes show, he planned to rewrite nearly all of it he had written.

We can say of *The Last Tycoon* that luck had given Fitzgerald the nearly perfect image for his feeling about experience, even if we have to say also that luck of another kind prevented his finishing the book. The essential quality of experience for him (I believe he thought it the essential quality of experience for all Americans) was the continual queerness and the occasional miracle of it, no less what they are for occurring always amidst commonplaceness, vulgarity, and a good deal of evil — and, perhaps it should be added, during a continuous earthquake. For this feeling, Hollywood provided him with an almost perfect image, and Cecilia, whose upbringing made her accept "Hollywood with the resignation of a ghost assigned to a haunted house," the perfect narrator.

The relevance of what Hollywood is to what Fitzgerald felt about experience is clearly illustrated by the crucial scene when Stahr first meets Kathleen. The scene begins in literal fact with an earthquake, during which, as Fitzgerald observes, "small hotels drifted out to sea" in the most ordinary way imaginable (small hotels, of course; we are not to exaggerate reality). This is no process shot, no distortion of actuality for symbolic effect; this is earthquake country, and earthquakes will do this kind of thing, though we may not always notice that they do. What an earthquake could not literally do anywhere except in Hollywood is what it does in the studio back lot. When Stahr and his assistants get there, they see "a huge head of the Goddess Siva . . . floating down the current of an impromptu river." Incongruously, "two refugees had found sanctuary along a scroll of curls on its bald forehead." The tone here — the ironic exaggeration of "refugees" and "sanctuary," the grotesque indignity of the goddess's "bald forehead" — is deliberate and characteristic. We are not allowed to forget for an instant the ordinary and even fake materials out of which this event is made, for all that it is very nearly a miracle. This point is driven home by Fitzgerald's adding that the head of the goddess "meandered earnestly on its way, stopping sometimes to waddle and bump in the shallows," like a frumpish old lady who means well but is badly muddled. Then Robbie, the cutter, says, "We ought to let 'em drift out to the waste pipe, but DeMille needs that head next week," and shouts at the refugees, "Put that head back! You think it's a souvenir?" In the midst of all this, off that ludicrously waddling head of the goddess of destruction and life, steps the living image of Stahr's dead wife. It is perhaps worth adding, as an illustration of the way Fitzgerald's imagination warms to its work, that he had originally planned to make the floating object "a property farmhouse"; that incongruous head of Siva was an invention of the moment of composition.

This kind of controlled and particularized realization of the miracle — the often absurd miracle — at the heart of ordinary experience is the essential achievement of Fitzgerald's mature fiction, and Hollywood made it possible for him to convey that feeling without forcing his material in the slightest. How strictly he held himself accountable for an accurate presentation of his material is suggested by the frequency with which those who know Hollywood assert that *The Last Tycoon* is the best novel we have about it. But this verisimilitude, though vital to the novel's success, is only an aspect, and a minor aspect, of its achievement, just as the brilliant account of Long Island society in *The Great Gatsby* is a vital but relatively minor aspect of its achievement. The wholly convincing representation of a world in *The Last Tycoon* is an image of experience, and the most important aspect of that image is the quality of experience it conveys.

This quality, the remarkable queerness of ordinary experience, is everywhere in the novel, inherent in the crass everyday life of Hollywood. With some irony but considerable seriousness, Fitzgerald had made the mad priest of "Absolution" say of the amusement park that was his image of the ideal life, "but don't get up close because if you do you'll only feel the heat and the sweat and the life." But the late Fitzgerald does not share Father Schwartz's sentimental regret for the distant prospect of the world's fair or his conviction that actual life consists wholly of unendurable heat and sweat. He has got up close to it and found that it is, if indeed thoroughly sweaty, also wonderfully strange and even absurd in a way that is sad enough but also genuinely funny. When Martha Dodd, the faded star of silent pictures, remembers her days of fame, she says with a wistfulness that is all the more moving for its comically incongruous expression: "I had a beautiful place in 1928 — thirty acres, with a miniature golf course and a pool and a gorgeous view. All spring I was up to my ass in daisies." When Cecilia, hearing someone moaning in the closet of her father's office, rushes over and opens the door, her father's secretary with the wonderful name of Birdy Peters "tumble[s] out stark naked — just like a corpse in the movies" — except that she is faint and covered with sweat from the heat of the closet.

This alertness for images of the queer commonplaceness of existence spreads out into the book's vision of life outside Hollywood. When the pilot in Nashville tells "the awful-looking yet discernibly attractive" drunk that they will not take him on the next flight, he says earnestly, "Only going up in ee *air*." "Not this time, old man." "In his disappointment the drunk fell off the bench," Cecilia says, "— and above the phonograph, the loudspeaker summoned us respectable people outside." When Kathleen, who has constantly disconcerted Stahr by her European, her almost peasant inclination to calculate openly what there is for her in their relation, finally tells Stahr her story, it turns out in the most plausible way in the world that she has spent a large part of her adult life as the mistress of a king.

But perhaps the most beautiful image of the book's sustained awareness of the ordinary queerness of experience is the scene of the consummation of Stahr and Kathleen's love. The scene makes clear another aspect of Fitzgerald's feeling, the aspect that led him to have the opening scene take place during an earthquake that sets everything visibly afloat and moving (so that "all the earth beyond the pond appeared like a thin crust insulated and floated," as Thoreau said about his flood). Everything in Fitzgerald's novel is afloat and moving, in an earnest and fumbling way that is at the same time a rapid drift toward the waste pipe. Nothing stands still and no one can afford to wait for things to be just right. Even while Stahr decides to wait a day before proposing to Kathleen, for instance, Kathleen's fiancé is unexpectedly on his way to marry her, and the next thing Stahr knows he is looking at a telegram that says: *"I was married at noon today. Goodbye;* and on a sticker attached, *Send your answer by Western Union Telegram"* — as soon, that is, as you can think of an answer to the unredeemable.

Stahr and Kathleen had consummated their love on a visit to a house Stahr was building at Malibu. Characteristically, it was only half finished, surrounded by concrete mixers, yellow wood, and builders' rubble. But Stahr had given "a premature luncheon" the week before and had "had some props brought out — some grass and things." Kathleen laughs and says, "Isn't that real grass?" "Oh, yes," Stahr says "— it's grass." Just before they leave this half-finished house with its temporary but quite real lawn and other appurtenances, Kathleen suggests to Stahr that perhaps he only thinks he loves her because she looks so astonishingly like his dead wife. He says simply, "You look more like she actually *looked* than how she was on the screen"; and at that Kathleen gets up, goes over to a closet, and comes back wearing an apron. "She stared around critically. 'Of course we've just moved in,' she said, '— and there's a sort of echo.' "

This queer, half-finished, floating world with its ghostly echoes constitutes the unavoidable condition of every man's life. Within it Stahr works to build something. Stahr, who had begun life as the leader of a street gang in the Bronx, dominates his world for a while by the exercise of imagination and will. Fitzgerald calls him "the last of the princes" and Stahr calls himself "chief clerk," and both are right. Stahr is the real aristocrat, the man who devotes himself to the service of the world he rules, in contrast to the phony aristocrats of Hollywood like Brady, who keeps a painting of Will Rogers in his office to suggest his "essential kinship with Hollywood's St. Francis," or the Café Society of Hollywood —"from Wall Street, Grand Street, Loudon County, Virginia, and Odessa, Russia." "[Stahr] had a long time ago run ahead through trackless wastes of perception into fields where very few men were able to follow him." He knows as only a few men at any time do what must be done, and knows too the unavoidable conditions in which it must be done. When Boxley, the British novelist Stahr has hired as a script-writer, says complainingly, "It's this mass production," Stahr says simply, "That's the condition. There's always some lousy condition." To using the complex technical process of the movies and the muddle of Hollywood to make something under this condition, Stahr devotes all his energies, as the wonderful scenes of one of his working days show.

But this is not the only condition, for Stahr had also to dominate an economic organization. On one side he is under attack from people like Brady who do not want to create something but only to get money and power. "I want," Fitzgerald said in one of his notes for the book, "to contrast [Stahr's attitude] sharply with the feeling of those who have merely gypped another person's empire away from them like the four great railroad kings of the coast." This note incidentally reveals that Fitzgerald meant the image in his book to suggest something significant about American society as a whole and about its history. On the other side, Stahr is under attack from organized labor and the Communists who support it. In part the two attacking groups work together: Brady's plot to murder Stahr includes Wylie White of the Writers' Guild and Robinson, the cutter.

But Brimmer, the Communist organizer and ruler, can understand Stahr and even feel a kind of sympathy with him, because his own problems are not unlike Stahr's. "I never thought that I had more brains than a writer has," Stahr tells him. "But I always thought that his brains *belonged* to me — because I knew how to use them. . . . Do you see? I don't say it's right. But it's the way I've always felt — since I was a boy." And Brimmer says, "You understand yourself very well, Mr. Stahr." When Stahr says to him, "You don't really think you're going to overthrow the government," Brimmer says, "No, Mr. Stahr. But we think perhaps you are." And Stahr, remembering all the Bradys in his world, the American business world, feels sure Brimmer is wrong only so long as he can feel sure that he and not the Bradys will dominate that world.

Stahr is a tycoon in the serious sense of the word — a great prince — because he is not a tycoon in *Time* magazine's sense, but an example of genuine authority in a democratic society. The particular form in which he exercises his gift for authority is the form imposed on that gift by the comparatively old-fashioned capitalism in which he grew up and which maintained itself in the Hollywood of his lifetime; that was the condition. Fitzgerald's novel suggests that he may well be the last tycoon, the last ruler of that particular kind there will be. But the essential qualities of the great prince which he possesses will be needed in any kind of society. Brimmer understands that; it is the source of his sympathy with Stahr. On the other hand, the lack of sympathy — so great that it issues in murder — between Brady and Stahr represents a contrast Fitzgerald plainly felt runs through modern American business society and, indeed, through the whole of American history.

His imagination was haunted by the difficulty and waste of creating over again in each generation of American history, in the face of a powerful alliance of acquisitive and genteel men, the tradition of responsibility that Stahr instinctively represents. The tradition is always there, but the few people in each generation who are capable of realizing it cannot see it because the fluidity of our floating American society keeps them unaware of it. They are thus forced to re-create it against heavy odds every generation. The irony in calling Stahr "the last tycoon" is central to the book. Stahr has the essential qualities of a great prince that are needed in any kind of society, though he is the last man to think of himself in these honorific terms ("I'm . . . a chief clerk. That's my gift, if I have one," he says quite honestly) because he is a great prince, not as the real tycoons were — that is, with the support of a whole society and its dominant tradition — but in spite of them.

The Last Tycoon opens with an example of what this isolation can mean. A producer called Manny Schwartz, who has been defeated in Hollywood as Stahr was to be defeated at the end of the book, arrives by accident on the steps of The Hermitage at the moment he has decided, in despair, to commit suicide. He too was once a prince, if a minor one. "I have decided," he says to Wylie White when he stays on at The Hermitage after the others leave. "Once I used to be a regular man of decision — you'd be surprised." And Fitzgerald adds:

> He had come a long way from some Ghetto to present himself at that raw shrine. Manny Schwartz and Andrew Jackson — it was hard to say them in the same sentence. It was doubtful if he knew who Andrew Jackson was as he wandered around, but

perhaps he figured that if people had preserved his house Andrew Jackson must have been someone who was large and merciful, able to understand.

The tradition is there in American society, but for the people who need it most it is very difficult to discover.

About a quarter of the way through the book, a Danish Prince who is visiting the studio sees an extra dressed as Lincoln in the studio commissary. "This, then, he thought, was what they all meant to be." Then, with Fitzgerald's unfailing awareness of the queer way the miracle lives in the commonplace in American society, he adds: "Lincoln suddenly raised a triangle of pie and jammed it in his mouth, and, a little frightened, Prince Agge hurried to join Stahr." "Stahr," as Boxley thinks later, "was an artist only, as Mr. Lincoln was a general, perforce and as a layman." Such, Fitzgerald implies, has always been the necessity of American society. About half way through the book, Stahr was to have visited Washington, but he has an attack of grippe there and moves around Washington in a high fever, so that he never gets acquainted with the meaning of America's center of authority as he wanted to, just as Schwartz never knew the meaning of Andrew Jackson.

Fitzgerald evidently meant to suggest in this part of the book that the moral and the economic conflict in Hollywood, which Stahr understands thoroughly, is an aspect of the moral and economic conflict of American society as a whole, and that if there are any men in Washington with the gift of authority, Stahr will find he has much in common with them. But Stahr does not, of course, find them; in the a-historical blindness to the tradition of authority that the fluidity of our society creates the man with the gift of authority is a great prince only perforce and as a layman, a self-made prince. Fitzgerald's plan to include episodes like these in the novel makes it clear that he intended Stahr's career in Hollywood to be an image of Amer-

202 The Sense of Life

ican experience; a conception of American experience as a whole was to constitute the framework of the novel, within which the immediate and detailed account of Stahr's experience in Hollywood was to be composed.

We cannot tell, of course, whether Fitzgerald would have brought off this ambitious compositional scheme or what the emphasis of the novel's conclusion would have been if he had. We do know that Stahr is a dying man all through the novel and was to be killed at the end in the crash of a transcontinental plane, after having lost his battle to retain control of the studio — though possibly not to have lost it forever. The epilogue of the novel, for which Fitzgerald left a rough sketch, has much the same implications that this planned ending has. Stahr's death is the death of the hero, of the superior man, of American culture.

In the superficial sense of the word also, he is the last tycoon, the last man who will exercise his gift of authority in the form authority takes in a paternalistic capitalistic society. Fitzgerald indicates very clearly the limitations — at least for a society moving as rapidly as ours is toward different forms of organization — of the form in which Stahr exercises his gift. Stahr's paternalism drives him with unavoidable logic to connive at the organization of a company union, despite his distaste for it, and reduces his conflict for power with Brady to murderous violence. These things suggest that the form within which Stahr, as a man of his time, has learned to exercise his gift, will no longer work. In this sense Stahr is the last tycoon, the last of the typical rulers of a doomed and on the whole unregretted social order.

But from Brimmer the Communist and Wylie White the intelligent and unscrupulous writer to Jim, the young boy of the epilogue, everyone of any intelligence recognizes how vital to any society Stahr's essential qualities are. In this sense, though Stahr is the last prince of this particular dynasty, he is only the latest ruler in a tradition that, despite the superficial differences of form American society gives it, runs back through Lincoln to Andrew Jackson and will produce other people who, in a different style, will become princes as Lincoln became a general, perforce and as a layman. For this, as Prince Agge saw, was what the best of them all meant to be. Perhaps, then, we may guess at the effect Fitzgerald would have aimed at in his treatment of Stahr's end. It would have been an effect not unlike the one he produced at the end of "Afternoon of an Author." Stahr would have been on the verge of losing his power completely. The flaw in the form of authority to which he had committed his gift would have led to his defeat and, without ceasing to feel how desperately his world needed the authority he could give it, he would have recognized the reasons for this defeat and even their rightness. The Bradys would have been about to take over power, and Stahr would have recognized without self-pity how disastrous this change would be. He would have been a very ill man, barely able, by a fierce effort of the will, to keep going, but he would be fighting for his now lost cause with all that was left of his diminished powers, perhaps even recognizing with a kind of amusement how absurdly diminished and inadequate these powers now were.

The Last Tycoon is the work of a writer who had, like Stahr, been through some trackless wastes of perception; unfinished though it is, it is an extended exercise of a perception of great range and refinement in marvelously close contact with actual life. In the notes Fitzgerald wrote to himself about the novel, he could formulate this perception only in the crudest and most general way, as he did for instance in his note about the railroad kings "who gypped another's empire away from them." These notes are only the roughest sort of shorthand, the result of a habit of mind not unlike the one that led Dr. Johnson to write a poem in his head, jotting down as he went along only the first part of each line. The important part had

to remain in his head until it became poetry. Shortly before
he died, Fitzgerald said of his own unwritten work that it
was "some unfinished/ Chaos in your head." It was only when
he created an action, a fiction, that his full perception was realized.

If we look at the perception that is realized in *The Last Tycoon* without allowing ourselves to be influenced by our judgment of Fitzgerald's personal life, I think we see a remarkable
awareness of the actual in all its ordinariness and all its strange-
ness, together with an acceptance of what we are so complete
and so unqualified by romantic irony that it can take even
the heroism of Stahr with mild amusement, as if it were some
sort of vice. What we are given by *The Last Tycoon*, with
an integrity very difficult for the American imagination to
achieve, is a mature perception of the American hero's life at
the apex of power in American society.

X

THE AMERICAN HERO AS LEATHERSTOCKING:

NICK ADAMS

HEMINGWAY is said to have disliked New York intensely and to have avoided it as much as possible. Certainly his tastes were not urban, and his image of the American hero is that of a man very much alone. He never exists as part of a community and on the rare occasions when Hemingway shows him in one — as he does in "Soldier's Home" — he finds it as alien as an African tribal village. Behind the cheerful assumption of family affection and solidarity in Marcelline Hemingway's *At the Hemingways'* there is a suggestion that Hemingway felt much the same way about Oak Park when he came home from the wars. All his life he seems to have been able to join in the casual gregariousness of conventional American life only by reverting to a high-school-boy self that can have expressed only his most superficial feelings: with rare exceptions he seems to have been unselfconsciously at home only with the humble — though not necessarily the unwise or even uncomplicated.

The Hemingway hero's real life is lived alone. His heroism is an action performed before the court of his own private judgment and, preferably, quite literally in private. If he shares it at all it is with a very few intimates who instinctively understand his values and never vulgarize them by describing them and thus associating them with the common values. ("Doesn't do to talk too much about all this. Talk the whole thing away. No pleasure in anything if you mouth it up too much," as Wilson, the

hunter in "The Short Happy Life of Francis Macomber," says.)
He would have been as puzzled as Ahab or Isabel Archer by
any feeling that glory, public reputation, is a necessary element
in the realization of heroism, that "fame, that all hunt after in
their lives," must "live register'd upon our brazen tombs" in
order to "grace us in the disgrace of death." Hemingway's
heroes seek grace under the pressure of death all right; Catherine Barkley speaks for them all when she says of dying, "I'm
not afraid. I just hate it." But the fame they seek, though a
plant that grows on mortal soil, does, indeed, not lie in broad
rumor but lives and spreads aloft by those pure eyes and perfect witness of the all-judging private consciousness, an ironic
romantic secularization of Milton's Puritan feeling that the
spirit of God dwells in the human heart. Hemingway's heroes
die as they live, in chosen isolation, and are buried in obscurity,
a host of unsung Hampdons whose heroism has, for all its occasional ostensible commitment to a cause, served no rebellion
but their own.

This hero is most himself up in Michigan or among the green
hills of Africa, where he pits his hunter's skill and courage
against an alien nature. When he does dwell " 'mid the din of
towns and cities," he lives in "lonely rooms" in foreign communities with which he cannot be expected to establish any
intimate contact. Here he struggles to make his soul in the
privacy of bedrooms where even having the light on all night
will not keep the wolves at bay. "There is no reason," he
thinks, "why because it is dark you should look at things differ-
ently from when it is light. The hell there isn't!" Instead of
imagining this hero as part of a community, Hemingway imagines him confronted by current events of public interest — the
Spanish Civil War, the First World War, the much publicized
Paris of the twenties. His role is that of the volunteer or the
newspaper man, one that leaves him essentially uncommitted to
the community and untouched by its pieties, aware of them
only as the uninvolved observer is.

He is as alone among large numbers of people as he is in the woods; in either situation what matters is his heroic struggle to maintain against attack, by his skill and courage alone, the privacy in which he realizes his image of himself. The people who confront his hero in cities, like the animals and fish that confront him in the woods, have for him the unsympathetic though respected remoteness of another species. At those moments when they have a part in the drama of the hero's self-realization, they take on an intense, temporary life, but most of the time they are objects of the brilliant journalism that can be written only by a man who can accept, as Hemingway could, the most advanced public attitudes of his time as if they were exclusively his own. The legendary joke, disseminated by Hemingway himself, about Fitzgerald illustrates Hemingway's journalistic skill. "The rich," said Fitzgerald, thinking of us all, even the rich, as individuals living as part of a community of their fellows, "are different from you and me." "Yes," Hemingway has himself reply, reducing the rich to a fashionable type, "they have more money."

There is something old-fashioned, even conventional about Hemingway's conception of the American hero. The most commonplace of all American impulses is to be "different," an impulse large numbers of us try to satisfy by doing exactly the same "unconventional" things; "differentness" comes so close to being mass-produced in America that we must surely be approaching a time when the really distinguished form of self-assertion will be a deliberately cultivated, a refined conventionality. "And the worst part is," as Franny says to Lane Coutell, "if you go bohemian or something crazy like that, you're conforming just as much as everybody else only in a different way." The commonness of this impulse does not make it less capable of heroic realization, but it does have its dangers. "I do not want," Fitzgerald warned himself in his notes for *The Last Tycoon*, "to be as intelligible to my contemporaries as Ernest who as Gertrude Stein said, is bound for the Museums."

Gertrude Stein had her reasons for being as unkind as possible about Hemingway, but she was too shrewd not to make what she said at least minimally true.

Edmund Wilson has made much the same point. "Bourdon Gauge of Morale," he once called Hemingway, as if his greatest talent was the sensitivity with which he responded to the tone of his time. His immediate success must have been partly due to his ability to adapt his feelings to those of the intellectual community with great precision and a conviction of complete personal independence. Perhaps it was some half-conscious discomfort about this adaptability — Gertrude Stein said it made him "bourgeois" — that led Hemingway to the unusually ostentatious unconventionality of his personal behavior. In any event, it makes judging Hemingway's work unusually difficult as long as we are at all involved in the period it deals with. At the same time it increases the importance of our doing so. Everyone knows how the reputation of Tennyson, a writer whose feelings were similarly responsive to those of his time, suffered because no one promptly distinguished his best work from his merely skilful popular work, in the way Coleridge and Arnold did Wordsworth's. If Hemingway is to have the reputation he deserves, we ought to begin now to set his best work apart from his museum pieces.

This task is not made easier by Hemingway's personal reputation. There is no doubt that we create great difficulties for famous writers in this country. Perhaps necessarily, the superficial nationwide cultural patterns in America, in which everyone of us knows how to play the part called for, are very crude. This crudeness frequently causes confusion, as when Europeans, seeing us all playing our parts in this public charade with ease and apparent satisfaction and perhaps wanting to think so, convince themselves that this is all there is to our lives; from the time of Wyndham Lewis' essay on, Hemingway was a particularly popular example among such an-

alysts of American culture. Not the least awkward consequence of our surface culture is the limitations it imposes on
our public men; few societies can have provided cruder public
personae for men to take on when they are forced into public
roles. These limitations may not bother most politicians or
bank presidents, who are either as simple as the available roles
and do not find them uncomfortable, or are so habituated to
living behind a manufactured, public-relations face that they
are no longer aware of their own discontinuity. But the
romantic modern writer is not, by temperament, a public man
and he is especially uncomfortable when he is thrust into the
world of newspapers and publicity. Hemingway, with his habit
of doing in isolation all the living that seemed real to him, must
have found himself acutely so.

Faced by fame, that he had not in any serious sense hunted
after, with the necessity of providing himself with a public
face, and pressed by his middle-western inheritance to remain a
solid, simple American (of the kind, he must occasionally have
remembered, who committed suicide, as his father did), Hemingway made for himself an absurd public self that was an
outrageous parody of his vision of the American hero. If we
are to see how magnificent a writer Hemingway was at his
best, we must get behind this public self. It is not easy to do.
The public Hemingway, old two-gun Ernie, was almost as well
known as a movie star or a professional athlete and during
his lifetime appeared at regular intervals in magazines like
Life in a Daniel Boone beard and outlandish clothes as an authority on fishing and hunting and a man who could talk in
their own language to all the wise fools among the natives everywhere.

This cross between Teddy Roosevelt and a character invented by Richard Harding Davis was particularly anxious that
no one should confuse him with the effeminate types who pass
as writers and intellectuals and, when he was forced to talk

about his art, treated it as if it were some athletic performance, perhaps a boxing match in which he had fought Stendhal to a draw. He presented himself as a man who had spent his youth in the rough, hearty comradeship of war, bullfighting, and prizefighting; devoted his middle years to the exercise of a special gift of sympathy for the Spanish earth; and lived out his last years among the peasants and cats of San Francisco de Paula. It is easy enough to sympathize with the annoyance that led Max Eastman to urge this Hemingway to take the false hair off his chest, and many readers must have been bothered by the care with which he shows the Hemingway hero avoiding tourist traps in Paris or sneering at defeated writers in Venetian hotels. But we ought never to forget that this public Hemingway is a persona for whose limitations we are all in part to blame — "certainly the worst invented character in the author's work," as Edmund Wilson once called him, a man who, as Scott Fitzgerald put it with sympathetic amusement, was, "contrary to popular opinion, . . . not as tall as Thomas Wolfe, standing only six feet five in his health belt."

Perhaps the worst effect on Hemingway the writer of the attitude of this public character was the encouragement it gave to a tendency in any event strong in American writers like Hemingway, a tendency to distrust the formulating intelligence. Much of the time Hemingway seems to have supposed that all intellectual activity does what the bad kind certainly does, that is, substitute second-hand ideas for felt responses. This bias was reenforced early in Hemingway's career by his adopting without much modification the disillusionment so widely advertised, if not experienced, by his contemporaries. Frederic Henry of *A Farewell to Arms*, that Childe Harold of the First World War, is the classic expression of his feeling.

I was always embarrassed by the words sacred, glorious, and sacrifice and the expression in vain. We had heard them, some-

times standing in the rain almost out of earshot, so that only the
shouted words came through, and had read them, on proclama-
tions that were slapped up by billposters over other proclama-
tions, now for a long time, and I had seen nothing sacred, and
the things that were glorious had no glory and the sacrifices
were like the stockyards at Chicago if nothing was done with
the meat except to bury it. There were many words that you
could not stand to hear and finally only the names of places had
dignity. . . . Abstract words such as glory, honor, courage, or
hallow were obscene. . . .

Abstract words had been made obscene by their accumulation
of socially acceptable and therefore false emotions; only names,
numbers, and other "unsocialized" terms could be trusted to
convey the true emotions of the private consciousness. There
is an aesthetic as well as a social theory here, and both are —
despite their common insistence that all theories be expressions
of sincere, individual feelings — second-hand theories. The social
theory is that of the popular disillusionment of the twenties;
the aesthetic theory is one that was almost as well advertised as
the social theory, by Pound's imagism, Eliot's objective cor-
relative, and a number of other prescriptions of dramatic representation for poetry and fiction.

The most dangerous consequence of Hemingway's distrust of
the abstracting intelligence is his unwillingness to think out the
meaning of what he feels and the form that meaning needs.
Witwoud says that Petulant did not think but trusted to his
natural parts. Hemingway's natural parts were very fine, but
there are limits to what even the most powerful unanalyzed
responses can do to give formal order. Nevertheless Hemingway insisted on trusting them in his work, just as all his heroes
trust them in their lives. But in a fiction of any size, a writer
must grasp with his intelligence at least the controlling elements
of each of the many local insights that make up his action;
otherwise he will not know how to order these insights or be

able to see what perfectly genuine ones are irrelevant to this occasion and what ones that do not arise spontaneously are nonetheless made obligatory by this occasion.

To make a true marriage between insight and intelligence and to prevent each from violating the other may well be the most difficult part of a writer's job. There is always a serious risk that the rational intelligence will impoverish the insight, possibly even reduce it to a commonplace, just as there is always a risk that the unreasoned insight will be inchoate or inadequate. The novel that is too much a conscious act of the intelligence will, like some of Edith Wharton's late work, be deficient in life; the novel that is insufficiently so will, like some of Faulkner's work, lack coherence. For historical reasons I have tried to indicate, American writers have mostly been inclined to trust unanalyzed insight, to assume that everything they feel about an occasion comes from the heart of their perception of it, and that all their feelings will, like the complicated factors of Adam Smith's vision of an economy, fall into accord by the mysterious operation of the Primary Imagination's unseen hand. Matthew Arnold argued that the great romantic poets thought too little, and at least in this sense most American writers have been romantics.

In Hemingway's finest work, such as *The Sun Also Rises* and *A Farewell to Arms*, the emotion evoked in him by the whole occasion of the novel is so intense that it dominates and controls his immediate responses to the individual episodes that make up the whole, and then the local feelings of each episode are united into a single, final feeling. *The Sun Also Rises* is a beautiful instance of coherence achieved in this way. We know that after Hemingway had spent a weekend with Fitzgerald at Juan-les-Pins going over what he presumably thought a completed text of the novel, he went back to Paris and cut a long passage that preceded the present opening. Clearly, then, the novel was not written to a carefully worked out plan, yet its only serious defects are failures of local insight like Brett's embarrassing description of one of Hemingway's strongest feelings, "not [being] a bitch," as she puts it, as "sort of what we have instead of God." The design of the novel is nevertheless very beautiful.

In the very first paragraph we learn that "in [Cohn's] last year at Princeton he read too much and took to wearing spectacles." In Hemingway that is, of course, a very bad sign, and we soon learn that Cohn is a great admirer of W. H. Hudson's *The Purple Land*, "a very sinister book if read too late in life. It recounts splendid imaginary amorous adventures of a perfect English gentleman in an intensely romantic land, the scenery of which is very well described. . . . Cohn, I believe, took every word of [it] as literally as though it had been an R. G. Dun report." Out of this apparently casual opening there emerges the whole action of the book.

Under the sinister influence of *The Purple Land* Cohn conceives a borrowed literary passion for Brett and persuades her to go off with him for a weekend. It is a perfectly casual experience for her, but Cohn, seeing himself as "the perfect English gentleman" in romantic circumstances, takes it very seriously and attempts to play the part of a Tennysonian Launcelot to the Guinevere he insists Brett is despite everything she does to dissuade him. To the amused despair of the self-aware characters in the book he calls her Circe. "He claims she turns men into swine," Mike Campbell says, "damn good. I wish I were one of these literary chaps." Confident in their conviction that only the attitudes you imagine are spontaneously produced by your own consciousness can be sincere, these characters are specially alert for the kind of self-deception Cohn represents.

In contrast to Cohn Hemingway sets Jake. Jake is in love with Brett, truly, as only the Hemingway hero can be. But this love will never be realized because a war injury has made him incapable of sexual intercourse. Their honor — its exercise is a daily necessity — is to confront their situation without behaving badly. "Why don't you get married, you two?" says the count. "We want to lead our own lives," says Jake, parodying one of the clichés of the period, and Brett, the disoriented girl who is marrying Mike Campbell in sheer desperation, adds, "We have our careers." Cohn has a passion for textbook information about architecture, but Jake trusts his instinctive responses to Spanish cathedrals. Cohn is much moved by literary descriptions of lush landscapes, but Jake loves — unostentatiously, of course — the bare, brown Spanish countryside. This contrast, at work in every episode of the book, comes to a climax when Cohn, carried away by shameful jealousy, beats everybody up. He knocks them all down — he is a semi-professional boxer — but he is morally defeated by Romero, the bullfighter, who keeps getting up until Cohn cannot bring himself to hit him again. Bill Gorton sums up Cohn perfectly for the good Americans of the book: "The funny thing is he's nice, too. I like him. But he's just so awful."

If the false American has an earnestly cultivated, fake sensibility, hopelessly mismanages the major human relations, and makes a general nuisance of himself, the good American lives by his genuine, natural feelings, keeps his love clear of ego, and behaves well no matter what it costs him. His object is not to learn what life is about — especially if that means learning from books — but to learn how to live. Living is overwhelmingly a matter of acting in ways that accord with one's deepest personal sincerities. It is therefore best done in direct, personal confrontation of danger, where the sincerity of the hero's commitments is tested, in action, under extreme pressure, or in the intimacies of passion, which provide a similar test. *The Sun Also Rises* is a beautifully organized representation of the American sense of experience as Hemingway understood it, at its best and at its worst.

Sometimes, however, a Hemingway novel has a merely mechanical unity, the limitations of which are made obvious by individual episodes so good that they separate out and become self-contained short stories. *For Whom the Bell Tolls* suffers in this way. It contains many fine episodes — the death of Sordo, Pilar's account of how the war began in her village, Andrés' journey with the message for Golz, the destruction of the bridge. Each of these episodes has its independent emotion, far too powerful to be contained by the form of the novel as a whole, a good journalist's political analysis of the Spanish Civil War. Like much journalism, this analysis has not worn well, and it has only the loosest relevance to the feelings of the separate episodes or the moving aspects of Robert Jordan's mind.

In Hemingway's less successful books, all sorts of random matter leaks in, perhaps worst of all the public Hemingway's views. *To Have and Have Not* is peppered with Marxist opinions, *The Green Hills of Africa* with ill-considered judgments of American writers, and *Across the River and into the Trees* with smart remarks about the generals of the last war — remarks that come with particularly bad grace from a man who always insisted that only writers should be allowed to criticize writing. Somewhere behind this public character, with his distrusted and therefore untrustworthy intelligence, who is so ready to give us his views, lay the fine consciousness that created the best of Hemingway's work, two novels, large parts of several others, a dozen or more short stories. In this considerable body of work Hemingway penetrated to the heart of American experience with a rightness few writers have equaled.

"The 'I' in this work," Wyndham Lewis said, "is the man that things are done to"; it would be juster to say "the man that things happen to." Hemingway was not, as Lewis' remark suggests, a passive and perhaps masochistic victim. He was the experiencing self. For him the individual consciousness,

with all its ultimately unsharable shades and distinctions of
feeling, is the significant reality, and he believes real only what
this consciousness knows from experience: "I know only what
I have seen," as Hemingway himself put it. His best work is
a biography of this self's confrontation of the things that happened to it, as his worst work is a display of the public self
he used when he could not conjure up this self.

This self was eager to experience the world; that was the
serious reason for Hemingway's notorious restlessness. But it
insisted on the right to make its own terms, and was always
ready to ignore society's claims and, like Frederic Henry, make
"a separate peace." The shaping effect on Hemingway's work
of his personal experience is so evident that it has disquieted
many readers, but from the early stories to *Across the River and
into the Trees* Hemingway's best work as well as his inferior
work grew out of his personal experience. If the journalism of
his inferior work was encouraged by his habit of depending for
stimulation on direct observation of dramatic public events, so
often was the kind of understanding he had in his best work.
That understanding was his immediate, personal sense of "the
way it was." A sense of the way things really are is possible
only to a man who is fully, perhaps even professionally involved in them; Hemingway's necessary, semi-professional involvement in the activities he wrote about is the serious aspect
of an impulse that made the public Hemingway childishly proud
of being in on the know. It also helps to explain why Hemingway's romantically exaggerated regard for love so often expressed itself as a minute concern with the sexual act. For
Hemingway, "love," as old Count Griffi says in *A Farewell to
Arms*, "is a religious feeling." But the abstractions of love,
especially when they are dressed up in the big words of idealizing novelists, are obscene; only the act of love itself and, if you
are very careful to remember the way it was, the words that
describe that act, can be trusted. Let the Robert Cohns imagine

they can learn about it from the folklore of the community's customary conception of it or the reflections of this folklore in books; Hemingway knows only what he has seen in bed, and his difficult task is to put that down in words, without distortion or additions.

Out of another order of things seen Hemingway has made some of the most moving descriptions of nature in American literature. Like his own Colonel Cantwell, he has lived much of his emotional life "by the accidents of terrain," and like Colonel Cantwell, he is sure the only way to express his emotional life is to put down these accidents with the accuracy of the professional observer.

> In the late summer of that year we lived in a house in a village that looked across the river and the plain to the mountains. In the bed of the river there were pebbles and boulders, dry and white in the sun, and the water was clear and swiftly moving and blue in the channels. Troops went by the house and down the road and the dust they raised powdered the leaves of the trees. The trunks of the trees too were dusty and the leaves fell early that year and we saw the troops marching along the road and the dust rising and the leaves, stirred by the breeze, falling and the soldiers marching and afterward the road bare and white except for the leaves.

Nothing could be more accurately observed than that, or more unadorned. Yet it is saturated with the horror of death. It would be interesting to know the reasons why the distinctive rhythm of this passage moved the people of its time so profoundly as it did. ". . . clear and swiftly moving and blue in the channels"; Ezra Pound uses it often in the *Cantos*, particularly the early cantos ("A sheep to Tiresias only, black and a bell-sheep"), and Archibald MacLeish, whose ear for the rhythm of his time must have been nearly the best there was uses it even more ("Big in the fault of the light and his men armed").

In a writer like Hemingway a clear paraphrasable content or penetrable symbols will almost certainly be a sign of inferior work, the relatively crude resources of a writer who has spoiled — by thinking and theorizing — what was initially felt with unadulterated purity. Hemingway seems to have allowed himself as few ideas as possible about the meaning of his stories. When Fitzgerald undertook to analyze a number of them, Hemingway told him that he was like a great mathematician who loved mathematics truly and always got the wrong answers. Possibly he did, but Hemingway added an observation that suggests there are no answers of this kind when he said of "Cat in the Rain" that it was just something that happened. If he could get down what happened exactly as he had perceived it, he believed the story would embody the feelings that made what happened matter to him, something that could only be falsified by being paraphrased.

The natural unit of fiction for a writer like this is a single occasion, usually one not very long or crowded with events. Hemingway in fact began as a writer with very brief pieces — sketches as the editors who wrongly rejected them rightly called them. Even the briefest of them have the major characteristics of a Hemingway story.

> We were in a garden at Mons. Young Buckley came in with his patrol from across the river. The first German I saw climbed up over the garden wall. We waited till he got one leg over and then potted him. He had so much equipment on and looked awfully surprised and fell down into the garden. Then three more came over further down the wall. We shot them. They all came just like that.

This is an unadorned presentation of the way it was; Hemingway gives us nothing that does not seem part of what a participant would have noticed when he was involved in the action itself and wholly preoccupied with practical things. We are made to feel that this was the way it was in the most literal sense, at the very moment the narrator lived through it.

At the same time the intense clarity of the narrator's perception suggests that his emotional response to the occasion was very powerful. He does not break down under its pressure or become inefficient; in fact, his efficiency appears to be a ritual for controlling his emotion. But the emotion is evident in the way the passage selects and emphasizes a small number of details out of the large number it might have reported; it is evident too in the way the passage shows us these details, not more or less simultaneously, in the tangle we are aware of in ordinary states of perception, but isolated, as a series of the cameo-like images characteristic of perception under great emotional stress. This way of presenting the event allows the description itself to suggest the horror that violent death should be so ordinary, so lacking in dignity, so nearly ludicrous. There is the German soldier, one leg over the garden wall like a small boy come to steal apples; there we are, "potting" him as if this were some game; there he finally is, humanly clumsy with his load of equipment, looking awfully surprised for just a moment before he falls down, altogether insignificantly dead.

What has determined the selection of details here, in short, is the heightened perception of a moment of great emotion, an emotion that is never stated directly or even hinted at with adjectives and similes. Hemingway's best long stories are exactly like this one. For example, the longest and one of the best ones, "Big Two-Hearted River," is a detailed description of a lonely fishing trip that is, as Malcolm Cowley has pointed out, the desperate effort of Nick Adams, just back from the war and on the edge of collapse, to lose himself in the homely but subtle ritual of fishing that he had learned before the war. This desperate purpose — again never stated in the story — makes the smallest act of the fisherman a gesture in a ceremony of salvation.

After long practice in the art of discovering what his private self truly felt, Hemingway came eventually to certain moral generalizations of his own. He had deliberately discarded the inherited ones; they were not to be trusted; his experience did not bear them out. What it did bear out was the moral satisfaction of Jake Barnes's stoicism, the effort to behave well and not make a nuisance of oneself no matter how painful the circumstances. This is Hemingway's "grace under pressure." If it is to be genuine, the circumstances that create the pressure must be fully experienced and completely understood, whether they are the circumstances of physical danger or high passion. Hemingway is as scornful of the opinions of those who have not been there as Faulkner is of "the hasty minds of those theoreticians who have no business of their own"; nobody ever allows poor Cohn to forget that, before he sees a bullfight, he says, "I'm not worried about how I'll stand it. I'm only afraid I may be bored."

The amount of importance attached to the testing occasion by conventional opinion counts for nothing, except that it can usually be assumed that conventional opinion is wrong. The occasion may be the frustration of love, as it is in *The Sun Also Rises*, the defeat of the individual's most sincere and innocent impulses by the sinister alliance of society and nature against him, as it is in *A Farewell to Arms*; it may be the death of a bullfighter, as in "The Undefeated," of the defeat of a prize fighter, as in "Fifty Grand." If you have become an expert in one of these specialized ways of life because you love it, you will live your life by the ritual of technical activities that are the natural manners of your profession and will behave according to its code whatever happens, simply because you cannot conceive life on any other terms. Manuelo, the old mediocre bullfighter of "The Undefeated," dies after his goring with only one thought; "I was going great," he says to his friend; "Wasn't I going good, Manos?" He had been, too, though out of sheer love of bullfighting, not because he was any good — " 'Why, that one's a great bullfighter,' Retana's man said. 'No, he's not,' said Zurito."

Hemingway took a special pleasure in finding this kind of purity and grace in characters like Manuelo, in whom the conventional mind is least likely to suspect it. An even better example is Jack Brennan, the aging fighter of "Fifty Grand." Apart from a little pride that he is champion, he thinks only about his wife and children and the money he wants for them. Hemingway is obviously thinking of the conventional motive of American businessmen who never tire of observing that they do it all for the wife and kiddies. Jack is a tough, independent professional with nothing of the good guy about him. When he enters the ring for his big fight, his opponent puts his hand on Jack's shoulder for a minute. "So you're going to be one of these popular champions," Jack says to him. "Take your goddam hand off my shoulder."

While he is training for this fight, Jack worries about his investments and misses his family. He has not been sleeping well — Hemingway's heroes seldom do — and as the fight draws near he is in bad shape. Then some gamblers offer him a chance to bet "fifty grand" on his opponent, and since he is sure he is going to lose the fight perfectly honestly, he makes the bet. The fight goes just as he has expected it to until, near the end, his opponent deliberately fouls him. Standing there in agony he realizes that the gamblers have double-crossed him. To increase the odds against him and thus increase what they can win by betting on him, they have tricked him into betting $50,000 on his opponent and then bribed the opponent to lose the fight by fouling Jack. With almost incredible courage, Jack stays on his feet and insists to the referee that he is all right. When the fight is resumed, he measures his opponent carefully and fouls him exactly as he had fouled Jack. The opponent goes down in agony and is awarded the fight, and

Jack wins $25,000 instead of losing $50,000. "It's funny how fast you can think," he says, "when it means that much money." "You're some boy, Jack," his manager says to him. "No," Jack says. "It was nothing." This is an echo of the modest disclaimer of the stock hero of the cheapest fiction. But it is not a modest disclaimer for Jack; it would never enter his mind to make one. It is the bald truth.

In a more complicated way the same purpose dominates one of Hemingway's best late stories, "The Gambler, the Nun, and the Radio." The central character of this story, Mr. Frazer, is in the hospital with a broken leg. He makes friends with one of the sisters who has hoped she was going to become a saint but thinks she has not. Such is her simplicity that she loves all good people without suspecting there is anything remarkable about herself. She is particularly concerned for a Mexican patient who has been shot twice in the stomach and is in great pain from a gangrened wound. Though he is expected to die, he refuses to identify his assailant, apologizes in embarrassment to the sister for the smell of his wound, and never utters a groan. "So many people in the ward," he explains deprecatingly after he has, to everyone's astonishment, recovered. He is a small-time professional gambler deeply in love with gambling. "I am a poor idealist," he says. "I am the victim of illusions. I am a professional gambler but I like to gamble. To really gamble. . . . When I make a sum of money I gamble and when I gamble I lose." So unillusioned about himself is this victim of illusions that he can even see the joke of the professional gambler's inability to win in an honest game. It is the purity of this devotion without illusion — to however incongruous an object — that enables him to behave well. It is what he has, to use Brett's expression, instead of the sister's love of God. But Mr. Frazer, who wants as much as they do to behave well, has nothing to love and must go it wholly alone. The story ends very late at night with Mr. Frazer lying awake, as he does every night. "He would have a little spot of the giant killer and play the radio, you could play the radio so that you could hardly hear it." "After all," as the waiter in "A Clean, Well-Lighted Place" says, "it is probably only insomnia. Many must have it."

Like these stories, all Hemingway's best work is about the difficult acceptance of what the self sees — for itself — to be the true nature of personal experience and about the achievement of grace under the pressure of that experience, if a man is lucky with the support of some devotion (no wonder Hemingway tried to think of himself as a Catholic), but if he is not lucky without any support whatsoever. When his novels succeed, they do so by making patterns of the same kind of heroism as "The Gambler, the Nun, and the Radio." *A Farewell to Arms*, for example, has a group of unlike characters who are alike in the important respect that they have learned, by loving something completely, all there is to know about it and have acquired the strength, the dignity, the grace of unillusioned dedication. Rinaldi, who believes in nothing except surgery, is as *croyant* as the shy priest who loves God or Frederic and Catherine who love one another. They are all, in their different ways, driven hard, and all of them, however much they may hate what they have to go through, are unafraid of it.

If we must recognize, as Hemingway in effect did in "The Snows of Kilimanjaro," that he often deceived himself into trusting his superficial feelings, we must also recognize that his best work is the consequence of a dedication as final and, in its less spectacular way, perhaps as heroic as Catherine's. Fitzgerald once observed that Hemingway's physical courage was not a natural but a painfully cultivated attitude; so was his artistic courage. The personal significance of "The Short Happy Life of Francis Macomber" is not so much the way it reflects the hunting exploits of the public Hemingway as the way it reflects the creative life of Hemingway's private self. To see what it tells us about that is to feel a deep respect for the Hemingway who produced his finest work by following his own nature into places that must have been, for his vanity, extremely dangerous.

"The Short Happy Life of Francis Macomber" is a remarkably complete and coherent representation of Hemingway's American hero. He begins as one of the rich who have more money than is good for them and have been insulated by it from experience all their lives; Francis "would stay adolescent until [he] became middle-aged" unless the test of reality was accidentally forced on him. He has never known passion; he and his wife "had a sound basis of union. Margot was too beautiful for Macomber to divorce her and Macomber had too much money for Margot ever to leave him." He has never known danger, never confronted death with only his hunter's skill and courage to aid him. He "kept himself very fit, was good at court games, had a number of big-game fishing records, and [when the story opens] had just shown himself, very publicly, to be a coward."

In Hemingway's terms Macomber's behavior is the result of inexperience and immaturity rather than of practiced cowardice. When the wounded lion charged he did not really know what was coming, what kind of self-control he needed, what knowing these things would make him. "[He] heard the blood-choked coughing grunt, and saw the swishing rush in the grass. The next thing he knew he was running; running wildly, in panic in the open. . . ." Like all men who have not been forced to outgrow the ignorance of immaturity, he was a coward upon instinct. That does not make him any the less a coward, but it does make him less irretrievably one, and in the buffalo hunt he is carried by the excitement of the occasion over the boundary of immaturity into the manhood that defines heroism for Hemingway and knows for the first time how to live: he "felt a wild unreasonable happiness that he had never known before" and became almost drunk with elation. "You know, I'd like to try another lion," he says. "I'm really not afraid of them now. After all, what can they do to you?" "That's it," says Wilson the hunter. "Worst one can do is kill you." Wilson is much moved by Macomber's self-realization; "he had seen men come of age before and it always moved him. It was not a matter of their twenty-first birthday." So moved, and in deep embarrassment, Wilson brings out a passage from Shakespeare he has spent his life earning the right to quote ("By my troth, I care not; a man can die but once, etc."), incidentally showing us what literature is really good for, as contrasted to the use "these literary chaps" like Cohn make of it.

Francis Macomber thus becomes Hemingway's hunter hero, but it is important to realize that, had he lived, he would also, as a consequence, have become Hemingway's heroic lover. Macomber's happy life is cut short by Margot Macomber, who shoots him. The story says she "had shot at the buffalo . . . as it seemed about to gore Macomber and had hit her husband"; Wilson implies she shot Macomber deliberately. It does not really matter because she was essentially responsible whether the act was intentional or not, just as Francis was essentially responsible when he ran away from the wounded lion. Francis has now been radically transformed; as Wilson puts it himself, Francis has gone through "More of a change than any loss of virginity. Fear gone like an operation. Something else grew in its place. Main thing a man had. Made him into a man. Women knew it too. No bloody fear." But Margot, though she does know it, remains what she had made herself in order to live with the immature Francis; "she had done the best she could for many years back and the way they were together now was no one person's fault." Regardless of who was to blame for the way they are, however, Francis is no longer the man who would not divorce Margot because she was too beautiful. "He *would* have left you too," Wilson says to her after she has shot Macomber. It is evident he would have. When he and Wilson discuss Macomber's transformation and Margot says they are talking rot ("She's worried about it already, [Wilson] thought") Francis says easily to her, "If you don't know what we're talking about why not keep out of it?" When Margot had slept with Wilson after Francis had publicly shown himself a coward, it was Francis who complained querulously and Margot who said, "We don't have to talk about it, do we?"

"The Short Happy Life of Francis Macomber" shows us the immature American boy-man who has been too long kept in ignorance by the civilizing Aunt Sally of American urban life, suddenly confronted by one of those occasions that constitute reality and call forth our essential moral natures and achieving the difficult, magnificent, and all too rare manhood that only Hemingway's hunter hero and heroic lover can fully experience.

XI

THE AMERICAN HERO AS POET:

SEYMOUR GLASS

J. D. SALINGER represents American writers a full generation younger than those discussed in the last four chapters, the generation of the second rather than the first World War. He is not — no one could be — entirely representative, of course; his generation contains a surprising number of writers who have, like Hemingway, made a separate peace and are busy making their souls in isolation from their society, some of them with a quite spectacular amount of social visibility. But there is a good deal of evidence that if Salinger does not represent all the writers of his generation he does represent his generation, that his hero is the hero of our time to a degree that none of the other heroes, however interesting, is.

The problem of the hero has not changed appreciably for Salinger, and in certain respects he is more nearly in the direct line of American literature of the nineteenth century than were the writers of the twenties, closer in attitude, that is, to writers like Thoreau, less obsessed than a great many writers of the twenties with direct dramatic representation and the image, more willing to narrate and comment, in a way only Faulkner among the writers of the twenties does. Unlike Faulkner, Salinger frequently uses a first-person narrator, and he has in effect told us that, even when a story shows no sign of having a narrator, he thinks of it as being told by one. But his narrator, Buddy Glass, is difficult to distinguish from Salinger

228 *The Sense of Life*

himself. In "Seymour: An Introduction" Buddy tells us that he gets "Get-Well-Soon notes from old readers of mine who have somewhere picked up the bogus information that I spend six months of the year in a Buddhist monastery and the other six in a mental institution." This allusion to a widespread rumor about Salinger himself invites us to identify Buddy and Salinger, as do many other particulars in the Glass stories, such as Buddy's assertion that he wrote the narratorless story "A Perfect Day for Bananafish" "just a couple of months after Seymour's death . . . using a very poorly rehabilitated, not to say unbalanced, German typewriter . . ." and "an ex*cep*tionally Haunting, Memorable, unpleasantly controversial, and thoroughly unsuccessful short story about a 'gifted' little boy aboard a transatlantic liner" who is clearly Teddy; since "Teddy" not only has no narrator but is not even a Glass story, Salinger is thus committed to the fiction that all his stories have been written by Buddy.

Faulkner usually uses a third-person narrator, but since Salinger's first-person narrator is nearly indistinguishable from the author, this difference is not significant. Salinger's real use for the first-person narrator is to give him an opportunity to introduce a voice, to allow him the passionate, colloquial, expansive rhetoric that characterizes his work; this rhetoric comes out of a different American tradition from Faulkner's, but it has many resemblances to Faulkner's and Salinger depends on it as much as Faulkner depends on his. Like Faulkner, too, Salinger likes to use dialogue for narration and comment. Except for Les Glass — who has so far made only a brief and bad-tempered appearance and seems baffled by his children (he proposes to offer Franny a tangerine when she is having a nervous breakdown) — and perhaps Boo Boo, all the Glasses are indefatigable talkers, ready at a moment's notice to explain anything or anybody "*in full*"; they are, as Buddy puts it in a typical Glass phrase, "experienced verbal stunt pilots."

Salinger's rhetoric is very important, then, to the expression of his meaning (and is, incidentally, a consciously cultivated thing; it hardly exists in the stories he wrote for *Collier's* in the early forties, and only gradually emerges in the stories of the forties like "The Varioni Brothers" and "Blue Melody"). Apart from its own intrinsic charms, this rhetoric is both characterizing and evaluating; Salinger is obviously very conscious of the way a person's style reflects his nature: "The expression is Franny's 'young man' . . . not her 'boy friend.' Why are you so out of date, Bessie? Why is that? Hm?" Even in the most fragmentary form his dialogue creates characters. "I wasn't supposed to come back after Christmas vacation, on account of I was flunking four subjects and not applying myself and all." "Everybody else on the train . . . looked very Smith, except for two absolutely Vassar types and one abso*lute*ly Bennington or Sarah Lawrence type. The Bennington-Sarah Lawrence type looked like she'd spent the whole train ride in the john, sculpting or painting or something, or as though she had a leotard on under her dress." "They got their *pores* open the whole time. That's their *nature*, for Chrissake. See what I mean?" "This here's officers' quarters, Mac."

Seymour Glass, Salinger's hero, is dead almost as soon as we get to know the Glasses and we are largely dependent for our understanding of him on the rest of the Glass family, as we would be to some extent even if Seymour were alive, especially since Salinger has now in effect denied the accuracy of the portrait of Seymour he gave us in "A Perfect Day for Bananafish." It is easy to understand why he wants to. The other members of the family have pointed out to Buddy that the "Seymour" of this story is "someone with a striking resemblance to — alley oop, I'm afraid — myself"; and as Buddy elsewhere reminds us, Seymour once said that "cleverness was my permanent affliction, my wooden leg, and that it was in the worst possible taste to draw . . . attention to it." The "Seymour" of

"A Perfect Day for Bananafish" is too clever and perhaps too unkind (to the woman in the elevator, for instance) to be the Seymour Salinger now sees. The trouble with his new Seymour, however, is that he hardly exists; in "Seymour: An Introduction" we catch a few brief, very badly lighted glimpses of him, leaping out of bed in the middle of the night, "yellow pajamas flashing in the dark," to tell Buddy something; "investigating loaded ashtrays with his index finger, clearing all the cigarette ends to the sides — smiling from ear to ear as he did it — as if he expected to see Christ himself curled up cherubically in the middle"; answering one of his father's questions "gravely and at once, and in the special way he always answered questions from Les"; playing stoopball or marbles with uncanny skill, or chasing Buddy, the Second-Fastest Boy Runner in the World, up Broadway. Even Seymour's allegedly marvelous poems reach us only in Buddy's bald narrative paraphrases. The only fully realized character in "Seymour: An Introduction," and the overt subject of at least half of it, is Buddy.

We are thus driven back on the other Glass children for knowledge of Seymour, especially on Buddy and Zooey, between whom and Seymour "the membrane is," as Seymour once said ". . . thin." Moreover, the Glass family as a whole offers Salinger a variety of instances of the exceptional man's difficulties with society that no single character could. He began to depend on this sort of group hero early in his career; a whole series of the stories he wrote in the forties deal with two related families, the Gladwallers and the Caulfields, who are connected by the friendship between John Gladwaller and Vincent Caulfield, the sons. These two families are not so fully developed as the later Glass family, but Salinger's most significant characters are beginning to appear in them — Vincent Caulfield, who "didn't believe in anything from the time little Kenneth Caulfield died"; Babe Gladwaller's younger sister, Mattie ("With her feet together she made the little jump from the curb to the street surface, then back again. Why was it such a beautiful thing to see?"); and, of course, Holden Caulfield himself. In these stories Holden dies, as Walt Glass does, in the Pacific in 1945, at the age of nineteen. (Curtis Caulfield, who was on *It's a Wise Child* with Seymour and Buddy, was "killed during one of the landings in the Pacific" — to add to the confusion.) The Gladwaller-Caulfield stories are scattered over several magazines and quite a few years but are nonetheless painstakingly precise about names, dates, and places, and, above all, the minute details of human relations. There are a few discrepancies — especially between the unrepublished stories of the series and *The Catcher in the Rye* — but they are clearly deliberate. Salinger locked in on Holden Caulfield only late in the series, in 1945, with "I'm Crazy"; much of the family detail from the first four stories of the series is kept in the two stories about Holden, but there are important changes, too. Holden is not killed; Vincent, who before the war had been a television writer, is replaced by D. B. Caulfield, who is, as Holden says, a prostitute in Hollywood; Babe Gladwaller disappears and his sister Mattie is transmuted into Phoebe Caulfield, who was barely mentioned in the first four stories. With some revisions, these two stories became chapters in *The Catcher in the Rye*. I think it is a fairly good guess that, after writing *The Catcher in the Rye*, Salinger decided that most of the things he now saw he wanted to do with the Gladwaller-Caulfield stories could be better done if he started afresh without some of the awkward commitments of these stories.

In any event, in 1948 he dropped the Gladwallers and the Caulfields and with "A Perfect Day for Bananafish" began to develop the Glass family. This is, in order of publication anyway, the first of the Glass stories, of which there have so far been eight. (We have Salinger's word for it that he has "several new Glass stories coming along.") It is anybody's guess, of course, whether Salinger had the whole, as yet unfinished history of the Glass family in mind when he wrote "A Perfect Day for Bananafish"; there is some suggestion in "Seymour: An Introduction," where Buddy substantially rejects the portrait of Seymour in "A Perfect Day for Bananafish," that Salinger now wishes he could change some of the qualities of the characters established in these early stories, if not the facts of their history. But it is a good guess that, much as Faulkner apparently always had at least the main outlines of the McCaslin family history in mind, Salinger has known about the Glasses from the start. At least, the order in which the Glass stories have appeared (and probably were written) has little relation to the chronological order of events in the family history, yet all the details of the family history are remarkably (if not perfectly) consistent. Next to the effects of his rhetoric, Salinger depends most on these details of the Glass family to convey what he means, and they are by now very numerous. At the same time they are widely scattered and easily lost track of in the baroque convolutions of Salinger's rhetoric, so that it may be useful to set down here an outline of the Glass family and its relations.

The parents, Les Glass (Jewish) and Bessie Gallagher Glass (a fat Irish Rose, as her youngest son lovingly calls her), were successful Pantage Circuit vaudevillians in the early twenties. But in the spring of 1925 Bessie Glass decided, for a variety of reasons, that they had to leave vaudeville, and Les "took a job in what he invariably referred to, for years and years, with no real fear of being contradicted around the house, as the administrative end of commercial radio, and Gallagher & Glass's extended tour was officially over." In the late twenties the Glasses lived in an apartment house on Riverside Drive at 110th Street. In the forties Les was "hustling talent for a motion picture studio in Los Angeles" and in the fifties he and Bessie were living, with their two youngest children, in "an old but, categorically, not unfashionable apartment house in the East Seventies" to which they had moved in 1929. They have had seven children.

The oldest of these children, Seymour, was born in February, 1917, entered Columbia at the age of fifteen, and took a Ph.D. in English. In 1940 he and his brother Buddy reluctantly gave up the room they had shared in the Glasses' apartment in the East Seventies for twelve years and moved into an apartment of their own near 79th and Madison. Seymour taught English for several years between taking his Ph.D. and being inducted into the service. While he was stationed at Fort Monmouth he met a girl named Muriel Fedder, whom he married on June 4, 1942, in New York, flying there from the B-17 base in California where he was then a corporal and acting company clerk (or maybe a buck sergeant). When the war ended he had himself psychoanalyzed — as he had promised Muriel and her mother he would — presumably by what Buddy calls one of those "*summa-cum-laude* Thinker[s] and intellectual men's-room attendant[s]" that people like Muriel's mother so admire. Possibly as a result, one day in 1948 he deliberately drove the Fedders' car into a tree, and it was decided that he and Muriel should take a vacation, in Florida of course, and at the place he and Muriel had spent their honeymoon. There, in room 507 of a fashionable beach hotel, on the afternoon of March 18th, Seymour made his second, successful attempt to commit suicide, by putting a bullet from an Orgies caliber 7.65 through his right temple. He had been Bessie Glass's "favorite, her most intricately calibrated, her kindest son."

The second child, Buddy Glass (whose given name is, I think, Webb) was born in 1919, as was Jerome David Salinger. Like Salinger (who tried three) he never finished college. *The Great Gatsby*, he says, was "[my] 'Tom Sawyer' when I was twelve." He entered the service early in 1942 and in June of that year was stationed at Fort Benning, from which he came to New York to attend the wedding of Seymour and Muriel Fedder (a ritual Seymour absented himself from). When Buddy got out of the service he became what he insists on calling "a writer-in-residence," teaching at several colleges; by 1955 he had settled at "a small girls' junior college in upper New York state. He lived alone in a small, unwinterized, unelectrified house about a quarter of a mile from a rather popular ski run." He mumbles in a disgruntled way about his students' stories, thirty-seven out of thirty-eight of which, he says, are always "about a shy, reclusive Pennsylvania Dutch lesbian who Wants To Write, told first-person by a lecherous hired hand. In dialect." But when he is off guard he admits that "by some good fortune I can't believe I've deserved, I've had one of [the] ebullient, cocksure, irritating, instructive, often charming girls or boys in every second or third class I've taught . . . [who] are the hope, always, I think, of blasé or vested-interested literary society the world over."

The third child and first girl in the family is Boo Boo Glass; we do not know her given name. "Her joke of a name aside, her general unprettiness aside, she [is] — in terms of permanently memorable, immoderately perceptive, small-area faces — a stunning and final girl." She seems to be more easily reconciled to the world as it is than the rest of the Glass children, though she agrees with the small child in *Kilvert's Diary* who, when asked by a Sunday-school teacher who made the world, promptly replied "Mr. Ashe" (Mr. Ashe is Kilvert's eccentric and tyrannical local squire). During the war Boo Boo was a Wave stationed, most of the time, at the Brooklyn Navy Yard and living in Seymour and Buddy's apartment. During that time she met "a very resolute-looking young man" named Tannenbaum, whom she later married. The Tannenbaums live in Tuckahoe and have a summer place in New England. By 1955 they had three children, the oldest of whom is named Lionel, the hero of a story called "Down at the Dinghy."

Boo Boo was followed by twins, Waker and — twelve minutes younger — Walt. Waker spent the war in a conscientious objectors' camp in Maryland and after the war became a Catholic priest. He was assigned to a parish in Astoria, but presently

became what Buddy calls an "impounded Carthusian"; he inherited the vaudeville talents that run in all the Glass children
and "Family rumor has it that he was originally cloistered off
. . . to free him of a persistent temptation to administer the
sacramental wafer to his parishioners' lips by standing back two
or three feet and trajecting it in a lovely arc over his left
shoulder." "If you tell Waker it looks like *rain*," his mother
says, "his eyes fill up with tears." Walt entered the service in
the spring of 1941 and by May of 1942 was in the Pacific. In
Japan, late in the autumn of 1945, a Japanese stove he was
packing as a souvenir for his commanding officer turned out to
be full of kerosene; it blew up and killed him. In 1941 this
"only truly lighthearted son" of Bessie Glass had a happy love
affair with a girl named Eloise; a few years later, married and a
helpless drunk, she can only say, remembering Walt, "I was a
nice girl, wasn't I?"

The Glasses' sixth child, Zachary Martin Glass, known in the
family as Zooey, was born in 1930. Zooey is startlingly handsome, or, as Boo Boo says, he looks like "the blue-eyed Jewish-
Irish Mohican scout who died in your arms at the roulette table
at Monte Carlo." After college, instead of going on to graduate
work, he became a television actor; by 1952 he was playing
leads. The youngest Glass child is a girl named Frances, born
in 1935. Like Zooey she is beautiful. In the summer between
her junior and senior years in college, she played summer stock.
Zooey, an enthusiastically severe judge of acting, saw her do
Pegeen in *The Playboy of the Western World* and says she is
a very good actress. By the next fall she was in the midst of an
affair with a boy named Lane Coutell, but in November of
1955 she was driven close to a nervous breakdown. "I'm just
sick of ego, ego, ego. My own and everybody else's. I'm sick
of everybody that wants to *get* somewhere, do something distinguished and all, be somebody interesting. It's disgusting —
it is, it *is*. I don't care what anybody says." After three

difficult days at home, she is saved from collapse by her brother Zooey, who possibly saves himself at the same time, and goes on into an acting career.

Salinger's hero, Seymour, and in fact all the Glass children, are, like Gavin Stevens, wrestling with the problem of how to be their very exceptional selves and still remain a part of their community. Salinger represents Seymour as a poet, but very much the poet as seer, "the heavenly fool who can and does produce beauty, [and] is mainly dazzled to death by his own scruples, the blinding shapes and colors of his own sacred human conscience." Seymour is preoccupied with the transcendental "poetry that flows through all things" and would no doubt feel — though not with so much unkindness — what Franny feels when she says, "If you're a poet, you do something beautiful. I mean you're supposed to *leave* something beautiful after you get off the page and everything. . . . All that maybe the slightly better ones do is sort of get inside your head and leave *some*thing there. . . . It may just be some kind of terribly fascinating syntax *droppings* — excuse the expression."

At the same time the Glass children recognized how necessary their community is to them and, indeed, are sure that the only way to fulfill the religious urge that is powerful in all of them is to love that community's members. Seymour will not publish his "un-Western" poetry because Miss Overman (the librarian of the public-library branch the Glass children used) "would have trouble turning to it with pleasure or involvement." "You can't," Buddy says, "argue with someone who believes, or just passionately suspects, that the poet's function is not to write what he must but, rather, to write what he would write if his life depended on his taking responsibility for writing what he must in a style designed to shut out as few of his old librarians as humanly possible." Their community is not the small-town, rural Southern one that Gavin Stevens clings to. It is ultimately the whole of the America that the Glass children address when they are performing on their quiz program known "with perhaps typically pungent Coast-to-Coast irony" as "It's a Wise Child." Immediately it is modern urban America, the New York of fashionable psychoanalysts, mixed-up scriptwriters from Des Moines, terrible and touching television producers, college students, and instructors.

Among the writers of his time, only Salinger seems to have fully understood the way the university has, during the last couple of decades, become a standard part of the conventional American world. Gavin Stevens with his Phi Beta Kappa key and his Heidelberg Ph.D. is an incomprehensible absurdity to the conventional people of Jefferson, but Salinger's conventional people admire Ph.D.'s and even the stupid ones boast about the papers they write on Flaubert. The ordinary member of the academic community is thus no less familiar an American type and no more easy to endure than any of the rest of the ordinary people the Glass children are up against. In her most self-destructively bitter mood Franny tells Lane Coutell he is like a section man and then tells him what a section man is like; "he comes in, in his little button-down-collar shirt and striped tie, and starts knocking Turgenev for about a half hour. . . . Where I go, the English Department has about ten little section men running around ruining things for people, and they're all so brilliant they can hardly open their mouths — pardon the contradiction. I mean if you get into an argument with them, all they do is get this terribly *benign* expression on their —"

Bessie Glass, whose mind often seems to her children "an impenetrable mass of prejudices, clichés, and bromides," has never reconciled herself to Zooey's going into television instead of taking his Ph.D. in Mathematics or in Greek, as he easily could have. (But Zooey did have a shot at translating the Mundaka Upanishad into classical Greek.) Seymour took a Ph.D., though not of course in quite the usual way, with a working wife, three children, a Woodrow Wilson Fellowship, and five or six years of part-time teaching; "Seymour had his Ph.D. at an age when most young Americans are just getting out of high school." The Glass children know full well the destructive conventionality — what Franny calls "just one more *dopey, inane* place in the world dedicated to piling up treasure on earth and everything" — the university is, "the dark, wordy, academic deaths we all sooner or later die," as Buddy, who is a teacher, says, and that "no doubt we all deserve."

But this death is no worse, if no better, than the other conventional lives open to the Glass children. What will Zooey's life as an actor be? —"playing Pierre or Andrey in a Technicolor production of War and Peace, with stunning battlefield scenes, and all the nuances of characterization left out (on the ground that they're novelistic and unphotogenic), and Anna Magnani daringly cast as Natasha (just to keep the production classy and Honest), and gorgeous incidental music by Dmitri Popkin, and all the male leads intermittently rippling their jaw muscles to show they're under great emotional stress, and a World Première at the Winter Garden. . . ." It is this Hobson's choice that brings Franny to the edge of despair, "All those egos running around feeling terribly *char*itable and *warm*." But the Glass children know too that their mother is right when she says, "You can't live in the world with such strong likes and dislikes" as these.

Thus the Glass children know everything there is to know about the deaths to which the conventional modes of life tempt us, which is perhaps more than can be said for Gavin Stevens in Jefferson, but that does not prevent their understanding how necessary it is to participate in the conventional life of their community, because they know equally well the kind of death "a separate peace" is, the kind their brother Buddy has all but made. "If [Buddy] were twenty *miles* in the woods, with both legs broken and a goddam *arrow* sticking out of his back," Zooey says, "he'd crawl back to his cave just to make certain

nobody sneaked in to try on his galoshes while he was out. . . .
Take my word for it. He cares too much about his goddam
privacy to die in any woods." New York is their home town,
quite as much as Jefferson is Gavin's. Even Buddy "after
thirteen years of country living [is] still a man who gauges
bucolic distances by New York City blocks."

Salinger's work shows us very clearly that the old American
longing for community has not been decreased by the urbaniza-
tion of America, that the people Faulkner calls "the coastal spew
of Europe . . . quarantined unrootable into rootless ephemeral
cities" (the Glass children are half Jewish and half Irish) are as
deeply rooted in their community as any Southern gentleman in
his. The Glass children understand that they exist in any proper
sense only in relation to their community, only when they succeed, at however great a cost, in loving it. "I say," says Buddy
Glass of his story "Zooey" — and Salinger could say it of all the
Glass stories — "that my current offering isn't a mystical story,
or a religiously mystifying story, at all. *I* say it is a compound,
or multiple, love story, pure and complicated." Salinger's constant allusions to Zen Buddhism, the Bhagavad Gita, Sri Rama-
krishna, and Chuang-tzu are only alternative ways of expressing what his stories express.

The Glass children cannot escape being the supremely aware
people they are, nor can they escape knowing that they must
be members of a particularly demanding and not very perceptive community; they are forced to live partly in the world of
ordinary American experience and partly in what may perhaps
fairly be called the transcendental world of extraordinary
American experience. Like Thoreau and Henry Adams, Huck
Finn and Ike McCaslin, Ishmael and Jay Gatsby, they are committed, involved, torn. "I'd enjoy [doing a movie in France],
yes," says Zooey. "*God*, yes. But I'd hate like hell to leave
New York. If you must know, I hate any kind of so-called
creative type who gets on any kind of ship. I don't give a god-

dam what his reasons are. I was *born* here. I went to school here. I've been *run over* here — *twice*, and on the same damned *street*. I have no business acting in Europe, for God's sake." This sounds not unlike the protagonist of Allen Tate's "Ode to the Confederate Dead," except that the voice is Northern and urban and is — for all its desperateness — less despairing.

It is the Glass children's effort to convey the full sense of their situation that leads them to talk the way they do. They must speak the language of the place where they were born, went to school, were run over; it is their native language, the only one wholly theirs, just as the place itself is. But they need to express in this language an understanding of experience which, if it is possessed in some degree by many Americans, is wholly clear to only a few of them; a similar insistence on making poetry out of the colloquial American speech of their communities is evident in Mark Twain and Ring Lardner. The well-worn and apparently limited phrases of this speech are made comic by the special quality of the feelings the Glass children use them for; at the same time, the common language holds them, for all the special quality of their feeling, in contact with ordinary people, just as their commitment to some ordinary profession like television does, just as their cultivation of conventional manners does. Zooey is a small man who makes a habit of smoking panatelas; like so many of the Glass children's activities, "the cigars are ballast, sweetheart. Sheer ballast. If he didn't have a cigar to hold on to, his feet would leave the ground. We'd never see our Zooey again."

The special quality of feeling, of insight, of the "artist-seer" that all the Glass children to some extent share is very uncommon, but what it sees into and requires its possessors to love is universal. It shows most obviously in children, but it is there in everyone, in "the very corny boy" who gave Franny the gold swizzle stick for a birthday present that she cannot bear to throw away; in Seymour's Miss Overman with her innocent love of Browning and Wordsworth who "had opened a book to a plate of Leonardo's catapult and placed it brightly before" Seymour his first day in the public library; in Zooey's producer, LeSage, who delights in scripts that are down-to-earth, simple, and untrue, but believes with beautiful innocence that his "really tired, bosomy, Persian-looking blonde" wife is a dead ringer for "the late Carole Lombard"; in Seymour's mother-in-law, Rhea Fedder, who might as well be dead, yet "goes on living, stopping off at delicatessens, seeing her analyst, consuming a novel every night, putting on her girdle, plotting for Muriel's health and prosperity" — "I love her," Seymour says. "I find her unimaginably brave."

The Glass children's most treasured jokes are an expression of their sense of the absurdity of what they know they must love. At the end of Buddy's trip to Florida after Seymour's suicide, when he had wept nearly all the way, he heard a woman back of him in the plane saying, "with all of Back Bay Boston and most of Harvard Square in her voice, '. . . and the *next morning*, mind you, they took a pint of pus out of that lovely young body of hers.' " As a result when he got off the plane and Muriel Fedder "the Bereaved Widow came toward me all in Bergdorf Goodman black, I had the Wrong Expression on my face. I was grinning." But if they can grin at the absurdity of what they must love, that absurdity is close to horror and is a quite terrible burden. "Smart men," as Dick Diver said a long time ago in *Tender Is the Night*, "play close to the line because they have to — some of them can't stand it so they quit." Dick says this about Abe North, who is modeled on Ring Lardner.

Like Abe, Seymour, the most gifted of the Glass children, kills himself. He knows that, in spite of — because of — the unusual depth and intensity of his insight, his need to be a part of the daily life of the ordinary world is very great. That is why he marries Muriel Fedder and tries to live her kind of life. This is no mere intellectual need; it is a desperate emotional necessity for him; "How I love and need her undiscriminating heart," he says of Muriel. But he finds it impossible to live the life of his own discriminating heart, so intense that on the day of his wedding he feels as if he had been born again and cannot go through the conventional marriage ceremony, and Muriel's life with its "primal urge to play house permanently . . . [to] go up to the desk clerk in some very posh hotel and ask if her Husband has picked up the mail yet . . . to shop for maternity clothes . . . [to have] her own Christmas-tree ornaments to unbox annually." He is torn apart by two incompatible worlds of feeling until he cannot endure it any longer.

This, then, is the hard thing, not to find out "what it [is] all about," a thing the Glass children have all known from very early in their lives, but "how to live it." Knowing what it is all about, in fact, is the burden. Seymour and Buddy taught Franny and Zooey what wisdom is very early, or, as Zooey, desperate over his inability to accept the world on its own terms, says, "Those two bastards got us nice and early and made us into freaks with freakish standards, that's all. We're the Tattooed Lady, and we're never going to have a minute's peace, the rest of our lives, till everybody else is tattooed, too. . . . The minute I'm in a room with somebody who has the usual number of ears, I either turn into a goddam *seer* or a human hatpin. The Prince of Bores." This, Zooey knows, is not a failure of love — he would not be concerned with his own freakishness if that had happened — but a distortion of it. If you take to somebody, his mother says to him:

> ". . . then you do all the talking and nobody can even get a word in edgewise. If you *don't* like somebody — which is most of the time — then you just sit around like death itself and let the person talk themself into a hole. I've seen you do it. . . . You do," she said, without accusation in her voice. "Neither you nor Buddy know how to talk to people you don't like." She thought it over. "Don't love, really," she amended.

"Which is most of the time" because, apart from children and the occasional very simple adult, the world is made up of people who are innocently imperceptive and emotionally dead. Of the drastic limitations of such people the Glass children have an almost unbearably lucid perception. Buddy's stories are filled with undergraduates "giving the impression of having at least three lighted cigarettes in each hand," of parents who say "I'll exquisite day *you*, buddy, if you don't get down off that bag this minute," of brassy women like Muriel's Maid of Honor with her "But my gosh. Honestly! I just can't stand to see somebody get away with absolute murder. It makes my blood boil." Such people, as Teddy says of his parents, "love their reasons for loving us almost as much as they love us, and most of the time more."

But even if the acts of such people are not consecrated by love, as are Bessie's and — to some extent — Muriel's, they must not be hated. "But what I don't like," Zooey tells Franny, ". . . is the way you talk about all these people. I mean you don't just despise what they represent — you despise them. It's too damn personal, Franny. You get a real little homicidal glint in your eye when you talk about this Tupper, for instance. All this business about his going into the men's room to muss his hair before he comes in to class. All that. He probably does — it goes with everything else you've told me about him. I'm not saying it doesn't. But it's *none of your business*, buddy, what he does with his hair." Franny really knows this well enough. When she remembers how she treated Lane Coutell about his pseudo-Freudian paper on Flaubert that his instructor thought might be publishable, she tells Zooey, "He'd written some perfectly harmless test-tubey paper on Flaubert that he was *so* proud of and wanted me to read, and it just sounded to me so strictly English Department and *pa*tronizing and campusy that all I did was . . . It's a wonder he didn't shoot me. . . . I'd have absolutely con*grat*ulated him if he had." As she remem-

bers how she acted about Lane's paper, Franny looked "even
paler, more post-operative, as it were, than she had on waking."

Even more harrowing to their consciences is their inability to
see past the irrelevance to the love of the acts of people like
Bessie and Les. Franny is driven nearly frantic by Bessie's insistence on nice cups of chicken soup when Franny is having her
crisis of the soul. But she knows perfectly well Zooey is right
when he points out that she is "missing out on every single goddam religious action that's going on around this house. You
don't even have sense enough," he says, "to *drink* when somebody brings you a cup of consecrated chicken soup—which is
the only kind of chicken soup Bessie ever brings to anybody
around this madhouse." This is Zooey's gloss on the text from
the Bhagavad Gita quoted on the beaverboard that is nailed to
the back of the door to Seymour and Buddy's bedroom: "Perform every action with your heart fixed on the Supreme Lord.
Renounce attachment to the fruits. Be even-tempered [under-
lined by one of the calligraphers] in success and failure; for it is
this evenness of temper which is meant by yoga." This is why
Zooey is so suspicious of Franny's breakdown. "I don't like this
Camille routine . . ." he says, "and if you don't know it yet,
you're beginning to give off a little stink of piousness. . . . I'd
like to be convinced — I'd *love* to be convinced — that you're
not using it as a substitute for doing whatever the hell your duty
is in life, or just your daily duty."

"The cards," as Buddy puts it for them all, "are stacked
(quite properly, I imagine) against all professional aesthetes."
The Glass children, unable not to see all the horror of a world
of Rhea Fedders and Professor Tuppers, are equally unable not
to see the horror of themselves becoming "like those dismal
bastards Seymour's beloved Chuang-tzu warned everybody
against. 'Beware when the so-called sagely men come limping
into sight.'" Not simply to see through but to dislike the
Rhea Fedders and the Le Sages, the affected undergraduates and

the "terribly sad old self-satisfied phon[ies]" who teach them is
to suffer the particularly ugly kind of wrongness that consists
in being right about people — even, possibly, clever about them.
All Salinger is talking about — and it is plenty but not a lot of
things it is easy to suppose — when he speaks of the religious life
is what Walt Glass once called "just something God sicks on
people who have the gall to accuse him of having created an
ugly world."

What Zooey is trying to tell Franny and himself they must
learn to do if they are to survive is, then, to love even what he
calls the fishy people, the walking wounded like Holden Caulfield's old Spencer who was "a nice guy that didn't know his
ass from his elbow," because they are the Fat Lady for whom
Seymour told Zooey to shine his shoes before going on the air.
"This terribly clear, clear picture of the Fat Lady formed in my
mind," he tells Franny. "I had her sitting on this porch all day,
swatting flies, with her radio going full-blast from morning till
night. I figured the heat was terrible, and she probably had
cancer and — I don't know. Anyway, it seemed goddam clear
why Seymour wanted me to shine my shoes when I went on the
air. It made *sense*." It made sense because it made clear Seymour's understanding that the highest standard of behavior a
man's personal understanding can establish for him must ultimately be embodied — however mystically — in the ordinary,
suffering members of the community of his fellows. Otherwise
there is no solution for the dilemma in which the Glass children,
along with all good Americans, are caught. Zooey puts this
point, logically enough, by making it the Incarnation itself at the
end of his telephone conversation with Franny,

I'll tell you a terrible secret — Are you listening to me? *There
isn't anyone out there who isn't Seymour's Fat Lady.* That includes your Professor Tupper, buddy. And all his goddam
cousins by the dozens. There isn't *any*where that isn't Sey-

mour's Fat Lady. Don't you know that? Don't you know that goddam secret yet? And don't you know — *listen* to me, now — *don't you know who that Fat Lady really is?* . . . Ah, buddy. Ah, buddy. It's Christ Himself. Christ Himself, buddy.

There is in Salinger's work every evidence that, like Seymour, he has written what he must; perhaps too much evidence — at least Buddy is constantly admonishing himself parenthetically to "*cut that out.* Just manage to nip that stuff in the bud, please." But he has certainly written it, if not "in a style designed to shut out as few of his old librarians as humanly possible," certainly with the Fat Lady always in mind. He has rediscovered, reimagined, made new, with loving attention to the precise way in which his community in its time knows its experience, the traditional American sense of experience: it is a significant coincidence that Seymour's beloved Chuang-tzu was Henry David Thoreau's beloved Chuang-tzu too.

Salinger's attempts to represent his hero Seymour have sometimes been baffled by his transcendentalist's feeling of ecstasy as he contemplates love incarnate, so that instead of a created character we get only Zui-Gan's "Yes, sir; yes, sir." But more than enough of what that perfection means for the ordinary experience of life comes clear in the minutely particularized less bafflingly perfect members of the Glass family like Franny and Buddy and Zooey. Salinger's vision of the heroic life is quite clear from the stories about the Glass family as a whole. It consists in a struggle that, with only minor modifications, American heroes have been going through for the last hundred years of our literature. That uncalculated coincidence helps us to see more clearly what our tradition is and how close to the center of it Salinger's work, for all its traditional novelty of observation and expression, really is.

XII

THE AMERICAN HERO AS HIGH-SCHOOL BOY:

PETER CALDWELL

JOHN UPDIKE belongs to the generation of American writers
that is a decade or so younger than Salinger (Updike is fourteen
years younger than Salinger), and the geographical circumstances as well as the social conditions of his upbringing were
very different from Salinger's. But the basic attitudes of their
work and the dilemmas of their heroes are very similar; both
writers have a strong impulse to mix memory and desire and to
make them come alive in the present. Behind this common impulse is a common concern for the double nature of reality —
as indeed, there is in Mr. Eliot, too, with his inability to think of
Lil without thinking of Philomela; but then, Mr. Eliot is also a
very American poet. The solid and grimy actualities of New
York and "Olinger" where the desires of Salinger and Updike
took shape as they grew up and attached themselves forever to
the particulars of the places, are the basic stuff of reality for
both of them. And for both of them the meaning of this actuality is some transcendent quality, some ineffable and gaudy
element that constitutes a larger and more permanent life that
inheres in the universe and is known to men — obscurely and
figuratively — in the slowly accumulated wisdom of myth and
religion. But this meaning can be experienced only at home.
Like Zooey Glass, who will not leave the New York in which
he grew up, went to school, and was run over, Peter Caldwell
(he is given different names but is the same high-school boy in

Updike's short stories) cannot keep away from Olinger for reasons that are made clear by one of Updike's finest stories called, appropriately enough for my purposes here, "The Persistence of Desire."

The Olinger of Updike's stories is evidently the Shillington, Pennsylvania, where Updike himself grew up. Shillington is a small town near Reading in the Pennsylvania Dutch country, "on the Western periphery" of the John O'Hara country, as Mr. Updike puts it. Like Peter Caldwell's father, Updike's was a high-school teacher and Updike himself, one can guess from his stories, was the brightest boy in the local high school. He went from there to Harvard, from which he was graduated *summa cum laude*. He had not yet given up an early ambition he shared with Peter Caldwell to become a painter, and after Harvard he spent a year at the Ruskin School of Drawing and Fine Art in London (it is called the Constable School in the story — "Still Life" — he later wrote about it). In 1955 he came back to New York, where he worked for two years on *The New Yorker* doing pieces for "The Talk of the Town" as well as writing short stories and poems and what his blurb writer calls "humor." In 1957 he left *The New Yorker* to write full time, moving to Ipswich, Massachusetts, where he lives with his wife and children in a seventeenth-century house from which he flees daily to what he calls "a sort of slum" in the center of Ipswich to do his writing.

Brief as this career has so far been, it shows the same divided ambition his work does, and in both its display of talent and energy and in its alternation between a desire for conventional success and a dedication to literature, it has a curious resemblance to the career of Archibald MacLeish. At Yale MacLeish was conventionally successful, an athlete and a Senior Society man, and also a serious poet. After a brilliant performance at the Harvard Law School, he began with great success to practice law in Boston; in 1924 he deserted Boston for the Paris of the expatriates, where he produced an impressive volume of poems, *Streets in the Moon.* At the end of the twenties he returned to New York to become an editor of *Fortune,* a position from which he retired to write poetry. In the late thirties he returned to public life and had, during the war, an impressive career in government service. After the war he became a professor.

Updike's alter ego is not, of course, a lawyer, an editor of *Fortune,* and an Assistant Secretary of State; he is a *New Yorker* staff writer. Like MacLeish he has, however, alternated between the opportunities for success in that direction his undoubted talents for it open up to him and the impulse to dedicate himself to the most serious kind of writing he can conceive. Like MacLeish, who did a small stint of teaching at Harvard in his early days, Updike has felt the appeal of the academic life as a possible way out of this dilemma. In the short story called "A Sense of Shelter," there is a beautifully sardonic account of the career a high-school boy very like Updike dreams of: he would be a professor, "brilliant in his forties, wise in his fifties, renowned in his sixties, revered in his seventies," and would die "like Tennyson, with a copy of *Cymbeline* beside him on the moon-drenched bed." "Consciousness of a special destiny," says a similar high-school boy in "Flight," "made me both arrogant and shy."

There are thus, as there are in so many American writers, two writers in Updike, the dazzlingly talented young man with the desire to become a conventional success — a *Time* Magazine professor or a cosmopolitan, urbane, *New Yorker* wit — and the romantic American haunted by a small-town childhood that glows in his memory with a unique intensity of felt reality. His work shows the struggle that has gone on between the sophisticated urban wit and the romantic with his transcendentalist feeling that the life of Shillington, Pennsylvania, he knew as a boy was lived in the light of eternity.

This division shows most clearly in the incongruity of form and substance in Updike's work. He is almost always dealing with the homely, everyday realities of small-town American life, but he can never resist dealing with them in a highly self-conscious literary way, in a form that is full of portentous symbolic implications, mythological analogies, and the latest thing in narrative techniques, and in a style of extreme rhetorical elegance. This apparent discontinuity of substance and style is one of the clearest marks of the American temper. Melville himself wrote much of the time about Nantucket sailing-ship life in a pastiche of styles borrowed from Shakespeare and Carlyle. These pastiches are over-elaborate and artificial in his work precisely because they were not produced by and are therefore not controlled by Melville's own sense of life but were taken second-hand from writers of a very different kind. To a considerable extent, therefore, they answer to a merely aesthetic response to language itself in Melville, and insofar as they do, they tend to obscure, or at least divert attention from, the sense of experience that makes Melville, in spite of this often irrelevant style, one of the great writers of the world. The later work of Henry James suffers from a similarly cancerous over-development of style, and so, in ways at least for the moment less complained of, do the styles of many great American writers.

For at least a hundred years — roughly since modern America came into existence around the time of the Civil War — there has been a discontinuity between the defining images of our writers and their manner of expression. This discontinuity is not merely a matter of individual temperament; it reflects something observable in American culture. We Americans, Mary McCarthy once said with both wit and justice, are a nation of twenty million bathtubs — with a humanist in every tub. Bathtubs are in themselves incongruous enough settings for humanists, and what is worse, the more luxuriously expressive of mere taste in plumbing the bathtubs become, the more they obscure the humanistic idealism of their occupants. Much the same thing could well be said of the other supposedly expressive objects of our society, from our clothes and our magazines to our automobiles and our architecture. They are all ostentatiously, even extravagantly tasteful, in a ready-made, ready-styled way that is hopelessly inexpressive of our inner selves, which dwell among them like embarrassed strangers caught sitting naked in luxurious bathtubs — which, taken merely as bathtubs, they very much enjoy. Nevertheless, we live all our lives among these objects, and our most highly metaphysical commitments are attached to them and must be expressed in terms of them.

Updike's sharp awareness of this American dilemma is everywhere in his work; returning from a year in Europe, one of his heroes finds the American cars, "bunched like grapes and as blatantly colored as birds of paradise . . . were outrageous, but made sense," and as he drives through the American countryside, "the dear stucco hot-dog stands, the beloved white frame houses, the fervently stocked and intimately cool drugstores unfurled behind car windows smeared with sullen implications of guilt, disappointment, apology, and lost time." This is where all Americans live; however jarring it may be, we have to love it. It is hardly to be wondered at, therefore, that within Updike there has been a kind of fighting between the aesthetic delight of his cultivated humanistic self in complex forms and ingenious verbal patterns and his commitment to the everyday, homely American life that is filled with inexpressible transcendent significance for him; he once told an interviewer that his favorite writers were Henry Green and Karl Barth. That fighting is no less severe because Updike's stylistic masters are more up-to-date than Melville's, are writers like Joyce rather than writers like Carlyle.

It may be that the precise, quiet, charged language in which Updike re-creates the Shillington of his boyhood owes something to the style Joyce developed for the re-creation of the Dublin of his boyhood. But a great many of Updike's Joycean ingenuities have — however serious the motive for them may be — the mechanical and dead effect of exercises for a creative writing course (as does the Joycean style of the story called "Wife-Wooing," where the imitation is frankly acknowledged). His virtuosity must have charmed his teachers all through his high-school and college career and they no doubt encouraged his natural delight in it. The results are, in their limited way, very attractive. They are most evidently so in his verse, for example, in the sheer verbal excitement of these lines from an alphabet poem written for his small son:

> Conceptually a blob,
> the knob
> is a smallish object which,
> hitched
> to a larger,
> acts as verger,

or in the cleverness with which he exploits an idea that his novel *The Centaur* shows really disturbs his imagination in his comment on the statement of the Rand McNally Atlas that the population of Argentina is fourteen million:

> Rand, recount; recount, McNally:
> There's been some slip-up in your tally;
>   Count Argentinian heads again.
> Search every cellar, scan each alley,
> And you'll discover Axis Sally
>   Playing poker with Hart Crane.

But cleverness of this kind tends to divert attention from the subject by its own charms. In even the best of his work Updike does not always resist the temptation to elaborate minor details with an excessive verbal elegance, as when, in "The Persistence of Desire," he says of a group of high-school girls that, "small-town perennials, they moved rather mournfully under their burdens of bloom," or in "Still Life," that "a remarkably complete set of casts taken from classical statuary swarmed down corridors and gestured under high archways in a kind of petrified riot," or in *The Centaur* that the pain of George Caldwell's injury "extended a feeler into his head and unfolded its wet wings along the walls of his thorax . . . [and] seemed to be displacing with its own hairy segments his heart and lungs."

This lovingly executed cosmatesque surface of irrelevant decorative details makes critics describe Updike as a poetic novelist, as indeed, he too often is. *The Poorhouse Fair*, his first novel, for instance, comes out of his haunted memory of childhood — the fair turns up in other stories — his deep involvement in the realities of that time. It plainly wants to say something about the conflict between the desires of the old people in the poorhouse and the earnest wrongheadedness of the social worker in charge of them. Less plainly but more movingly, it wants to say something about the unique sense of experience of these old people, their precise and — to Updike's memory — priceless understanding. How close this subject is to his heart we know from the other stories he has written about them, how central it must have been to the purpose of this novel we can guess from the fact that the main character, John Hook, seems to combine the characteristics of his father and his grandfather. Far too little of this intention, however, gets realized in the novel because so much of it is taken up with working out "poetic" symbols like the violently independent, half-dead tomcat, or with ostentatious phrases like, "self-denying by doctrine, he walked against the slope of his desire."

This conflict between subject and style is so striking because Updike's essential subject, though it calls for a certain amount of romantic irony, is uncomfortable with symbolic elaboration that has the slightest amount of self-conscious literary elegance about it. What it requires is sincerity, earnestness — however eloquent — because Updike is a romantic for whom the instinctive, unselfconscious grasp of "what feels right," not the self-conscious sophistication of the "educated" sensibility, is the source of life and the means of salvation. Rabbit Angstrom, the hero of *Rabbit, Run,* often inadvertently does harm, causes pain; he bumps and blunders through his life in a pitiful way because he has almost no sophisticated capacity for constructing intellectual explanations of himself and his experience. But he does know "what feels right." "I once played a game real well," he says. "I really did. And after you're first-rate at something, no matter what, it kind of takes the kick out of being second-rate. And that little thing Janice and I had going, boy, it was really second-rate." "I don't know," he says to the girl he takes up with when he runs away from his wife. "I don't know any of these answers. All I know is what feels right. You feel right to me. Sometimes Janice used to. Sometimes nothing does." Rabbit, we are to believe, has what the old lady at the end of the novel tells him "is a strange gift and I don't know how we're supposed to use it but I know it's the only gift we get and it's a good one." She calls it "life." When Rabbit runs away a second time at the end of the novel it is a desperate, instinctive act, undoubtedly futile and in some ways, perhaps, cowardly, but at least a continuation of the fight for life as Updike understands it. Rabbit, run; it is the author's urgent, ironic advice to his hero, an imperative cry from the heart.

The pathos of one-time star athletes is real enough; "they are ex-heroes of the type who, for many years, until a wife or ritual drunkenness or distant employment carries them off, continue to appear at high school athletic events, like dogs tormented by a site where they imagine they have buried something precious." The occasion of athletic achievement, too, is a patriotic one and may no doubt evoke the unselfish impulse to excellence that a war may. To have been excellent in these circumstances, as Rabbit Angstrom was when he played high-school basketball, may give a man a sense of impersonal achievement. But there are difficulties with what Updike wants to make of this sense of achievement. In the first place, the occasion is a mock one. No matter how much hysteria the crowd generates, nothing of real importance is at stake even for the participants; Roman gladiators were only a circus, too, but at least their own lives depended on their skills, if nothing else did. True as it is that there is no tragedy without heroic excellence, it is also true that there is none without a significant occasion, and there is nothing significant about a basketball game.

In the second place, however much we may believe in the intrinsic value of the nine and ninetieth sheep, we do not necessarily believe in his self-awareness. In an unrealistic action, it is probably possible to stretch a good deal the limits of the hero's probable self-awareness: Othello knows that when things go wrong between him and Desdemona, "Othello's occupation's gone." But to do so in a realistic fiction is to betray the convention to which you are committed, or if you are not committed to it, to mix genres in an awkward and unpersuasive way. It is one thing for Rabbit to join the kids playing basketball and to feel "like he's reaching down through years to touch this tautness" as he takes a shot. It is another for him to understand himself so well that he can reach from his athlete's experience of excellence to an understanding of what is wrong between him and his wife Janice. This is to pile onto a character a burden of transcendental perception greater than he can bear. The difficulty is that, for the sophisticated understanding of Updike, this achieved sense of the promises of life and its constant redefinitions throughout the history of Western culture are the chief meaning of Rabbit's story, and Updike has to get them in somehow; this is his way of mixing memory and desire, of showing the way tradition and the individual talent combine.

Updike is a romantic in a second and more important sense;

he is preoccupied with a feeling about the past that is characteristic of the nineteenth-century romantics; Wordsworth
might be talking about Updike rather than himself when he says
in *The Prelude:*

> I am lost, but see
> In simple childhood something of the base
> On which thy greatness stands; . . . The days gone by
> Return upon me almost from the dawn
> Of life: the hiding places of man's power
> Open; I would approach them, but they close.
> I see by glimpses now; when age comes on,
> May scarcely see at all; and I would give,
> While yet we may, as far as words can give,
> Substance and life to what I feel, enshrining,
> Such is my hope, the spirit of the Past
> For future restoration.

This is a classic statement of the romantic attitude; it is also a
precise description of Mr. Updike's almost irresistible impulse to
go home again in memory to find himself. Most of his stories
and all three of his novels are about the same town. The rest of
his stories are memories, too, but of the more recent past, of his
own marriage, for instance, as is the opening story of *Pigeon
Feathers,* called "Walter Briggs." This is a story in which a
husband and wife, driving home with their sleeping child, play
a memory game, trying to recall the names and all the particulars they can of the people they had known at the summer camp
where they spent their honeymoon. There is one man whose
name neither of them can remember. But as the husband is falling asleep that night, remembering exactly what his wife had
been like and how much he had loved her on that honeymoon,
he finds what he wants. He raises himself on his elbow and calls
his wife's name, "softly, knowing he wouldn't wake her, and
[says] 'Briggs. Walter Briggs.' "

Not that the past need be happy; what matters is that it is

made real by the intensity of feeling that has accumulated around it, as nothing else is real. Thus, in a story called "Wife-Wooing" the hero remembers, in a moment of intense desire for his wife, another detail from that honeymoon, of how in the cabin where they slept a "great rose window was projected upward through the petal-shaped perforations in the top of the black kerosene stove, which we stood in the center of the floor. As the flame on the circular wick flickered, the wide soft star of interlocked penumbrae moved and waved as if printed on a silk cloth being gently tugged or slowly blown. Its color soft blurred blood. We pay dear in blood for our peaceful homes." Here we can catch a glimpse of why Updike is so deadly serious about his literary elaborations of homely experience; that red reflection cast by the kerosene stove on the simple cabin roof is the image of his deflowered wife and his cathedral's rose window, the image of the price we pay for our homes, here and in the eternity we know because it is here. In Shillington, Pennsylvania, as Peter Caldwell knows, "we lived in God's sight."

In this way the glow of joy and pain, of intensely felt experience, together with all its transcendent implications, gathers around the particulars of the past for Mr. Updike, whether he is writing about his childhood and parents or about his wife and their children, or about both, as he is in "Home." The epigraphs of his very first collection of stories, *The Same Door*, are a quotation from Bergson that discusses the importance of memory to desire ("What would there be left of many of our emotions, were we to reduce them to the exact quantum of pure feeling they contain by subtracting from them all that is merely reminiscence"), and a passage from T. S. Eliot about family love, "within the light of which/ All else is seen." Precise recollection, then, especially of family love, is vital to him; it is the actual experience in which the saving truth is incarnate, and it worries him to lose the least fragment of it, as he seems to feel he is gradually losing his understanding of the past; the epigraph of his latest book of stories is from Kafka, and begins: "In revenge, however, my memory of the past has closed the door against me more and more." This anxiety, if it is real, appears premature, for *Pigeon Feathers* is filled with prodigies of recollection from that time.

In "The Persistence of Desire," for example, a young man very like Peter Caldwell returns to Olinger to see his eye doctor, and finds himself in the doctor's waiting room with a girl very like Peter's girl Penny. They are both now married, but he cannot resist the desire that comes flooding back with memory, and he begins to woo her again. "Aren't you happy?" the girl says, and the young man replies " 'I am, I am; but' — the rest was so purely inspired its utterance only grazed his lips — 'happiness isn't everything.' " When he comes out of the doctor's office, his eyes dilated and unfocused from the drops the doctor has used in checking his vision, the girl is waiting for him. She slips a note into the pocket of his shirt. He cannot focus his eyes to read it, but in his shirt pocket it "made a shield for his heart. In this armor he stepped into the familiar street. The maples, macadam, houses, cement, were to his violated eyes as brilliant as a scene remembered; he became a child again in this town, where life was a distant adventure, a rumor, an always imminent joy."

The hero of "Flight" remembers with minute psychological realism a high-school love affair with a very similar girl and builds up around their story a world of remembered details of his grandmother and grandfather, his mother's shocking jealousy of the girl, the high-school debates and dances of his courting. It is a loving and meticulous re-creation of the past and Updike's mind probes it with the delicacy of a surgeon, seeking what makes it in memory so preternaturally alive and meaningful. Even the knowledge that the past is not a shelter from lifelessness, as it now seems to be, comes to him, in a story

called "A Sense of Shelter," as a memory. What he remembers
is how he achieved the courage to tell the most mature and mysterious of his high-school classmates that he loved her, only to
discover that she was having a bitterly unhappy affair with an
older man. "You never loved anybody," she said. "You
don't know what it is." He knows now that she was right,
knows enough to remember what he thought then with a
schoolboy's uncertain insight — "after all, it was just a disposi-
tion of his heart, nothing permanent or expensive" — as true in
a sense more terrible than he could then have imagined.

It always seems to Updike, as he says of his grandmother
whom he recalls again and again, "necessary and holy, to tell
how once there had been a woman who now was no more," to
tell everything, "all set sequentially down with the bald simplicity of intrinsic blessing, thousands upon thousands of pages;
ecstatically uneventful; divinely and defiantly dull." He feels
this way because, in memory, the transcendental value of the
people he loved as a child inheres in them, an intrinsic blessing.
This motive comes out very clearly in one of the experimental
stories in *Pigeon Feathers*, "Packed Dirt, Churchgoing, a Dying
Cat, a Traded Car." In it the narrator brings together a series
of ostensibly unconnected recollections, because in each he discovers some object that has been humanized and thus has acquired intrinsic blessing that he can, in memory, recognize. He
opens the story with a statement of this point: "I . . . am always affected — reassured, nostalgically pleased, even, as a
member of my animal species, made proud — by the sight of
bare earth that has been smoothed and packed firm by the passage of human feet . . . the more matter is outwardly mastered,
the more it overwhelms us in our hearts." Churchgoing is for
him "to sit and stand in unison and sing and recite creeds and
petitions that are like paths worn smooth in the raw terrain of
our hearts," and "the expectantly hushed shelter of the church
is like one of those spots worn bare by a softball game in a

weed-filled vacant lot." The incident of the cat, as the narrator
says, "had the signature: decisive but illegible." While he is
wandering about waiting for his child to be born, he finds a
dying cat in the street and puts it behind the hedge of the nearest
house "to be safe," though he is sure it is dying. "It suffered
my intrusion a trifle stiffly. It suggested I was making too much
fuss, and seemed to say to me, *Run on Home.*" A few hours
later he calls the hospital and, "after some rummaging in the
records," they are able to tell him his daughter has been born.
Something far more complicated gathers for him around the
car he cannot bring himself to trade in — lust and love and all
kinds of death. "Not only sand and candy wrappers accumu-
late in a car's interior, but heroisms and instants of communion."
The packed dirt, the dying cat, the churchgoing, the car have
become, each in its different way, a part of some heroism or
some moment of communion; they have been mastered; they
are intrinsically blessed. That is all that ever matters for Updike
about any object or event. "The Blessed Man of Boston, My
Grandmother's Thimble, and Fanning Island" is a similar collection of moments of intrinsic blessing, images that, if he could
properly evoke them, would be full of joy, "just as a piece of
turf torn from a meadow becomes a *gloria* when drawn by
Dürer." But he despairs of ever realizing life that fully. "As it
is," he says to his reader, "you, like me, must take it on faith."

This is a feeling for the sacredness of life itself, and it is accompanied by a real horror of death. The narrator of "Packed
Dirt" has to wake his wife up in the middle of the night, so
great is his horror of dying, and Updike deals with this horror at
length in a much too brilliant symbolic story called "Lifeguard." The lifeguard is real enough, in his way; a divinity
student during the winter, "in the summer," as he says, "I dis-
guise myself in my skin and become a lifeguard." It is a dis-
guise, the skin — real enough as far as it goes, but not the important reality. Walking around in our skins we are all to

Updike what his lifeguard is, dying animals with the capacity to love. "Young as I am," the lifeguard remarks, "I can hear in myself the protein acids ticking; I wake at odd hours and in the shuddering dark and silence feel my death rushing toward me like an express train." The psychological process is like swimming: "We struggle and thrash, and drown; we succumb, even in despair, and float, and are saved" — by human love that, like the rest of life, walks around dressed in flesh and blood, or, as the lifeguard puts it, "our chivalric impulses go clanking in encumbering biological armor." It may be an awkward kind of equipment for a chivalric knight to wear while he is saving the princess, but we have to use it if we are going to guard life: "every seduction is a conversion." The story ends with an image of great ingenuity that catches up the whole significance of Updike's humanist parable. This lifeguard has never been called on to save a life, but "someday," he thinks, "my alertness will bear fruit; from near the horizon there will arise, delicious, translucent, like a green bell above the water, the call for help, the call, a call, it saddens me to confess, that I have yet to hear."

This is a metaphysical call that can be answered only by a chivalric impulse clanking in encumbering biological armor, and its full meaning is seldom heard except in memory, where its divine ordinariness becomes wholly clear. It is the divineness of the ordinary calling so imperatively to writers like Salinger and Updike that leads them to their complications, both structural and rhetorical. The elaborate machinery of reference, quotation, and allusion they pile up around their realistic narratives often looks artificial and affected, and to some extent it is. It is a fairly safe guess that Salinger did not grow up, as did the Glass children, surrounded by Zen koans and having Taoist stories read to him in his cradle when he was ten months old, and if churchgoing was a commonplace of Updike's childhood, the remoter reaches of Greek mythology

cannot have been. For both, these languages, however necessary they may be to express the implications of actuality, are
acquired languages. As a consequence nothing angers Salinger
more than to be told he has an inferior accent and cannot be distinguished from fashionable Zen Buddhists, the very thought of
whom drives him to hard words in "Seymour: An Introduction." It is made similarly clear by Updike's devotion to it that
complex perspectives and elaborate symbols are not just literary ingenuities to him. This is most evident in *The Centaur*, in
which the structure is, cleverly and unsuccessfully, made extremely complicated and the symbols are mythological characters.

The Centaur has, to begin with, a narrative frame; it is nominally being told by Peter Caldwell, who is fifteen in the story,
years later when he is a painter living in New York with a
Negro girl. Only once in the novel are we in the actual presence of these two, as they lie in bed together — and then the
girl is asleep. But three or four times a phrase such as "My
love, listen" is introduced to remind us that this is all the recollection of a man lying sleepless. At the same time, the story is
told only a small part of the time as a recollection. As in
Ulysses, other needs that can be satisfied only by other modes
of narration — the anonymous voice of "The Cyclops" or the
parodied voice of "Nausicaa" in *Ulysses*, the obituary writer of
Chapter V or the frequently omniscient third-person in *The
Centaur* — cause other voices to obtrude and make this framework nominal and ineffective.

It would seem almost enough for the purpose that the
story of Peter Caldwell and his father, the bright high-school
boy and the teacher of science in Olinger, has been supplied
with an elaborate system of mythological parallels: Updike has
even written an index that lists some seventy mythological figures that are either directly represented in the novel or indirectly represented by some native of Olinger.

One might well argue that all this machinery is the excess of a writer too clever for his own good who has lived too long near some awe-inspiring research library. To some extent it probably is; there are some combinations of myth and actuality in the book that are more like the work of John Erskine than anything else — for example, the representation of Dionysos by a drunken homosexual bum. Yet the motive behind this mythological machinery, in spite of its occasional irritating cleverness, is certainly a serious one and ought to remind us of Ezra Pound's *Cantos* rather than John Erskine.

"The first myths arose," says Pound,

> when a man walked sheer into "nonsense," that is to say, when some very vivid and undeniable adventure befell him, and he told someone else who called him a liar. Thereupon, after bitter experience, perceiving that no one could understand what he meant when he said that he "turned into a tree," he made a myth — a work of art that is — an impersonal or objective story woven out of his own emotion, as the nearest equation he was capable of putting into words.

Conceiving myths in this way, Pound can connect them with his own personal experience conceived in the same way. The vivid and undeniable adventures of his own moments of insight and the images he constructs for them are of the same order as the myths, and he can therefore go back to the early literature of western culture for wisdom exactly as did Renaissance humanists like Poggio Bracciolini or as Odysseus, seeking an earlier wisdom by descending to the dead to consult Tiresias, did. Thus Pound can make all of mythology an integral part of his poem of experience. Moreover, he does make it so; when the gods appear in the *Cantos* we are lifted out of our chairs:

> Gods float in the azure air,
> Bright gods and Tuscan, back before dew was shed.
> Light: and the first light, before ever dew was fallen.

Panisks, and from the oak, dryas,
And from the apple, mælid,
Through all the woods, and the leaves are full of voices,
A-whisper, and the clouds bowe over the lake,
And there are gods upon them,
And in the water, the almond-white swimmers,
The silvery water glazes the upturned nipple,
          As Poggio has remarked.

"And we *have* heard the fauns chiding Proteus/ in the smell of hay under the olive-trees."

But Updike's gods are at best figures from some handbook of mythology and at worst (as when Chiron addresses Aphrodite gallantly as "Milady Venus") sound like Charlton Heston in some multimillion-dollar production of *The Metamorphoses.* Moreover, the story of George Caldwell the high-school teacher and his talented son Peter is altogether too well done as a realistic fiction to be connected in any but the most sterile and mechanical ways with these mythological figures. There has not been a more completely realized and moving character of his kind than George Caldwell since the Dr. Bull of Cozzens' *The Last Adam.* All his wisdom and his compassion and his self-awareness are made beautifully clear within the terms of his actual life. There is not anything we do not understand about his disenchantment with his students and his devotion to them. "Off to the slaughterhouse," he says as he starts for school. "Those damned kids have put their hate right into my bowels," or "Kill or be killed, that's my motto. Those bastards don't give me any quarter and I don't give them any." "Rounding the corner [of a high school corridor, he] surprises Gloria Davis the hopped-up bitch leaning against a wall allowing young Kegerise to rub his knee between her legs. With his I.Q. he ought to know better." All through the book we watch him devoting his life to these same "little monsters." When he thinks he is dying he puts all his school records in order and says, "If I don't show up tomorrow, the new teacher can step right in and take over, poor devil. Biff, bang; move over, buddy, next stop the dump." When his friend, the French teacher, says she has always lived by the sentence "Dieu est très fin," George says, "That's right. He certainly is. He's a wonderful old gentleman. I don't know where the hell we'd be without Him." With a character as fully and beautifully realized as this one is by the novel as a whole, the parade of a lot of mythological symbols that conduct themselves with no more life than the characters of Bulfinch's mythology is an annoying intrusion.

The same thing is true of Peter Caldwell's fully realized life at Olinger High School. We can see clearly, without mythological parallels, how he suffers. "That my existence at one extreme should be tangent to Vermeer and at the other to the hitchhiker seemed an unendurable strain," as he once puts it himself; "in that year, the year I was fifteen, if I had not wanted so badly to be Vermeer, I would have tried to be Johnny Dedman" (Johnny Dedman is Peter's high-school hero, a boy who "performed exquisitely all the meaningless deeds of coördination, jitterbugging and playing pinball and tossing salted nuts into his mouth").

It is not Updike's fault if so many of the acts that are exquisitely performed in the actual world his memory has preserved — the world of high-school basketball games and jitterbugging and pinball machines — are meaningless deeds to which he feels he can give meaning only by an elaborate philosophical analysis that he can get into his story only by making the meaningless deeds symbols of it or by adding symbols of it from mythology. It is perhaps a matter of taste whether the meaning that does inhere in the lives of George Caldwell and his son is adequate to our conceptions of the human situation. What is not a matter of taste in this sense is the incoherence between the realistic novel that constitutes the heart of *The Centaur* and the mythology that is attached to it, an incoherence that would exist even if the mythology were successfully represented. This mixture of genres might possibly be given coherence by a narrator whose character justified his telling us both his memories and myths. But the narrator of *The Centaur* barely exists in the novel and has no character at all.

In Allen Tate's *The Fathers*, the narrator, in a moment of extreme exhaustion, has an hallucination in which his grandfather sits with him on a pile of fence rails beside a Virginia road and tells him the story of Jason and Medea in such a way as to make Jason a counterpart of the novel's hero, George Posey. This episode is managed with great care for the conventions of the realistic novel of which it is a part — for the physical condition of the narrator that allows him to imagine it, for the neoclassical bias of his culture that makes the story of Jason familiar to him, for the family piety that makes the portrait of his grandfather hanging "in the front parlor" of the house he grew up in a living memory for him; and it is an episode Mr. Tate has thought a mistake ever since the novel was published, a way of extending its meaning that is tricky and ineffective, easy and false.

XIII

THE REALISTIC NOVEL AS SYMBOL

E. M. FORSTER once remarked that, alas, the one indispensable element of the novel is the story. He said he wished it were melody, or perception of the truth, but in fact it was not. There may be considerable irony in these remarks, but they constitute, without irony, a very characteristic twentieth-century complaint, implicit in many novels and explicit in many critical essays. No one in his right mind is likely to belittle what we have gained from the experiments of the twentieth-century novelists or to contemplate without dismay the loss of their novels. But in a period when any failure to be experimental is taken as proof of a black and reactionary despair of the human enterprise it is probably a good idea to remind ourselves from time to time that all innovations in literature are in effect new conventions or ways of proceeding that may, if the author is lucky, become traditional and customary; if they do not, they will in the long run make the writer's work as incomprehensible as if he had taken the risk of writing in a newly developed language, as Chaucer took the risk of writing in English, only to have the language fail to survive.

The traditional mode of fiction, as of the drama and the epic to which it is related, is the conventionalized representation of nature that is usually called realism. This is the form from which all the experimental novels of the twentieth century have deviated into experiment, and in the cases of great ones like

Ulysses, not deviated very radically at that. The established conventions of the realistic novel and its familiar variations offer innumerable opportunities beyond those for mere verisimilitude and recognition which are often hastily said to be their only excuse for existence. The very survival over such a consider- able period of time of realism as the normal mode of the novel suggests that in giving it up the novelist may be sacrificing the one indispensable element of the novel, out of a conviction that the representation of nature makes it impossible for him to express without falsification his strongest feelings — as it may if he cultivates long enough the kind of feelings thinking this way encourages.

Francis Bacon's description of poetry as that which "sub- mits the shows of things to the desires of the mind" may be too rationalistic; Bacon is always supposed to be suspect in that way. But it has the great virtue of stressing for poetry the shows of things; it prevents our forgetting that we accept poetry, especially the kind of poetry we call the novel, because it *shows* us life. This vision, it suggests, is indispensable (alas or not). Everything else fiction gives us lives for our imagina- tions in its representation of life, so that verisimilitude is not just a trick of the trade, a means of providing the simple pleasures of recognition; it is the body of the fiction's life, without which the poet's meaning, if it does not — to avoid the mortalist her- esy — die, at least becomes as invisible as a disembodied spirit. It is, of course, a representation; we do not suppose it is literally "true to life." But it is a representation we see as probable, whether we see its meaning or not. A realistic novel can be read nearly as literally as history (much more literally than a great many history books). Neither can be read absolutely lit- erally; both are partly a matter of probability and partly a matter of myth. All this is, or is supposed to be, commonplace enough; it is to say that a fiction is an imitation of life.

To sacrifice a probable presentation of the shows of things to the direct expression of what the novelist thinks the things mean is for the novelist — and probably the novelist alone — to gain his own soul and lose the world, which is perhaps a satisfactory enough outcome for saints and angels, but not for novelists who may wish to be read. Older fiction offers innumerable examples of how the author's feelings are given life by his representation of a conventionalized actuality. Mr. Joseph Frank, an admirer of what he calls "Spatial Form in Modern Literature," says that we accept a Shakespeare play "as we accept an abstract painting." This is surely a very bold denial of the fact that Shakespeare's plays are, within the limits of the established theatrical conventions of their day, above all realistic depictions of people and events; there have even been those — James Joyce among them — who argued that Shakespeare occasionally showed a deplorable tendency to pander to the vulgar taste for sensational verisimilitude. Even if that possibility be ignored, there can be few people ready to assert with Mr. Frank that Shakespeare's plays work the way abstract paintings do. But everyone can probably cite Shakespeare for his purposes. It will be better to cite here a fiction that is modern, but at the same time not so recent that we have not had time to live with it, as an illustration of what wonderful life the realistic novel can give to the kind of meaning it is often argued only the nonrealistic novel can express. Allen Tate's *The Fathers*, published in 1938, has the further advantage for this purpose that it has not been so frequently analyzed that its interest has been exhausted.

The occasion of *The Fathers* is a public one, the achievement and the destruction of Virginia's antebellum civilization. Within that occasion the novel discovers the conflict between two fundamental and irreconcilable modes of existence that has obsessed American novelists and haunted American experience. *The Fathers* moves between the public and the private aspects of this conflict with an ease very unusual in American novels, and this ease is the most obvious evidence of the novel's remarkable unity of meaning and form. The action of the novel not only communicates the novelist's meaning; it is that meaning, is made with a careful respect for both the author's expressive needs and the conventions of realism that bring alive for the reader what the author expresses. This is the aesthetic aspect of the novel's meaning, the social aspect of which may be briefly described as the idea that "the belief widely held to-day, that men may live apart from the political order, that in-deed the only humane and honorable satisfactions must be gained in spite of the public order," is a destructive delusion.

The formal ordering of the novel is quite deliberate. "I wished," Mr. Tate has written —

> to retain the great gains in sensuous immediacy won by the Jamesian or impressionist branch of the naturalistic tradition, and to eliminate its hocus-pocus of "motivation" and cause and ef-fect, along with its reliance upon "recognition" or mere detailed photography of the scene for effect upon the reader . . . to do this I constructed an artifice which would permit the reader to experience meaning rather than recognition; or put otherwise, I tried to make the whole structure symbolic in terms of realistic detail, so that you could subtract the symbolism, or remain un-aware of it, without losing the literal level of meaning . . . but if you subtract the literal or realistic detail, the symbolic struc-ture disappears.

What makes this effect possible is the novel's narrator. Lacy Buchan is an old man who had, as a boy, participated in the events he is describing. As narrator he thus has a double per-spective on the events of the novel, and allows Mr. Tate to move back and forth between the now mature but uninvolved judgment of the old man and the partial understanding but di-rect sensuous response of the boy whom the old man remem-bers. "In my feelings of that time," Lacy says, "there is a new element — my feelings now about that time . . . the emotions have ordered themselves in memory, and that memory is not what happened in the year 1860 but rather a few symbols, a voice, a tree, a gun shining on the wall. . . ."

Thus every event in the novel is given "the sensuous immediacy" as well as the probability of the modern realistic novel, and at the same time, because the events have ordered themselves in the old man's memory as his growing understanding of them has led him unconsciously to select and arrange them, each event has become symbolic — "a voice, a tree, a gun shining on the wall." With an almost Jamesian neatness and economy, the novel makes the very process by which Lacy's apprehension changes from the sensuous immediacy of boyhood's experience to the quiet wisdom of his old age an example of its theme. The quiet wisdom of Lacy's old age is not a natural product of merely growing old; the idea that old men grow wise merely by growing old would, I think, be as firmly rejected by Mr. Tate as it is by his poetic master, Mr. Eliot; in fact, even when men do grow old wisely, there is a limitation on wisdom that is complementary to the limitation on the passionate immediacy of youth's response to experience, compared to which in old age "The serenity [is] only a deliberate hebetude,/ The wisdom only the knowledge of dead secrets/ Useless in the darkness into which they peered/ Or from which they turned their eyes." In *The Fathers* Lacy's growing up is a particular example of the civilizing process through which the Virginia society, represented in the novel by Pleasant Hill, puts its citizens; the process has been only half completed with the boy Lacy whom the old Lacy is remembering; it is one of the central points of the novel that it never occurs at all with Lacy's brother-in-law, George Posey. As a boy, Lacy remembers, "I shared [George Posey's] impatience with the world as it was, as indeed every child must whose discipline is incomplete."

The novel's narrator, with his old man's wisdom and his memory of his boyhood experience, will be expected by the reader to present the events of the novel as they "have ordered themselves in memory," and this expectation makes it possible for the novelist to present the events, without loss of probability, in the order that will bring out their meaning rather than in the order of chronology. The novel opens on the day of Mrs. Buchan's funeral at Pleasant Hill in April 1860. After the narrator has told us how his brother-in-law, George Posey, refused to attend the funeral, his mind jumps, almost inevitably, back to the point two years before when George Posey was wooing Susan Buchan and about to become an in-law of the Buchans. The narrator continues to recall the events that occurred after George began to woo Susan until he has filled in for us the two years between that time and the day of Mrs. Buchan's funeral. But this recollection is in its turn thrice interrupted by his recollection of events that occurred on the day of the funeral; they come naturally to his mind as he is remembering, and they are thus communicated to us in conjunction with those events of the previous two years to which they are most significantly related.

During the whole of this double narration we are aware that Mrs. Buchan's funeral occurred fifty years ago and that what we are hearing is not a contemporary account of it but the recollection of an old man, an old man who happens to have been her son. Complex as this narrative procedure may sound when it is described, it does not create the slightest confusion for the reader because it is essentially a very familiar one, an adaptation to the demands of the realistic novel of epic narrative structure. Its purpose is to give the novelist a chance to arrange his events in the non-chronological order his novel's meaning calls for without destroying our sense that we are observing actual events occurring in actual time. In this way the novel's meaning is made something we discover in the verisimilar, represented life of the novel, not something we are told by the author; we are, as Mr. Tate put it, given a chance "to experience meaning."

Because we do experience meaning as we read *The Fathers* we are likely to be particularly conscious of the loss the novel's meaning suffers when it is paraphrased, but paraphrased it must be, however crudely, if it is to be discussed. (This is the point at which novelists, to a man, rise to assure the critic with all the considerable passion at their command that for this reason and a good many others they have right at their fingertips it would be better if the novel were not discussed.) The central tension of meaning in *The Fathers*, like that of its formal presentation, is a tension between the individual's public and his private sense of experience, between his commitment to the order of civilization — always artificial, imposed on men by discipline, and at the mercy of its own inherent imperfections — and his commitment to the disorder of the private feelings — always sincere, imposed upon by circumstances, and at the mercy of impulse. We are made to see, on the one hand, the static condition a society reaches when it has been fully civilized, when, by slow steps, it has disciplined all the personal feelings of its members to established and customary modes of feeling so that the individual no longer exists apart from the ritual of society and the ritual of society expresses all the feelings the individual knows. We are made to see, on the other hand, the forces that exist (because time does not stand still and both rituals and individuals change), both within and without the people who constitute the society, that will break down the discipline of its civilization and leave the individual naked, alone, and lost. "People living in formal societies," says the narrator who himself once lived in such a society but does not now, "lacking the historical imagination, can imagine for themselves only a timeless existence." So it is with Major Buchan. But George Posey, for all his great personal gifts — his generosity, his kindness, his charm — must receive "the shock of the world at the end of his nerves" because he does not live in any society, least of all the one he exists in, but is alone and unprotected. He is a man who, having nothing to tell him how to act in order to express his feelings, is always in violent motion; as a boy, when he could not wholly understand why, Lacy Buchan saw George as "a horseman riding over a precipice." Remembering as an old man the differences between the Posey family and his own, he thinks, "Excessively refined persons have a communion with the abyss; but is not civilization the agreement, slowly arrived at, to let the abyss alone?"

The richness of life with which *The Fathers* realizes both aspects of this theme is remarkable; it makes one suspect that, if *The Fathers* is ever read with attention in the South, Mr. Tate may become as unpopular with the voting public there as Faulkner would be if his work were read attentively. Mr. Tate knows all too well that Pleasant Hill is gone forever and that he is not Major Buchan and never can be, knows that he is as completely excluded from the world of Pleasant Hill as George Posey was, and cannot avoid sharing George's feeling that it is radically absurd. But if he cannot avoid feeling Pleasant Hill's absurdity, he understands very well what it was and sees that, though time has — inevitably, perhaps even rightly — destroyed it, it was civilized in a way his and our life is not.

This attitude is very like the attitude of the speaker in Mr. Tate's "Ode to the Confederate Dead." It is possible, by reading that poem and Mr. Tate's essay about it, "Narcissus on Narcissus," to guess the extent to which Mr. Tate considers the personal situation of us all in the contemporary world like the situation of George Posey in the Virginia world of a hundred years ago. The integrity of *The Fathers* is never, even indirectly, violated by a personal intrusion of the author or a lecture on the disjointedness of our times, but it is not impossible to guess that the raw material out of which George Posey is made is the author's conception of himself: "George Posey, c'est moi." If this be so, it is only the perfectly maintained narrative integrity of the novel that conceals the extent to which an important part of its life, like the life of other American novels of its time, derives from the author's "inebriated *sense of self*," from his heightened, private sensitivity that invents many promises for life that he recognizes with something like despair life cannot possibly realize.

The difference between the attitude of *The Fathers* and that of most other American novels of its time — and it is a significant difference — is that *The Fathers* can, like "The Ode to the Confederate Dead," imagine an order of society and a conception of the self that do not commit the self to impossible hopes or society to their destruction. It can

> praise the arrogant circumstance
> Of those who fall
> Rank upon rank, hurried beyond decision

even though it knows that we ourselves — like the George Posey who is forever excluded from Major Buchan's world by the very nature of his own consciousness — remain "Here by the sagging gate, stopped by the wall." Almost the most impressive thing about *The Fathers* is that, despite its awareness of what the civilization of Virginia did for its members that our society does not do for us, it does not yield to the temptation to romanticize in a nostalgic way the life of Pleasant Hill. The antebellum South of *The Fathers* is a believable world, drastically limited in many ways, full of evils very imperfectly controlled, and subject like all civilizations to the destruction of time and change. Neither its virtues nor its defects are magnified by the Gothic exaggeration of event or the romantic extravagance of rhetoric that Faulkner so frequently resorts to in describing his South.

Thus the attitude of *The Fathers* can do justice to the nature of its very American hero, but, unlike most novels of its time, can also do justice to the world that does not — cannot — sat-

isfy the hero's demands upon it. This attitude extends the range
of the modern American novel's feelings considerably, and *The
Fathers* realizes this extended range of feelings even in the smallest of its occasions. When, for example, Major Buchan leads his
family, single file, into a hotel and says to the clerk, "We need
rain, sir!" we are at once charmed by the perfection of his manners, astonished by the innocent confidence in the coherence
of society with which he performs them, and amused by his
simplicity — not very creditably, for it is this same simplicity
of feeling and directness of performance that make him leave
his place in his wife's funeral procession to take the "brown
hand [of his wife's personal maid] to lead her into the line and
make her take her place ahead of us just behind the body of her
mistress." It is an irresponsible — if uncontrollable — indul-
gence of the romantic irony habitual to the private American
self and its unlimited demands on the social order to find such
acts simple. Major Buchan's manners are a complete expression
of his nature; they are at the same time like Cousin Custis' literary effusions. Major Buchan himself realizes that in these com-
positions "the tropes become more tropical every year," but he
nevertheless observes quite sincerely that "Custis is a most accom-
plished gentleman. A very fine artist, sir! In the heroic style.
And an elegant speaker." There is no doubt that the author's
feelings color this passage; however much it makes us respect
Major Buchan, it also makes us feel he is comically innocent. Dr.
Cartwright, the Episcopal clergyman of *The Fathers*, seems to
Lacy Buchan "to be just a voice, in the *ore rotundo* of imperson-
ality, no feeling but in the words themselves." This is the quality
of Cousin John Semmes' orations in the novel, and it is the quality of Major Buchan's habitual mode of speech. Mr. Tate's essay
"The Profession of Letters in the South" shows the same double
feeling about this style, and in "What Is a Traditional Society?"
he speaks in the same way about the *ore rotundo*.
   This complexity of feeling is equally evident in the pattern of

incidents in *The Fathers*, just as it is in the novel's main design. Consider, for example, what we are made to feel when the drunken John Langton challenges George Posey after the tournament. As Major Buchan is an embodiment of the best possibilities of his civilization, so John Langton is an embodiment of its worst, "a bold and insolent man who deemed himself an aristocrat beyond any consideration for other people." When he and George meet on the field of honor, George first makes a magnificent practice shot and then, suddenly, throws his pistol away and knocks Langton down. "I never did like Langton, from the time we were boys," says Jim Mason, his second, "But that ain't the point. . . . Mr. Posey agreed to come out here and there was only one thing to come for. Not for this." He is right. As always, George cannot realize his feelings in the humane and honorable terms established by the world he exists in, because he does not live in that world. Living in the isolation of his own consciousness, he lives with the illusion that will destroy any man, that "the only humane and honorable satisfactions must be gained in spite of public order." The very qualities that gave him his personal splendor, "the heightened vitality possessed by a man who knows no bounds," make him reject the modes of behavior provided by the public order of his time and place, leaving him with no meaningful way of realizing his feelings at all.

The implications of this scene are extended by the fact that we watch it with Lacy Buchan from under the pavilion set up for the tournament. There Lacy has found a contemporary, Wink Broadacre.

> "God damn," he said. "Son of a bitch. Bastard. Say, Buchan, cain't you cuss? Jesus Christ." He lay on his elbow gazing at me with a smirk. "You want some of it?"

And he points to a "half-grown mulatto girl with kinky red hair and muddy green eyes in a pretty, Caucasian face" who is

lying on her back a short distance away. This episode is a prologue to the duel. Its sexual and social evil is fully realized; it
is, like Langton's malicious arrogance, a part of this civilization, and the novel faces that fact squarely. At the same time
there is something comic, in a Tom Sawyerish way, about
Wink Broadacre ("Say, Buchan, cain't you cuss?"), as if this
evil were limited in a customary society: John Langton can
be insolently arrogant only within the bounds of the customary
ways of behavior of his society, and Wink Broadacre is rebel-
ling against the bounds of polite conversation and polite sexual
conduct in ways that are themselves customary and familiar to
his society. This does not make these evils any less evil, but it
does make them evils that are held within limits by an otherwise
orderly world. Before we condemn that world for containing
such evils, we must consider the unintended but unbounded
evil produced by the wholly personal sincerity of George
Posey's love for Susan Buchan that involved him in the duel
which shares our attention with Wink Broadacre's dalliance
beneath the pavilion. "There is no doubt," as the narrator says,
"that [George] loved Susan too much; by that I mean he was
too personal, and with his exacerbated nerves he was constantly
receiving impressions out of the chasm that yawns beneath
lovers; therefore he must have had a secret brutality for her
when they were alone." In the end George drives Susan mad.

The first third or so of *The Fathers* is a sustained contrast between the old and still dominant way of life of Major Buchan and
his family and the new way of George Posey and his family.
In it, because the narrator's mind moves back and forth among
the events that belong for him to the changeless period of
childhood, time seems nearly to stand still, as it does for those
who are part of the society it is describing (who "can imagine for themselves only a timeless existence"). Because we
all know, as the Buchans cannot, that the Civil War is about to
break out, we are aware of how short a lease on life this time-

less existence has, and that in turn alerts us to the evidence that the forces of change, unobserved by everyone except George Posey, who embodies them, had already undermined the Virginia way of life before the outbreak of the war — which was only a manifestation on the national political level of a change that had begun a long time before at the roots of our social life. This is what Mr. Tate calls, in the comment quoted earlier, "the literal level of meaning in the novel," the historical meaning it is, as a realistic fiction, bound to have. As such, the novel constitutes an example of how time, working within a civilization and the individuals who make it up, destroys them.

The novel's contrast between the old way of life and the new comes to a climax in the scene where George comes, not to ask Major Buchan for Susan's hand, but to announce his intention. "Major Buchan," he says, "I intend to marry your daughter." A whole civilization is denied by that mode of approach to Susan's father. Major Buchan had begun this scene with George by putting George as firmly in his place as he knew how to; he had failed to ask after George's family, "the first thing he always did when he met anybody, black or white," and he tells George that "I don't know that we are entitled to your kindness — no, sir, I don't know that we are." But George is unaware that he has been put in his place because he is quite unconscious of the customary patterns that give these gestures their force; "he was incredibly at his ease, the way a man is at ease when he is alone." Confronted by this imperviousness to the most violent rebuff his system of manners allowed him to administer, Major Buchan could only look astonished, "as if someone entitled to know all about it had denied the heliocentric theory or argued that there were no Abolitionists in Boston."

This is comedy, but high comedy, filled with tragic possibilities. Major Buchan is a man who exists in terms of this game, whose consciousness has wholly identified itself with the moves laid down by his society's system of manners for the expression of every feeling. "Our lives," Lacy thinks, "were eternally balanced upon a pedestal below which lay an abyss I could not name. Within that invisible tension my father knew the moves of an intricate game that he expected everybody else to play. That, I think, was because everything he was and felt was in the game itself." The possibility that an individual life might be lived without regard for this system of manners was incomprehensible to him, and he is baffled and helpless before the anarchic, impulsive, personal conduct of George Posey. The scene reminds Lacy of "the only time I had ever seen my father blush; somebody had tried to tell him his private affairs, beginning, 'If you will allow me to be personal,' and papa blushed because he could never allow anybody to be personal."

Because such men cannot conceive of themselves except as members of a society, they simply do not understand individualism, and Major Buchan never comprehends at all the individual competition for power that is rapidly taking control of the political and economic life of his country.

> Your pa — says shrewd cousin John Semmes to Lacy — thinks the government is a group of high-minded gentlemen who are trying to yield everything to one another. Damn it, Lacy, it's just men like your pa who are the glory of the Old Dominion, and the surest proof of her greatness, that are going to ruin us. . . . They won't let themselves see what's going on.

It is not so much that they won't as that they cannot, not without ceasing forever to be what they are; they and their society can be saved from ruin at the hands of the new way of life only by ceasing to be what they are and becoming something like the new men and the new society that are bringing them to ruin.

In Major Buchan's world property is not conceived financially; it is a final reality in itself and it never occurs to Major Buchan to think of property in monetary terms, as something that may be sold, exchanged for amounts of money. This attitude makes the slave-holding of Pleasant Hill, with all its defects, something very different from what it appears to those who do think of property in monetary terms. Major Buchan would no more think of selling a slave than of selling his wife or his daughter. He neither loves nor hates money; it simply does not exist for him. George Posey does hate money, and it is the nearest thing to a final reality he knows, almost the only thing that gives him a sense that other things exist. He even thinks of Yellow Jim, his Negro half-brother and slave, as "liquid capital," an attitude that shocks the Buchans almost as much as does George's refusal to pay his "labor enough to buy bacon and meal," though he will, on an impulse, in all the confusion and embarrassment of this naked exposure of personal feeling, give a beggar woman ten dollars. George is neither parsimonious nor uncharitable; he is simply, as people like him presently learned to say, "practical."

The profound effect of this difference comes out clearly in the history of Pleasant Hill, the novel's particularized image of Virginia's antebellum civilization. Throughout the novel the way of conducting the everyday life of Pleasant Hill that Major Buchan follows without conceiving that any other is possible gradually becomes unworkable as the larger society of which it is a part changes over from the principles and practices of the eighteenth century to the finance capitalism of the late nineteenth century. The seeds of that change are present from the start of the novel. The unfamiliar silence of Pleasant Hill on the day of his mother's funeral makes Lacy think of it for a moment empty of life "if we went to town." They do have to go to town a little later, and George Posey, who grew up in a town, where civilization as the Buchans understand it does not exist, takes over Pleasant Hill in order to preserve its financial value for the heirs. Almost like a well-to-do retired New Yorker today taking over an eighteenth-century country house (near Charlottesville?), he repairs and repaints the house and puts the plantation on a business basis. Cousin John Semmes thinks it is "a piece of damned impertinence for George Posey to mind Lew's business for him" in this way "because," as Lacy says, "he allowed himself to see not what George was doing but only the way he did it." This objection to Cousin John's criticism is justified enough; Major Buchan would not have long continued to have a business to mind if he had continued to run Pleasant Hill himself. Nevertheless, George saves Pleasant Hill, at least temporarily, only by destroying everything in its life that made it Pleasant Hill.

George's contribution to the Confederate cause is smuggled goods, which he purchases with great shrewdness in the North, brings in himself, and sells for cash on the barrel head, very cheaply and also at a profit, to the Confederates. Holding his satchel of money in his hand after one such transaction he says to Cousin John, "Mr. Semmes, your people are about to fight a war. They remind me of a passel of young 'uns playing prisoners' base." So far as the war they are about to fight is concerned, anyone like Major Buchan is a young 'un playing a game. Yet the man like George Posey who belongs to no community — "*your* people" he calls his fellow Virginians — and does not recognize the rules of Major Buchan's game, or some such game, is at the mercy of exposed nerve ends and random impulses.

Lacy once recalls for us how his mother dealt with a child's question about why a bull had been brought to Pleasant Hill. " 'He's here on business,' my mother said, and looking back to that remark I know that she was a person for whom her small world held life in its entirety, and who, through that knowledge, knew all that was necessary of the world at large." But when George Posey, walking with Major Buchan about Pleasant Hill, comes on a young bull who has been turned into a pasture with a herd of cows —

I looked at George Posey. He was blushing to the roots of his hair. He looked helpless and betrayed. I saw papa give him a sharp, critical glance, and then he said, "Mr. Posey, excuse me, I have some business with Mr. Higgins. I will ask Lacy here to take you back to the house." Papa's eyes were on the ground while George Posey mastered himself.

". . . the Poseys," as the narrator remarks elsewhere, "were more refined than the Buchans, but less civilized."

The Buchans and the Poseys differ in the same way when confronted by death. Major Buchan "was crushed [by his wife's death] but in his sorrow he knew what everybody else was feeling, and in his high innocence he required that they know it too and be as polite as he." So great is his sense of dignity and honor that he is even polite to George when George first rudely refuses to attend the funeral and then suddenly turns up again. His father's conduct teaches young Lacy a great lesson.

. . . it seemed plain [at my age] that a great many people had to be treated, not as you felt about yourself, but as they deserved. How could you decide what people deserved? That was the trouble — you couldn't decide. So you came to believe in honor and dignity for their own sake since all proper men knew what honor was and could recognize dignity; but nobody knew what human nature was or could presume to mete out justice to others.

George had fled the funeral because he "needed intensely . . . to escape from the forms of death which were, to us, only the completion of life, and in which there could be nothing personal." The intensity of George's need to escape is made clear by the agonized brutality with which he greets Semmes Buchan — a medical student — on his return; "I reckon you'll be cutting up your cadavers again this time next week," he says to Semmes. In speaking to Lacy he brings together the two

things that exasperate him most about Major Buchan's way of
life, its unwillingness — in his exasperation George thinks of it
as a stupid refusal — to see what he believes is obvious, the hard
but real financial aspect of life and the shocking but real cadav-
erous aspect of death. " 'And by God they'll all starve to
death, that's what they'll do. They do nothing but die and
marry and think about the honor of Virginia.' He rammed his
hands into his pockets and shouted: 'I want to be thrown to the
hogs. I tell you I want to be thrown to the hogs!' " ("and the
sacrifices were like the stockyards at Chicago if nothing was
done with the meat except to bury it.") In the wild confusion
of the destruction of Pleasant Hill at the end of *The Fathers*,
only the devoted propriety of Mr. Higgins saves the body of
Major Buchan from the hogs.

"As to all unprotected persons," Lacy thinks later when he
understands George better, "death was horrible to him; therefore he faced it in its aspect of greatest horror — the corrupt
body." So great is this private horror that he cannot even pay
his respects — as the old phrase goes — to his own dead mother.
When his uncle greets him at the door of the parlor where she is
laid out, he says, "Nephew, it pains me to greet you in these
melancholy circumstances. . . . Your mother —" But George,
"looking at him as if he were a child," interrupts him: "She's
dead, ain't she?" — and then turns abruptly away without ever
seeing her. "As Brother George threw back the door to the steps
down to the kitchen," says the narrator, "I believed that he was
imponderable, that I could have put my finger through him.
When death could be like this, nobody was living. If [the
Poseys] had not been of their Church, they would have thrown
one another at death into the river." George does in fact throw
his half-brother, Yellow Jim, into the river after Semmes has shot
him. This is what it is to live a life "in which the social acts are
privacies." In the Posey household the last fragment of social existence is old Aunt Milly Jane's spying through the crack of her

bedroom door at everyone who passes in the hall. "People have got to get life where they can," Susan says of her. ". . . it makes her live."

It makes it far worse for George Posey that, being the kind of man he is, he must live in a world made for men like Major Buchan. "In a world in which all men were like him, George would not have suffered — and he did suffer — the shock of communion with a world that he could not recover; while that world existed, its piety, its order, its elaborate rigamarole — his own forfeited heritage — teased him like a nightmare. . . ." It is this that so exasperates him and drives him to his acts of wanton and shocking impropriety, as it does when he participates in the elaborate Strawberry Hill-Gothic ritual of the tournament. We know from Brother Semmes' conduct how much the serious feelings of the participants were embodied in this ritual. "I knew," says Lacy, "that [Brother Semmes] didn't mind bringing [Minta Lewis] to the tournament because everybody knew that [she] was his cousin, not his choice; but he'd be damned if he'd ride, win the prize, and crown her queen." George does ride, wins the "small wreath of laurel that somebody must have made a trip to the Bull Run Mountains to get," and then, on an irresistible impulse to laugh at these "antic people," "as Susan leaned forward to receive [the wreath], according to custom, on her head, he hesitated, looked around him, and then dropped [it] into her lap."

Thus George, who cannot recover the existing world of custom and ceremony that would give objective existence and order to his feelings, is always trying to invent, on the spur of the moment, ad hoc, sincere gestures of his own. His feelings are always undisciplined and the only way he can attain even an illusion of self-realization is in improvised and violent action. "He is alone," as grandfather Buchan says, "like a tornado." He has nothing but his terrifying personal sincerity with which to meet experience, with the result that he cannot face death at

all, makes a tragic mess of his passion for Susan, and — having
shot Semmes Buchan on an impulse that astonishes even him —
actually attempts to explain to Major Buchan why he did it.
"Brother George," Lacy thinks, "had been sincere . . . had
been appallingly too sincere."

Between George Posey and Major Buchan stands Susan,
George's wife and the major's daughter. "There can be no
question but that Susan had been fascinated by George's mysterious power, by his secrecy and his violence," Lacy knows
(he has been fascinated by it himself), "but . . . she could not
have known that George was outside life, or had a secret life
that no one had heard of at Pleasant Hill. To Susan the life
around her in childhood had been final." But after Susan has
lived with George and his family — each of them isolated in
his room and the shell of himself, hardly knowing, as
George's uncle does not, whether it is night or day — she learns
that these are not just eccentric old people; they are not really
old at all. They are people who have dropped out of life,
walked through the looking-glass and forgotten the trick of
getting back, like the Alice of Mr. Tate's "Last Days of Alice."
This discovery makes Susan determined to prevent her brother
Semmes from marrying Jane Posey. She does so by allowing
— in fact almost forcing — George's colored half-brother to
attack Jane. As a consequence, Semmes, like a good Buchan,
shoots Yellow Jim; George, like himself, shoots Semmes; and
Susan goes mad.

"Why," the narrator wonders, "cannot life change without
tangling the lives of innocent persons? Why do innocent persons cease their innocence and become violent and evil in themselves that such great changes may take place?" For they had
all been innocent and they had all become, in different ways,
more or less evil. Either because of changes in themselves that
made the world unbearable to them, as with George, or because
of changes in the world about them that made their heroism at

best irrelevant and at worst disastrous, as with Major Buchan, or because of both, as with Susan, time has its way with them all. At the end of the novel George and Lacy stand beside the smoldering ruins of Pleasant Hill and Lacy says, "Can't we do something?" And George says what is true: "I have done too much."

The Fathers is essentially a very American novel; it deals with the dilemma of the American hero in very much the same way American novels always have, but its author, if he has something in common with that hero, is not like him by any choice of his own. If he is too intelligent and unsentimental to suppose he and George Posey can ever go back, can ever recover their forfeited heritage, or even to suppose that, being what he is, he can really desire to, he is also too intelligent to think a man can commit himself wholly to the private consciousness and live without a community and its customs and ceremonies. As a consequence, if he has the American sense that the meaning of a novel, like the meaning of life itself, transcends the "literal level of meaning" immediately implied by the realistic novel's image of life, he also knows that the best means the novelist has for embodying that meaning and giving it life is the realistic novel's conventionalized representation of nature. *The Fathers* is an action of a certain magnitude that is at once verisimilar and a symbol. Because it is, its meaning does not remain some merely airy nothing that is constantly evoked by the author but never materializes, and its realistic narrative is not a photograph that exists merely to be recognized. Its meaning ceases to be imponderable, as George Posey was, and takes on the full life of recognizable action that Major Buchan had. Its motive is a meaning, and the life of that meaning is an action. It is an imitation of life.

INDEX

Adams, John, 108
Adams, Robert, 14-15
Adams, Samuel Hopkins, 120
Aristotle, 18, 161, 287
Arnold, Matthew, 55, 105, 139, 212
Aubrey, John, 82, 97
Auchincloss, Louis, 178
Auden, W. H., 153
Austen, Jane, 6, 22, 25-26, 28-29, 31, 43

Bacon, Francis, 268
Basso, Hamilton, 175
Bellow, Saul, 114
Benét, Stephen Vincent, 120
Bennett, Arnold, 141
Bewley, Marius, 105-10, 111
Blackmur, Richard, 4
Booth, Wayne, 1, 14
Brackett, Charles, 120
Broun, Heywood, 140
Browning, Robert, 56-58
Burnham, David, 120

Carroll, Lewis, 13
Chandler, Raymond, 129
Chase, Richard, 106, 107, 110
Coleridge, Samuel Taylor, 22
Congreve, William, 22
Conrad, Joseph, 110, 114, 144-47, 158, 159

Cooper, James Fenimore, 107-10, 125-26, 169-70
Cowie, Alexander, 106
Cowley, Malcolm, 149, 219
Cozzens, James Gould, 78, 85-89, 119, 122, 123, 127, 129, 136-37, 175

Dell, Floyd, 144
Dickens, Charles, 31
Donne, John, 22
Dos Passos, John, 21, 119, 127, 130-131, 135, 142, 144, 145, 148-54, 155, 157-60
Dreiser, Theodore, 9-11, 55, 141, 143

Eliot, T. S., 23, 25, 121, 193, 211, 247
Emerson, Ralph Waldo, 166-67
Empson, William, 33

Farrell, James T., 129
Faulkner, William, 102, 110, 114, 117, 122, 127-28, 129, 135-36, 159, 160-81, 212, 227, 228
Feidelson, Charles, 106
Fiedler, Leslie, 106
Fielding, Henry, 7, 12, 16, 22
Firbank, Ronald, 22

Fitzgerald, F. Scott, 110, 123, 127, 129, 135, 140, 147, 151-60, 183-204, 207; *The Great Gatsby*, 115, 125-27, 133-35, 178, 180-81, 186; *The Last Tycoon*, 185, 194-204; *Tender Is the Night*, 114, 121-22, 135, 141, 156-57; *This Side of Paradise*, 121, 123, 140
Flaubert, Gustave, 114
Forster, E. M., 2, 56, 267
Frank, Joseph, 269

Gerould, Winifred and James Thayer, 40
Gold, Michael, 121
Grossman, James, 169

Hardy, Florence, 57
Hardy, Thomas, 55-77, 78, 112
Hawthorne, Nathaniel, 22, 54, 110-112, 115, 124
Hemingway, Ernest, 6, 110, 121, 127, 133, 134, 135, 150, 152, 160, 178, 180, 205-226; *A Farewell to Arms*, 135, 153, 223; *For Whom the Bell Tolls*, 131, 133, 160, 215; *The Sun Also Rises*, 114, 121, 122, 129, 131-33, 212-14; "The Gambler, the Nun, and the Radio," 222-23; "Fifty Grand," 221-222; "The Killers," 17; "The Short Happy Life of Francis Macomber," 223-26
Hemingway, Marcelline, 205
Hergesheimer, Joseph, 140
Homer, 19
Hume, Cyril, 120

James, Henry, 2-3, 4-5, 22, 23-24, 26, 27-28, 105, 107, 113-14, 120, 123, 124-25, 158, 159, 168, 250; *The Ambassadors*, 5, 17; *The Golden Bowl*, 5, 24, 111, 115, 125; *The Portrait of a Lady*, 115;

The Spoils of Poynton, 5; *The Wings of the Dove*, 5, 111
James, William, 124-25, 168
Johnson, Samuel, 26-27
Joyce, James, 14-15, 21, 114, 141, 268

Lawrence, D. H., 107
Levin, Harry, 106, 107
Lewis, R. B. W., 106
Lewis, Sinclair, 122, 128
Lewis, Wyndham, 208, 215
Loeb, Harold, 133
Lubbock, Percy, 2

Mackenzie, Compton, 143-44, 147
MacLeish, Archibald, 120, 217, 248-49
Marks, Percy, 120
Marquand, J. P., 122, 128, 129, 178
Matthiessen, F. O., 106
Melville, Herman, 22, 110, 124, 250; *Moby Dick*, 112

Newman, Frances, 143-44
New Masses, The, 121, 141
New Republic, The, 121

O'Hara, John, 128, 129

Pater, Walter, 142
Perkins, Maxwell, 140
Pope, Alexander, 12, 22
Pound, Ezra, 108, 211, 217, 263-64
Powell, Anthony, 78-103; *The Music of Time*, 82-85, 87-103

Richardson, Samuel, 12

Salinger, J. D., 227-46, 247, 261
Saunders, John Monk, 120
Scott, Sir Walter, 107
Shakespeare, William, 22, 63, 64-65, 70, 269

Southern Review, The, 121
Speare, Dorothy, 120
Stearns, Harold, 123-24
Stein, Gertrude, 119, 141, 208
Steinbeck, John, 6, 20, 128
Stendhal, 8
Strachey, John, 121
Swinburne, Algernon, 142-43

Tate, Allen, 58, 67, 114, 136, 266, 267-87
Tennyson, Alfred, Lord, 56, 140, 208
Thackeray, William, 28
Thoreau, Henry David, 166, 167-68, 246
Tolstoy, Leo, 8-9, 23-24
Trilling, Lionel, 154, 155, 179, 184

Trollope, Anthony, 16, 22, 25-54, 55, 109
Troy, William, 156
Twain, Mark, 176-77, 178-81

Updike, John, 247-66

Warren, Robert Penn, 17, 114, 175
Weatherwax, Clara, 121
Wells, H. G., 143-45, 148, 158, 159
Wescott, Glenway, 122, 184
Wharton, Edith, 178, 212
Whitman, Walt, 115, 168
Wilder, Thornton, 121
Wilson, Edmund, 121, 127, 142, 144, 147, 154, 176, 208, 210
Woolf, Virginia, 141-42, 143
Wordsworth, William, 12, 256